FREEDOM'S MOMENT

PAUL M. COHEN

FREEDOM'S MOMENT

AN ESSAY ON THE FRENCH IDEA OF

 LIBERTY FROM ROUSSEAU TO FOUCAULT

THE UNIVERSITY OF CHICAGO PRESS / CHICAGO AND LONDON

Paul M. Cohen is professor of history at Lawrence University. He is the author of *Piety and Politics: Catholic Revival and the Generation of 1905–14 in France* (1987).

The University of Chicago Press, Chicago 60637
The University of Chicago Press, Ltd., London
© 1997 by The University of Chicago
All rights reserved. Published 1997
Printed in the United States of America
04 03 02 01 00 99 98 97   1 2 3 4 5
ISBN: 0-226-11285-3 (cloth)
        0-226-11286-1 (paper)

Library of Congress Cataloging-in-Publication Data

Cohen, Paul M. (Paul Michael), 1955–
    Freedom's moment : an essay on the French idea of liberty from
Rousseau to Foucault / Paul M. Cohen.
        p. cm.
    Includes bibliographical references and index.
    ISBN 0-226-11285-3 (cloth: alk. paper).—ISBN 0-226-11286-1
(paper: alk. paper)
        1. Liberty—History. 2. Philosophy, French. I. Title.
B105.L45C64 1997
123'.5'0944—dc20   96-17928
                                                              CIP

⊗ The paper used in this publication meets the minimum requirements of the
American National Standard for Information Sciences—Permanence of Paper for
Printed Library Materials, ANSI Z39.48-1984

CONTENTS

ACKNOWLEDGMENTS

The essay that follows has not always aroused the unwavering support and enthusiasm of would-be publishers, reviewers, and readers. One editor at a major press, for example, literally laughed aloud at the thought—pursued herein—that the likes of Rousseau, Stendhal, Sartre, and Foucault might have performed variations on a single cultural narrative with a single theme. A senior colleague, likewise, fearing that the book might aggrandize the French radical tradition and its luminaries, accused its prospective author of having "stars in his eyes." No less forthrightly have devotees of France's radical intelligentsia, above all of Foucault, apprised me of the reductionism, injustice, and outright violence that this volume will inflict upon their heroes. In short, the unwitting—and perhaps even the witting—historian who seeks to navigate the still live political minefield implanted around the modern French intellectual does so at his or her own risk.

I feel all the more grateful, in this light, to those who have offered this book their early and active support—moral, intellectual, and otherwise. Foremost among these is Bliss Cohen, who has not only read every word of every draft of *Freedom's Moment,* but has also survived the ups and downs of its author with characteristic good humor and equanimity. Trained as a chemist, Ms. Cohen now knows much more than she ever wished to about modern French intellectuals and their ideas—surely more, in any case, than I will ever know about chemistry. To the extent that this book remains clear and accessible to the nonspecialist, it is owing to her unfailingly gentle criticisms and intelligent, commonsense readings, for whatever Ms. Cohen could not immediately grasp, I dutifully rewrote.

I owe an almost equal debt of gratitude to my good friend and colleague Professor Susan Rosa, who bolstered my courage from the outset and read drafts of nearly every chapter. Apart from her unflagging enthusiasm for the project, which often rekindled my own, and her ever-stimulating and incisive questioning of it, Professor Rosa offered her expertise as a specialist on the thought and literature of premodern France, a field that is not my own. Her corrections and recommendations—bibliographical, factual, and conceptual—have, I hope, both rectified my most egregious misconceptions concerning that epoch and deepened my understanding of it. Any errors that remain are, of course, mine and not hers.

There are three other individuals to whom this book is materially and intellectually indebted: Professor Mark Poster, whose affirmative review of an early chapter helped clear the path to its publication, and whose fair-minded appraisal of the completed manuscript—with which he did not, and still does not, entirely agree—has certainly made *Freedom's Moment* a better book; Professor Jeremy Popkin, whose generous, sympathetic, and insightful assessment of the manuscript not only helped me to redress some of its major defects, but epitomizes the kind of reading I hope the book will receive; and my editor, Doug Mitchell, who first recognized the potential merit of a rather unorthodox piece of intellectual history from an unknown author, and then—with requisite patience, empathy, and good cheer—shepherded both manuscript and author through the occasionally harrowing process of writing and publication.

To David Jordan and Basil Guy, who read and commented on early drafts of chapter 2, I feel particular gratitude both for helping me to clarify and enrich that chapter and for magnanimously allotting time and energy to a budding historian whom they did not know. I am no less grateful to my old teacher and friend, George Billias, who commented on an early draft of chapter 1 and warmly supported the book and its author from the outset. For early and much needed words of encouragement on this undertaking, I am indebted to Frank Doeringer, Paul Mazgaj, Vinni Data, David Wright, John Hellman, David Schalk, Dale Van Kley, and Larry Schehr; and to my friends at the Newberry Library in Chicago—especially Ruth Hamilton, Harvey Markowitz, Bill Sklar, Beth Newman, and Bruce Levy—I am equally thankful for providing the rare and somewhat magical academic community of support wherein it could take root and grow. Before leaving the topic of "magical communities of support," I would also like to acknowledge my mother and father, my sisters Jody, Carol, and Wendy, and each of their respective mates for the love as well as the proverbial "Cohen family yack," which helped sustain this project and its framer through good times and bad.

I feel quite a literal debt to my home institution, Lawrence University; without its financing of a year's sabbatical as well as necessary travel and books, the present work could not have appeared for quite some time, if at all. I would also like to thank those Lawrence students—especially Alexis Stokes, Ubah Hussein, Sarah Hopper, Jeff Campbell, and Jeannine Marks—whose industrious and intelligent engagement in my seminar "The French Idea of Freedom" helped me work through the book's fundamental ideas. I am also most grateful to Vicki Koessl, whose uncanny skill, knowledge, and imagination in the domain of WordPerfect helped generate the manuscript's sundry drafts, and especially its notes and bibliography; to Hrushit Bhatt, for his help on the index; and to Louise Cameron Maynard for her deft and discrete copyediting.

The most obvious intellectual forebear of this essay is the late Leonard Krieger, whose classic work *The German Idea of Freedom* I read and appreciated during my graduate studies with him at the University of Chicago. But its most profound and abiding intellectual debt is to Professor Paul Lucas of Clark University, to whom *Freedom's Moment* is dedicated. It was Lucas who first introduced me to "the life of the mind"—and indeed, more specifically, to the mind of Rousseau; and it was he who first imparted to me what I still consider to be the fundamental goal and ethos of historical inquiry: the need to grasp and appreciate "otherness" on its own terms. While I can no more than hope that what follows will approach his exacting standards of historical imagination, integrity, and lucidity—Professor Lucas correctly, and with all due consideration, dispatched an early draft of chapter 1 to the drawing board—I feel certain that it remains true to his tenets in at least one regard: he always said that historians, having meticulously scrutinized both their sources and themselves, should have the courage to "take a flier." Here it is.

A NOTE ON TRANSLATIONS

While all translations from works in French are my own, I have, wherever possible, consulted standard English translations in making them; the latter are therefore cited with their French counterparts in the bibliography.

ONE

INTRODUCTION

I. LIBERTY AND THE "FRENCH PROBLEM"

It might be argued that the modern West has generated essentially three schools of thought on the subject of liberty. The first and currently most prominent of these, generally associated by scholars with Great Britain and the United States, arose out of the intellectual tradition of John Locke, Adam Smith, and John Stuart Mill, and is distinguished by what Isaiah Berlin famously termed "negative liberty," insofar as it defines freedom as "the absence of external obstacles." Seeking to establish, that is, a legal sphere wherein individuals would remain unobstructed by the external authorities of church and state, it has constituted the moral foundation of classical liberalism, which has looked to laissez-faire capitalism for its fundamental mythos and values. Thus emphasizing the independence of the individual—and above all the "rational," middle-class individual—from political, social, and economic constraints, this school has characteristically celebrated the free pursuit of private gain in the open marketplace of material and spiritual goods. While compatible with a less than fully democratic politics, it has historically inclined toward representative government and universal suffrage—that is, toward liberal democracy.[1]

A second school, commonly linked by scholars with the German humanist tradition of Wilhelm von Humboldt, Kant, and Hegel, has espoused what Berlin labeled "positive liberty," or the achievement of "self-mastery" on both an individual and communal level. Liberty, in this tradition, is identified not with the individual's freedom from such societal institutions as church and state so much as his or her "self-realization"—the attainment of a "higher self"—above all through the agency of the state. Such "positive liberty" in general, and its German variant in particular, have become identified in the twentieth century with the rise of Nazi Germany and the totalitarian state. In his classic study *The German Idea of Freedom,* for example, Leonard Krieger argues precisely that the "German problem," or Germany's failure to achieve "a liberal democracy in the western sense," reflected not merely "the triumph of conservatism over generic liberalism" but also "a peculiar German attitude toward liberty." For while "individual rights were recognized" in the German liberal tradition, they were characteristically "absorbed" into "the moral power of the state."[2]

Scholars have conventionally identified a third school of liberty with modern France but have tended to exclude from it such French and Francophone thinkers as Montesquieu, Voltaire, Condorcet, Benjamin Constant, and Madame de Staël, whom they deport into the classical liberal camp. Rooted instead in the political philosophy of the Swiss-born Jean-Jacques Rousseau and in the French Revolution itself—especially its radical Jacobin phase of 1793–94—this school has conceived liberty neither as the "absence of external obstacles" nor as individual or communal "self-realization," but rather, in the words of political philosopher J. G. Merquior, as the democratic "self-rule" both of the individual citizen and of civil society as a whole. It proposes, in other words, to substitute the "general will" of "the people" for the particular will of a monarch, and thereby to redeploy the authority of the state so as to secure "autonomous selfhood" for each member of civil society. At first glance, then, this "radical school," as it might be labeled, would seem to mirror its German humanist counterpart in emphasizing the government's role in helping to generate societal freedom. For the former, however, the state is empowered not to engineer a "higher self" so much as to guarantee autonomy for all citizens through their ongoing participation in the "general will."[3]

The affiliation of the French radical school with Rousseau and the Jacobin terrorist regime of 1793–94—and its coinciding exclusion of several eminent liberal theorists who are indisputably French—underscores what scholars of modern France might term the "French problem": the chronic failure of modern France not so much to achieve a liberal democracy as to sustain one. Plagued by periodic political upheavals since the Revolution, the French body politic has characteristically oscillated, as historian Dale Van Kley has put it, between "order and freedom"[4]—between such "authoritarian" regimes as the Jacobin dictatorship of 1793–94, the Bonapartist empires of 1804 and 1852, and the "National Revolution" of Vichy; and such "liberal" ones as the constitutional monarchy of 1789, the July Monarchy of 1830, and the Third Republic of 1871. More than a few scholars, in fact, have gone so far as to identify the radical school of liberty with a singularly authoritarian strain in French political culture and, furthermore, with the advent of "totalitarian democracy" in the modern age.[5] For with its aspiration to achieve both individual and collective "self-rule" through the power of the state, the radical school would seem more a variant, in Berlin's terms, of positive than of negative liberty. In fact, by Berlin's own account, Rousseauian liberty comprised not "the 'negative' freedom of the individual" from interference "within a defined area," but rather the participation of all members of society in a "public power which is entitled to interfere with every aspect of every citizen's life." The French Revolution itself, Berlin contends, especially in its Jacobin phase, represented "an eruption of the desire for 'positive' freedom of collective self-assertion on the part of a large body of Frenchmen."[6]

Thus, the "French problem," as posed by modern scholarship, might be reformulated in the following questions: Is there a peculiarly French concept of freedom, which might be traced back to the political discourse of Rousseau and the revolutionary Jacobins? If so, how is it related to the legendary instability of modern French politics—indeed, to the apparent resistance of modern France to liberal democracy as an established form of government? Finally, does that mental construct carry within it the seeds of twentieth-century totalitarianism?

This book will assume that the answer to the first of these questions is "yes," there is indeed a "radical" or Rousseauian intellectual tradition that is both peculiar and integral to the political culture of modern France. It will seek to address the related issues of modern France's political volatility, its apparent ambivalence toward liberal democracy, and the putative link between its political culture and totalitarianism by examining the motif of liberty in the public biographies and most celebrated texts of Rousseau and seven other culturally prominent members of France's intelligentsia who span the period between the Revolution and the present day. They are as follows: the Jacobin chieftain and proponent of "the Terror," Maximilien Robespierre (1758–94); the Restoration novelist, Stendhal (1783–1842);* the anticlerical historian, Jules Michelet (1798–1874); the philosophical vitalist, Henri Bergson (1859–1941); the essayist and Catholic convert, Charles Péguy (1882–1914); the left-wing existentialist, Jean-Paul Sartre (1905–80); and the poststructuralist luminary, Michel Foucault (1926–84).

II. THE CONSECRATED HERETICS

At first glance, Rousseau and the seven designated figures succeeding him would scarcely seem to form a single cultural tradition at all, either professionally or politically. All, except for Robespierre, who was the only one among them literally to have exercised political power, were "men of letters" or "intellectuals" who produced works of recognized merit and originality within modern French culture; yet even these seven cover an undeniably wide literary range. Two of them—Rousseau and Sartre—produced celebrated works of fiction and philosophy as well as political theory, and two more—Michelet and Foucault— are known primarily for their works of history and historical criticism. Stendhal's fame rests almost entirely on his literary oeuvre—and most especially, as shall be seen, the novel *Le Rouge et le noir*—while Bergson's hinges on his achievement as a philosopher. Péguy, while a poet of some renown, became celebrated in the main for a series of critical essays on French politics, culture, and religion, which he penned during the decade before World War I.

The eight would seem to vary no less both in the style and substance of their politics. If Péguy, Sartre, and Foucault, for example, were ardent advocates of direct political engagement during their respective epochs, Bergson, whose numerous devotees at the turn of the century ranged from the revolutionary left to the protofascist right, steadfastly refused to engage in politics of any sort. Moreover, if most of the eight

---

*Stendhal, as shall be seen, constitutes a special case: his fictional masterpiece *Le Rouge et le noir* and its celebrated hero, Julien Sorel, will be treated here as opposed to their creator. See below, pp. 17–18.

might safely be classified on the ideological or political "left," they surely form no unified party. While both Robespierre and Michelet, for instance, were fervent republicans and French nationalists, the latter, in his classic *History of the French Revolution* (1847–53), reserved some of his harshest criticism for the revolutionary Jacobins of 1793–94 and above all for Robespierre himself. And while Sartre famously championed Marxist internationalism and revolutionary socialism during the 1960s and 1970s, Foucault—who once described himself as "an anarchist of the left"[7]—directly repudiated both Marxism and its Sartrean incarnation during the 1970s and 1980s. Even, finally, on the topic of religion there would seem no firm consensus among the eight: while Rousseau, Stendhal, Michelet, Sartre, and Foucault were notorious critics of the Catholic Church, Péguy was among the several intellectuals at the turn of the century who found in Bergson's philosophy a road back to Catholic faith.*

Notwithstanding such conspicuous divergences, however, all eight of these men share a single—not to say singular—standing within the political culture of modern France. That is to say, each achieved popular acclaim in his day for having denounced the "established order" and its values. Moreover, their vocabulary of cultural opposition, whether directly imbibed by a majority of the French populace or not, helped construct worlds of meaning for their respective generations. Such celebrated Rousseauian idioms as "natural liberty," "social contract," and "general will" came powerfully, if problematically, to life in the revolutionary discourse of Robespierre, who notoriously championed the "natural virtue" and "general will" of "the people." Julien Sorel, by the same token, the protagonist of Stendhal's Restoration novel *Le Rouge et le noir* (1830), breathed fictional and even mythic vitality into that postrevolutionary French culture-hero, the militant iconoclast. Similarly Michelet, through his acclaimed commemorations of "the people" and the French Revolution itself during the waning days the July Monarchy, helped provide the intellectual framework for the coming revolution of 1848. So too did Bergson, through such renowned metaphysical motifs as "pure duration [*la durée*]" and "the vital force [*élan vital*]," help incite an intellectual revolt in fin-de-siècle France against philosophical positivism and political liberalism. Péguy,

---

*Péguy, in fact, would seem by himself to have embraced a bewildering and contradictory array of political affiliations: a zealous defender of Dreyfus at the turn of the century, he remained a self-proclaimed republican and socialist thereafter, even while espousing both Catholic belief and an increasingly xenophobic French nationalism.

likewise, through his celebrated distinction of 1910 between the sacred "mystiques" of modern France and the inexorable "politiques" that debase them, helped frame not only a widespread cultural critique of France's Third Republic but ultimately the political discourse both of Vichy and the Resistance.[8] And finally, while Sartre, through such widely disseminated concepts as "bad faith," "authenticity," and "commitment [*engagement*]," furnished postwar France with its grammar of cultural opposition, Foucault did the same for the succeeding generation through his famous denunciation of modern "panopticism" and the oppressive "society of normalization" it generated. In short, each of these figures successfully incarnated—or, as in the case of Stendhal, helped delineate—a uniquely exalted and authoritative persona within the political culture of modern France: that, in sociologist Pierre Bourdieu's characteristically ironic formulation, of the "consecrated heretic."[9]

Bourdieu, of course, is hardly the first scholar to focus upon the singular stature of the intellectual in modern France. Indeed, the persona of the critical, autonomous, and even "aristocratic" intellectual—whether revered or reviled—emerges regularly in scholarly accounts of modern France. Defined both by his role as "the sovereign dispenser of new norms" and by his stance of "permanent opposition" or "protest intellectualism," this figure is typically cast as "a sort of missionary and, if need be, a confessor or martyr on behalf of great principles." Thus, he—the aristocratic intellectual of the modern age would seem all but invariably a masculine character*—is said to represent "the

---

*The degree to which women have or have not participated in the modern French intellectual tradition—and more particularly that of consecrated heresy—is an important historical question, which has been broached recently, at least in part, by historian Mona Ozouf in *Les Mots des femmes* (Paris: Fayard, 1995). Surveying ten women writers from Madame du Deffand and Madame de Charrière in the eighteenth century through such nineteenth- and twentieth-century luminaries as Madame de Staël, George Sand, Simone Weil, and Simone de Beauvoir, Ozouf seeks to disclose what she calls "the singularity" of modern French women: their simultaneous centrality in French culture and characteristic "timidity" regarding militant feminism of the Anglo-American variety. She contends, on the one hand, that women in modern France have traditionally participated as the virtual equals of men in the universe of civilized intellectual discourse symbolized by the Enlightenment salon. On the other hand, she suggests that it was not until the twentieth century that such women as "the two Simones" could have been publicly "consecrated" at all, much less as intellectual heretics; for only then were women admitted as the equals of men at every level of the national system of education. But even in the twentieth century, Ozouf argues, women intellectuals in France have tended to identify with the radical-masculine discourse of Rousseau and the Jacobins— at times to the detriment of their feminism. Hence, modern French women, she writes, typically view themselves "first and foremost as free and equal individuals" rather than

incarnation of the critical spirit . . . armed against all conformisms." A self-appointed "'frontiersman' of the ideal," writes one contemporary scholar, the French intellectual "propose[s] to the world a model of intransigence which [forbids] all compromise." In fact, concludes another, he is "happier in opposition" than "sullying" himself "with the exercise of power." [10]

In defining this renowned persona, however, Bourdieu goes a step further than most: he maintains that cultural "heresy" has become literally "consecrated" within the institutional framework of modern France. In other words, he situates his consecrated heretics firmly within that famously centralized state sieve of primary schools, lycées, and universities through which all modern French citizens must pass on their way to power or obscurity. Distinguishing them from the intellectuals at the official apex of the academic pyramid—from the "philosophical high priests," who occupy professorial posts at the Sorbonne (the University of Paris) and those select grandes écoles that propagate France's professional elite—Bourdieu locates his heretics, rather, "on the margins or in the marginalia" of that "academic empire," an empire, which, in point of fact, had once served as their training ground. Indeed, while noting their gravitation toward privately directed "avant-garde reviews," Bourdieu underscores the characteristic affiliation of his consecrated heretics with two elite state institutions at the center of Paris's Latin Quarter: the École Normale Supérieure, which they would most likely have attended as students, and the Collège de France, which represents, for Bourdieu, the foremost among a choice group of "peripheral institutions" that have achieved an exalted cultural stature outside the official university system. [11]

The École Normale—or, as Bourdieu labels it sardonically, the "'great lay seminary'"—was initially founded in 1795 to furnish revolutionary France with a secular priesthood of teachers. Subsequently commandeered by Napoleon, it became one of the aforementioned grandes écoles, which were meant to supply the Empire with a meritocracy of enlightened officials. But the school was destined to outlast both the Empire and the Restoration. Reflecting the secular classicism and critical spirit of its Enlightenment roots, it increasingly earned a

---

as members of an oppressed group; and even such feminist icons as Simone de Beauvoir have therefore envisioned the liberation of women as part of the more general emancipation of humankind that they associate with "the ultimate revolution" (see Les Mots des femmes, 11, 371, 383, 392–93). Intelligent and provocative as it is, of course, Ozouf's work constitutes only the barest introduction to a significant historical topic that remains open to future scholarship.

reputation both for political liberalism and intellectual independence. By 1848, its members and graduates included some of the July Monarchy's most celebrated patrons and politicians: the philosopher Victor Cousin, for example, and the historian-prime minister, François Guizot. Thereafter, even following its annexation to the Sorbonne in 1903, the École Normale became celebrated as the hatchery of France's political and cultural elite, producing such party leaders, prime ministers, and presidents as Jean Jaurès, Léon Blum, and Georges Pompidou, as well as such writers and intellectuals as Romain Rolland and Claude Lévi-Strauss. "France," summarizes Theodore Zeldin, "was the only country in Europe to make philosophizing a career, paying a good salary, and to have enough of these philosophers, distributed over the whole country, for them to form a significant social and intellectual force."[12]

The Collège de France also evolved, since its foundation in 1530 to "advance humane studies and the spirit of the Renaissance," into a cultural symbol of sorts—indeed, into "the holy of holies," as one contemporary writer has put it—within the French educational hierarchy. As a state institution devoted to research but entirely independent of the university system, it has offered complete academic autonomy to its members, who are elected by their peers and are therefore, in Bourdieu's words, "more or less totally deprived of, or liberated from," both the powers and "the responsibilities of the ordinary professor." While requiring no diplomas of its professors and granting no degrees to its students, the Collège expects the former to offer annual courses on subjects of their own choosing and to present their lectures to the public at large. The professor at the Collège de France, then, holds a position both unique to modern French culture and of unparalleled prestige within it: he is an anointed philosophe supported by the state but responsible to the public alone, and he is hence entirely free, if he so chooses, to criticize the established order. Thus, the Collège, as shall shortly be seen, has periodically provided the stage for legendary episodes of cultural heresy that have shaken the Parisian establishment literally from within the corridors of its own power.[13]

It is through such institutional affiliations as these, suggests Bourdieu, that the consecrated heretic has demarcated and reinforced his paradoxical posture within the political culture of modern France— his public "contempt and . . . rejection" of an elite, state-sponsored intellectual establishment that once "attracted and even consecrated" him. The heretic is able, thereby, to manifest before the public "the freedom and audacity of the artist's life" rather than the "somewhat circumscribed rigor of *homo academicus.*" Thus, "beyond the differences, the divergences, and sometimes the conflicts which separate them," Bourdieu concludes, the consecrated heretics share "a sort of *anti-institutional mood*" (Bourdieu's emphasis). And it is for this very reason, in the final analysis, that they possess "a renown which . . . considerably transcends the frontiers of the academic field"—that they so often accumulate "the most prestigious titles of academic recognition" as well as the "indices of 'intellectual' consecration most recognized by the general public."[14] In sum, through the term "consecrated heretic," Bourdieu conveys both the cultural ambiguity and the multilayered irony of his archetype; employing a pointedly religious taxonomy to characterize conspicuously secular luminaries, he portrays the latter as at once culturally "consecrated" (the secular "church's" consummate insiders) and "heretical" (its equally quintessential adversaries).

Among the eight previously designated figures, those who achieved prominence after modern France's academic pyramid was firmly in place—Michelet, Bergson, Péguy, Sartre, and Foucault—quite clearly embody, within their respective eras, Bourdieu's paradoxical archetype. All five, whether as students, teachers, or both, were initially affiliated with the École Normale Supérieure, and three of them (Michelet, Bergson, and Foucault) achieved wide public notoriety following their election to the Collège de France. Thus, Michelet, a former professor of history at the École Normale, ascended to the Collège in 1838 and went on to generate a succession of iconoclastic best-sellers—the ferociously anticlerical *Du Prêtre, de la femme, et de la famille* (1845), *Le Peuple* (1846), and the first two volumes of the aforementioned *Histoire de la révolution française* (1847)—as well as a "dangerous" and widely attended lecture series at the Collège, which the government abruptly suspended on the eve of the 1848 revolution. Similarly Bergson, who had both matriculated and taught philosophy at the École Normale, gained a remarkable celebrity following his appointment to the Collège de France in 1900. Again through such best-selling works as *L'Évolution créatrice* (1907) and, above all, a much celebrated series of public lectures at the Collège, the philosopher captivated an ever-expanding Parisian audience with his ongoing critique of the intellectual foundations of the Third Republic. Likewise Foucault, also a former student and professor at the École Normale, achieved an unsurpassed renown following his appointment to the Collège in 1970: it was thereafter that he launched such heretical best-sellers as *Surveiller et punir* (1975) and *La Volonté de savoir* (1976) as well as his own cycle of public lectures, which achieved no less a vogue in Paris than had those of Bergson and Michelet. Bourdieu, in fact, cites Foucault as "no doubt the most representative" model of consecrated heresy in the modern age; for while remaining "almost entirely bereft of specifically academic powers," his ultimate "fame" afforded him "considerable power . . . over the whole field of cultural production."[15]

While neither ever held a chair at the Collège de France, Péguy and Sartre fit the mold of consecrated heresy no less conspicuously than the three who did. A former student of Bergson's at the École Normale, Péguy left school in 1898 to join the then raging battle on behalf of Dreyfus and against the powers of the Third Republic. Two years later, however, he founded his own Parisian journal, *Les Cahiers de la Quinzaine,* which became the very prototype of Bourdieu's "avant-garde review." For it was from this independent and academically "marginal" launching pad that the former Dreyfusard fired a barrage of journalistic missiles—most notably, his 1910 essay, *Notre jeunesse*—wherein he denounced the "new Sorbonne" as well as that "anticlerical church," which, in his view, had risen to power following the Dreyfusard victory. Sartre, by the same token, even while establishing himself as yet another heretical ex-normalien through such subversive literary works as *La Nausée* (1938), *Les Mouches* (1943), *Huis clos* (1944), and *Les Chemins de la liberté* (1945–49), as well as the philosophical tome *L'Etre et le néant* (1943), pioneered his own renegade review in 1944, *Les Temps modernes,* from which to launch periodic offensives against the established order. In 1949, moreover, he actually *declined* an appointment to the Collège de France. By refusing an official affiliation even with the institutional embodiment of intellectual autonomy—and indeed heresy—in modern France, Sartre reconfirmed his public standing as consecrated heretic all the more.[16]

III. ROUSSEAU AND THE ESTABLISHED ANTI-ESTABLISHMENT

If such public intellectuals as Foucault, Sartre, and Péguy would seem to epitomize the institutional consecration of cultural heresy in modern France, each would appear also to re-enact a role first demarcated in the mid-eighteenth century by Rousseau. For it was during that epoch that France's "Republic of Letters"—the self-proclaimed polity of scholars and writers, which had emerged out of the royal and aristocratic courts of the seventeenth century—first successfully acquired that peculiar combination of cultural centrality and opposition that it has maintained ever since.[17]

The precipitous ascent of the Republic of Letters during the eighteenth century reflected an expanding constitutional crisis within the absolute monarchy of France's Old Regime. Not only had the crown, as Alexis de Tocqueville famously argues, undermined its own authority through a longstanding policy of centralization, which had rendered the realm's intricate hierarchy of legally privileged corporations both empty and onerous to much of French society; it stood perched, by midcentury, on the brink of financial insolvency. Unable to contain discussion of the resulting crisis within the traditional corporate vessels of the Old Regime, the crown allowed political contestation to spill out during the 1750s and 1760s into the newly invented realm of "public opinion," which the century's self-styled men of letters, or philosophes, were in the process of staking out as their own. In other words, even while finding an audience for its escalating cascade of pamphlets, treatises, and literary works primarily in the narrow domain of noble and bourgeois Paris, France's budding Republic of Letters claimed nonetheless to speak on behalf of "the public" or "the nation" as a whole; and it thereby increasingly appropriated, in Keith Baker's words, the "new public space" opened up by the breakdown of "monocratic authority."[18] Indeed, Baker is one among several contemporary historians to suggest that, in the final analysis, the French Revolution itself amounted to a competition over which among the Enlightenment's "prerevolutionary discourses" would successfully claim the "linguistic authority" to reconstitute the universe of meaning left in disarray by the collapse of royal authority.[19]

Formed initially in royal academies of the sciences and arts, the Republic of Letters had shifted its institutional locus by the 1750s to the newly fashionable—and more socially egalitarian—universe of the Parisian salon. There, in the words of Jürgen Habermas, the "sons of princes and counts associated with [the] sons of watchmakers and shopkeepers." The Republic's intellectual base of operations, furthermore, had become the notorious *Encyclopédie,* published between 1751 and 1772 by Dénis Diderot, the son of a provincial cutler, and Jean d'Alembert, the illegitimate son of a noble. As "a systematic universal dictionary of the arts and sciences," prophesies Diderot, which aspires to compile "the unity of knowledge" and establish "the definitions of words," the *Encyclopédie* will possess "the power to change men's common way of thinking." Such a "power" implied for Diderot a utilitarian and scientific critique of Old Regime French society, including the church and the government itself. The *Encyclopédie,* he proclaims, must "expose errors" and "skillfully discredit prejudices"; indeed, through its very structure it must "undermine and secretly overthrow certain ridiculous opinions, which no one would dare to oppose openly." Only by so reforming "the national spirit" might one offer a "general education of mankind," which would have worldly "happiness and virtue" as its goal. Explicitly repudiating the Académie Française and the other royal academies as too specialized and dependent to carry out such a project—and the nobility as too frivolous— Diderot entrusts the task to a "society of men of letters and skilled workmen." The project, he explains, must be left entirely independent of "the authorities," which should do no more than "encourage its completion." Such an autonomous "society of letters," remaining untainted by the "sordid self-interest" that motivates "any work that a king has commissioned," would be solely *"bound together by zeal for the best interests of the human race"* (Diderot's emphasis).[20]

Jean d'Alembert reiterated and further refined these claims in his "Essai sur la société des gens de lettres et des grands" of 1753. Opening with an ironic expression of gratitude to the nobility (*les grands*) for enhancing the social status and reputation of letters since the time of Louis XIV, he turns quickly to the "society of men of letters" itself, which he finds "truly the most useful and noble that a thinking man could desire." After all, d'Alembert contends, the "good of the nation" depends more on the talents of men than their birth or fortune, and men of letters possess such "probity and talents" in abundance. Indeed the latter, whose role of "instructing and enlightening men" he finds "the most noble lot of the human condition" excepting "the art of good government," should both familiarize themselves with society and keep their distance from it. "[M]ade for studying, for knowing, and for fixing the use of language," men of letters should "live united" in a modest independence befitting their proper function, which is "to legislate to the rest of the nation on matters of taste and philosophy." D'Alembert, moreover, at the end of his treatise, attests to his own qualifications for such a calling. Mine "are the reflections and views," he claims, "of a writer without family, connections, or support, and consequently without expectations—and also without cares and desires." In short, the founders of the *Encyclopédie,* not only asserted the authority of their newly constituted "society of letters" to "legislate to the rest of the nation" concerning questions of language and meaning, but also declared both its independence from the established order of the Old Regime and its right—even its duty—to criticize that order on behalf of the public good.[21]

And indeed, from its perpetual perch just beyond the established corridors of power this newly self-fashioned Republic of Letters could plausibly claim to impose upon the Old Regime a "Reign of Critique," in Voltaire's felicitous phrase. For it quickly came to occupy within that world a singular if not paradoxical institutional terrain: subject still to royal censorship, the men of letters were at the same time persecuted and sustained by a central government, which, beset by crisis, was seeking simultaneously to fend off their criticisms and enlist their support. Thus, while Diderot, for example, was imprisoned several times for his writings, and Voltaire was ultimately forced into exile for his, both men enjoyed the discreet patronage of government officials. Others, such as Turgot who had made anonymous contributions to the *Encyclopédie* before his royal appointment in 1774 to the monarchy's highest official post, were at once members of the government and the Republic of Letters. Accordingly, as Reinhart Koselleck has put it, the Republic of Letters could claim to be "nonpartisan" and "above politics" even while "it was in fact political." Taking refuge in his outsider's status but always cognizant of his proximity to power, the new man of letters could portray his "all-encompassing critique" of the state as a disinterested service to society. In fact, "[p]ushing criticism to its utmost limits," he could construct himself before his chosen public as "the king of kings, the true sovereign." [22]

The French men of letters, in sum, successfully constituted themselves as a shadow government of words in permanent and public-spirited opposition to the established order—that is, as a veritable established anti-establishment. In so doing, they would seem to have appropriated already under the Old Regime that privileged access to "cultural capital"—to employ Pierre Bourdieu's ironic terminology—which has since defined the stature of the intelligentsia in modern France.[23] Indeed, such previously cited institutions as the University of Paris and the École Normale Supérieure would appear to function, in this light, as nothing less than a permanent, state-sponsored "society of letters" embedded within the cultural infrastructure of modern France.

Within the eighteenth-century Republic of Letters itself, however, which was so uniquely located both at the core and the periphery of the monarchy, an equally paradoxical cultural space came to be occupied during the 1750s and 1760s by the idiosyncratic figure of Rousseau. A friend of Diderot's and an early contributor to the *Encyclopédie*, Rousseau, as is well known, gained notoriety through his scathing denunciation of civilized society, first in his *Discours sur les sciences et les arts* (1750), and then again in his *Discours sur l'origine et les fondements de l'inégalité parmi les hommes* (1754). While both works condemned the corrupting influence of the arts and sciences, and hence implicitly of the Republic of Letters itself,[24] it was only in his *Lettre à d'Alembert sur les spectacles* (1758) that Rousseau broke publicly, as Robert Darnton has put it, "with the literary system of his time." Addressing himself not only to the Encyclopedists, but "to a whole people . . . to the public," Rousseau frames his work as a defense of his native Geneva—whose "ancient liberty" he likens to that of Sparta—against the morally debasing character of the theater. But discernable just beneath its surface is an assault both upon the cultivated society of Paris, "where everything is judged by appearances," and upon "the literary men who shine" within it. Rousseau, in effect, denounced the French Enlightenment's new world of letters for its deleterious effect on morals.[25]

If the *Lettre* helped precipitate Rousseau's notorious public rift with Diderot, d'Alembert, and "the party of the philosophes," the publication in 1761 of his novel, *La Nouvelle Héloïse,* rendered the rupture permanent. Before what would become one of the largest reading publics of the eighteenth century, Rousseau reiterated his critique of "the fashionable world [*le beau monde*]." "This book," he warns his reader, "is not made to circulate in society [*le monde*]. . . . It will displease religious bigots, libertines, and philosophes." Indeed, he assures his audience that the novel's principals "are not French, not sophisticates, not academicians nor philosophes but rather provincials, foreigners, recluses, young people." Thus, in both of these works, Rousseau, no less than his Enlightenment peers, addresses "the public" on its own behalf. Yet in each he links the Republic of Letters and its patrons inextricably to the high society of the Old Regime, which he condemns as corrupt and detrimental to the public good. Thereby Rousseau became, in Koselleck's words, the first philosophe "to direct his criticism with equal vehemence against the existing state and its social critics."[26]

Rousseau's self-anointment as the official "antiphilosophe" of the Republic of Letters[27] would appear all the more conspicuous when placed alongside its living antithesis in Voltaire, who had successfully cast himself as the Republic's "leading citizen" and "patriarch."[28] For Rousseau's *Lettre à d'Alembert* had constituted not only a broad swipe at the "party of the philosophes," but a transparent indictment of the illustrious poet and playwright who was then crown prince of the Genevan stage. The ensuing and increasingly public quarrel between Rousseau and Voltaire has continued to reverberate in French political culture ever since.[29]

Symbolically speaking, the contrast between the two could hardly be more marked. Voltaire, the *haute-bourgeois* son of a prominent government official in Paris, became the city's most renowned expatriate in 1726 after being caned by street thugs in the hire of a noble whom he had dared to insult. In 1734, after he had returned from exile in England, the French reading public was treated to a pirated French version of his *Letters on England,* which championed Newtonian science and Lockeian "negative liberty"—civic, religious, and economic—against the iniquities of the established church and absolutist state.[30] Thereafter, whether from the provincial estate of his aristocratic mistress Madame du Châtelet, the royal court of Frederick the Great in Prussia, or the pages of the *Encyclopédie,* Voltaire proceeded to inflict his previously cited "reign of critique" upon France's Old Order. Yet he scarcely renounced "civilization" as such. Even while launching his poisonous literary arrows at the Old Regime's social and ecclesiastical hierarchy, Voltaire steadfastly promoted the ostensibly more civil and egalitarian society now embodied in the Parisian salon and the Republic of Letters itself. In principle, neither material prosperity nor even the institutional trappings of crown and court incited the moral outrage of the Republic's first citizen. On the contrary, Voltaire remained distinctly unabashed by his own considerable private fortune as well as the numerous public honors conferred on him both by the French monarchy and his fellow philosophes. A proud member since 1745, for example, of the Académie Française, he lived to see a full-length statue of himself erected in 1770 by his apostles in the Republic of Letters. Eight years later, when the 84-year-old patriarch triumphantly re-entered the city of his birth and subsequent exile to attend a staging of one of his plays, he was greeted by overflowing crowds and the cry of "Vive le roi Voltaire." Following the play, he was mobbed by admirers and literally crowned with a wreath of laurels.[31]

In breaking with this living icon of the Republic of Letters, then, Rousseau broke equally with the proto-"liberal bourgeois"—but hardly democratic or revolutionary—social vision that he personified. And surely no man was better placed to do so than this gifted prodigal son of a Swiss clockmaker. Rousseau, as shall be seen, in seeking to make plausible his ever-expanding condemnation of civilized society, could and did exploit his autobiographical credentials as an indigenous outsider both to France's established order and to the new "established anti-establishment" at its core. Indeed, his schism with Voltaire and the Republic of Letters enabled him ultimately to forge "his own myth," in Dena Goodman's words, "of the solitary seeker of truth, the lone man of virtue in a corrupt world."[32]

In other words, if Voltaire would seem to have been a forerunner of Bourdieu's university-based "philosophical high priest," who stands both critically detached from and entrenched within the established order, Rousseau represents the very prototype of the consecrated heretic, who earns his paradoxical renown by virtue of publicly denouncing both the established order and its established critics. In fact, the notorious Enlightenment rift between Rousseau and Voltaire has since helped mark the cultural divide between the previously cited "radical intellectual tradition" in modern France, and its less radical, or more "liberal," intellectual counterparts.[33]

Reflecting their Rousseauian heritage, modern France's consecrated heretics have characteristically opposed themselves—or been placed in public opposition—to intellectual rivals of a more "authorized" persuasion. A particularly vivid case in point is that of Bergson and the eminent sociologist Émile Durkheim, two figures who constituted, as had Voltaire and Rousseau in their day, the intellectual giants of the French Republic of Letters at the turn of the century. By 1902, these former normalien classmates stood symbolically face to face atop the academic pyramid of Paris: Durkheim, the official sociologist of republican "solidarity," in a chair at the Sorbonne expressly created for him by the state; and Bergson, his official Rousseauian nemesis, contesting the Third Republic's philosophical order from his chair at the Collège de France. Similarly—and at approximately the same time—Péguy found and denounced his own Voltaire in Jean Jaurès, a fellow normalien, would-be revolutionary socialist, and former Dreyfusard comrade-in-arms, after the latter had allegedly engineered a series of parliamentary compromises with the Republic. And Sartre, by the same token, publicly severed relations with (among others) Raymond Aron—who was, like Durkheim, a distinguished liberal intellectual and erstwhile normalien classmate—for his failure to repudiate the "bourgeois West" in favor of communist revolution.[34]

Such latter-day heretics as Michelet, Bergson, Péguy, Sartre, and Foucault may be viewed, in sum, as the institutionalized Rousseaus of modern France—as intellectuals who, whether under the conscious sway of the Genevan antiphilosophe or not, became publicly cast in his self-fashioned role of internal opposition to the established social order and the Republic of Letters that produced him. On the other hand, such revolutionary-era figures as Robespierre and Stendhal were Rousseauians of a more conscious and immediate sort. The former, while producing no distinctive literary or philosophical works of note, remained—in the apt formulation of David Jordan—a "literary intellectual" nonetheless, who was steeped in the revolutionary cult of Rousseau. A founding and ultimately leading member of the Jacobin Club, the most radical among those extraparliamentary societies that were to the Revolution what literary salons had been to the Enlightenment, Robespierre modeled his public persona directly after his idol's by then acclaimed autobiography, *Les Confessions*. It was above all through that work, in fact, that Rousseau had established himself posthumously before the French reading public as an island of virtue amidst a sea of vice. Hence, even at the height of his power, as shall shortly be seen, Rousseau's most famous disciple continued to pose as the righteous public gadfly within an ever-degenerating social order. Indeed, Robespierre has remained "an immortal figure" within French political culture, in the words of François Furet, not by virtue of his philosophical originality or even his brief hour of political ascendancy, but rather "because he was the mouthpiece" of the Revolution's "purest and most tragic discourse."[35]

Stendhal, on the other hand, represents a more ambiguous case. In his own public person, first of all, the novelist scarcely cut the figure of the Rousseauian heretic. A Napoleonic soldier and official in his youth, Stendhal was at most, thereafter, a self-described "fanatical republican" who remained aloof nevertheless from political engagement and outspoken cultural radicalism. During his own lifetime, in fact, he was neither particularly well known nor widely read. As a writer Stendhal sought expressly to "de-Rousseauify himself"—to escape from the "pedantry," "bombast," "insincerity," and "artificiality" with which, in his autobiographical *Vie de Henri Brulard* (1836), he saddled his illustrious Genevan predecessor.[36]

Yet Stendhal's oeuvre, both fictional and autobiographical, betrays an unmistakable and enduring debt to Rousseau—especially to *La Nouvelle Héloïse, Émile,* and *Les Confessions*. In fact, contemporary scholarship depicts a Stendhal ensnared despite himself within the Rousseauian web. Michel Crouzet suggests, for example, that the novelist found not an "influence" in the eighteenth-century antiphilosophe so much as "a model man . . . whom the more one imitates or contests, the more carries within oneself." Moreover, it is above all *Le Rouge et le noir,* Stendhal's masterpiece of 1830, that most clearly sustains the novelist's own once professed belief that his fictions were nothing but "the works of Rousseau." The renowned tale of Julien Sorel, who ascends from provincial lower-class origins to the heights of success and scandal in Paris, would seem a conspicuous recasting of Rousseau's legendary saga. It is not surprising, then, to find more than one literary critic echoing Marjorie Taylor's contention that Julien was meant to personify "Rousseau's 'homme naturel' or 'libre.'"[37] Indeed, Stendhal's own rise to cultural prominence following his death in 1842 has derived largely from *Le Rouge et le noir* and its subversive hero. For Julien Sorel stands among the most notorious and revered characters in modern French fiction—the very incarnation, in Nancy Rosenblum's terms, of that "romantic militancy" that emerged both within and against the corrupt, egoistic universe of the Restoration that supplanted the Revolution.[38] For the purposes of this essay, therefore, Stendhal's master work will be regarded as an archetypal myth of consecrated heresy within modern France, and its celebrated protagonist, rather than its author, will be treated as a representative Rousseauian prophet.

IV. THE HERETICAL NARRATIVE

If these eight figures—Rousseau, Robespierre, Michelet, Bergson, Péguy, Sartre, Foucault, and Stendhal's alter-ego, Julien Sorel—would seem culturally and even institutionally entrenched within modern France as consecrated heretics,[39] what exactly constitutes their heresy? Or, to recast the question in the poststructuralist idiom of the most recent heretic Foucault, what accepted "linguistic practices," or "discourses of truth," within modern French political culture have "privileged" the intellectual insurrections of Foucault and his ilk as opposed to "marginalizing" them?[40]

What follows here will seek to answer these questions precisely by distilling from the public biographies and the most celebrated texts and motifs of the consecrated heretics a relatively fixed intellectual tradition or "master narrative"[41]—that is, a common saga of freedom which has helped structure their public personas and discourse and, by consequence, the political culture of modern France. Hence, special— though not exclusive—attention will be paid to Rousseau's previously mentioned discourses of 1750 and 1754, which first established his celebrity, and to his *Lettre à d'Alembert sur les spectacles* (1758), *La Nouvelle Héloïse* (1761), *Émile* (1762), *Du Contrat social* (1762), and *Les Confessions* (1781) thereafter; to Robespierre's speeches before the National Convention following his rise to political prominence in the spring of 1791; to Michelet's best-sellers *Du Prêtre, de la femme, et de la famille* (1845), *Le Peuple* (1846), and *Histoire de la revolution française* (1847–53), which appeared following his appointment to the Collège de France in 1838, as well as his posthumous autobiographical works, *Ma jeunesse* and *Mémorial;*[42] to Bergson's works of the pre-

1914 era, above all *Essai sur les données immédiates de la conscience* (1889) and *L'Évolution créatrice* (1907), which reflect his philosophical stance during his own tenure at the Collège de France; to Péguy's essays of the 1905–14 period, and especially his much acclaimed *Notre jeunesse* of 1910; to Sartre's oeuvre between the publication of *La Nausée* (1938) and his autobiographical *Les Mots* (1963), most notably to his acclaimed wartime plays, *Les Mouches* (1943) and *Huis clos* (1944), his three-part novel *Les Chemins de la liberté* (1945–47), and his philosophical tomes, *L'Etre et le néant* (1943) and *Critique de la raison dialectique* (1960); and to Foucault's major works and published interviews between 1968 and the early 1980s,[43] particularly *Surveiller et punir* (1975) and *La Volonté de savoir* (1976), which both appeared subsequent to his own appointment to the Collège de France in 1970.* Finally, Stendhal's *Le Rouge et le noir* will be treated here quite literally as a "master fiction." For the purposes of clarity—if not correct historical sequence—it will serve to delineate at the outset of each chapter that aspect of the heretical narrative to be addressed therein.

The following analysis, then, constitutes neither a series of intellectual biographies nor of "great works" and seminal ideas placed into their respective historical contexts.[44] Indeed, making no attempt to evoke the multifaceted particularity either of its *dramatis personae* or their texts, it deliberately de-emphasizes what is historically unique, contradictory, or evolving in their personal biographies and oeuvre in favor of that which is structurally constant or repeated both within their works and the "heretical community" as a whole. Underscoring not the complex and enigmatic intellectual itineraries of those individuals who have imparted the heretical tradition in modern France so much as that tradition's fixed cultural architecture, it is organized thematically rather than chronologically. Its chapters, accordingly, are arranged so as to reflect the narrative structures, tropes, and repeated motifs that have characterized the community as a whole. Thus, chapter 2 addresses the biographical saga of the consecrated heretic and its cultural "moral"; chapter 3 investigates the theme of personal freedom and dependency in the heretical narrative; chapter 4 examines the motif of social subjugation and the coinciding critique of "civilized society" in same; and chapter 5 explores the dynamics of liberation—

---

*The autobiographical writings of the consecrated heretics will be supplemented, as shall shortly be seen, by popular biographical and historical accounts culled from the French academic world and beyond.

both individual and communal—within the heretical narrative, and their ultimate political ramifications. What follows, in sum, is an attempt to assemble an historical portrait of consecrated heresy in modern France—of its values, assumptions, and above all its vision of freedom—and to reconstruct thereby that historical mythos, or "master fiction," of revolutionary liberty that would seem to have resonated so powerfully within French political culture from the eighteenth century to the present day.

TWO

THE MYTH OF THE
CONSECRATED HERETIC

I. THE MASTER FICTION: JULIEN SOREL

Joseph Campbell once maintained that, until the modern

age, myths and legends the world over portrayed a single

"hero with a thousand faces." Beneath any number of pre-

modern myths both in the West and beyond, he argued,

might be discerned a common narrative structure consisting

of the hero's "Departure," "Initiation," and "Return." Hav-

ing ventured forth, that is, "from the world of common day

into a region of supernatural wonder," Campbell's universal

hero ultimately wins "a decisive victory," which enables him

to return to the realm of the commonplace "with power to

bestow on his fellow man."[1]

Campbell lamented the disappearance of such heroic

myths under the harsh light of the secular revolutions—sci-

entific, economic, and political—that heralded the modern

age in the West. But a glance at contemporary biographi-

cal accounts of such "consecrated heretics" as Sartre and Foucault suggests that Campbell's death notice for the mythic hero was perhaps
premature. Placing Sartre, for example, at the head of a list including
Rousseau, Hugo, and Zola, Annie Cohen-Solal cites "the charismatic,
symbolic, and mythological aura of the intellectual in French history."
Another of Sartre's biographers, Ronald Hayman, concludes that his
subject has achieved immortality through "giving his own experiences
the quality of myth." And James Miller, by the same token, has recently
suggested that Foucault, at the time of his death, "was universally regarded" in France "as *un maître à penser*—a master of thought, the
affectionate phrase the French use for the handful of Olympian figures
they invest with sovereign authority."[2]

Through detailing the universal outcry at their deaths, moreover—
a recitation which seems to have become a convention of the genre—
the public portraits of these "Olympian figures" traditionally evoke the
broad popular following they commanded. "Traffic was halted," writes
Hayman, setting the scene of Sartre's public funeral,

> as the procession, moving slowly through the streets, doubled in
> size and went on growing till about 50,000 people were following
> the coffin. It was like a demonstration, bigger than any he had
> attended while alive. For days the newspapers had been publishing
> articles about Sartre, and the Parisians who had not turned out
> into the streets were watching the procession on television.[3]

Priscilla Clark likens the same spectacle to the popular American out-
pouring following the assassination of John F. Kennedy. Corresponding accounts of the public mourning on behalf of other modern French
"Olympians" would seem cast in no less legendary a mold. Thus Rousseau, writes Daniel Mornet for example, while passing away in solitude, "was buried like a poet, like a prophet," and his grave attracted
crowds and public "pilgrimages" thereafter. And despite what one of
them describes as "the voluntarily discreet, even half-secret nature" of
Foucault's funeral, the philosopher's memorialists are agreed that at his
passing "[t]he chorus enshrined Foucault as another exemplary French
intellectual." James Miller, for one, citing the eulogies which "flooded
the media" from "all corners of the country," concludes that in France
Foucault "was regarded as a kind of national treasure."[4]

Campbell's lament notwithstanding, then, such public elegies suggest that the era of the French Revolution, one of modernity's defining moments, gave birth to a new hero in France—the intellectual
heretic—and that the latter would seem culturally invested, in his own

way, with mythic powers to "bestow" on "his fellow man" in "the world of common day." But if so, if certain French intellectuals have in fact acquired such a "mythological aura," what constitutes their mythology, and what "mythic powers" do these modern, secular heroes claim to manifest? By what common narrative, in other words, may the consecrated heretic be recognized, and which cultural values does that narrative advance?

Such a mythos may be sought at least in part through the public self-portraits of the intellectuals themselves; for the tradition of public autobiography has been powerfully represented in France since the eighteenth century. Indeed, Philippe Lejeune has gone so far as to contend that modern autobiography itself, reflecting such new eighteenth-century discursive categories as "the person" and "the public," begins with Rousseau's *Les Confessions,* the first six volumes of which appeared in 1781. Thereafter, he concludes, autobiographical discourse both in France and beyond has remained an attempt "to construct oneself" before the public as a coherent whole, to elaborate one's "personal myth [*synthèse du moi*]" as a self-revelatory narrative, which, departing from the earliest years of childhood, seeks to establish "the deep unity of a life" and hence its authentic "meaning." [5]

The immediate authority of this Rousseauian model over the likes of Robespierre and Stendhal has already been established. The former, while composing no finished autobiographical text himself, found in *Les Confessions* the "unequivocal and courageous emanation of the purest soul." The Jacobin leader, therefore, all but embraced Rousseau's autobiography as his own, shaping his public career according to the narrative scheme of his idol. "Divine man," he exclaims in his *Dedication à Rousseau,* "you have taught me to know myself." Indeed, David Jordan goes so far as to suggest that Robespierre's metamorphosis from obscure provincial into "self-conscious revolutionary," his willful construction of a Rousseauian revolutionary persona—itself the product not of heroic deeds but "verbal acts"—was his "most enduring creation." [6] Stendhal, likewise, notwithstanding his previously cited wish to "de-Rousseauify" himself, confessed to writing his own memoirs in the shadow of *Les Confessions,* cringing at any comparison between his own autobiography and "the masterpiece of that great writer." Furthermore, *Le Rouge et le noir* itself, as suggested above, may be viewed as a reframing of Rousseau's autobiographical melodrama against the backdrop of the Revolution and its aftermath, a reformulation of *Les Confessions* as postrevolutionary myth. [7]

While not always so conspicuously, the Rousseauian autobiographical model remains discernable in nearly all the consecrated heretics of later generations. Michelet and Péguy, as shall be seen, continued to view *Les Confessions* as a frame of reference for their own autobiographical writings, and Sartre, while fashioning *Les Mots*—in Lejeune's words—"as a critique of the myth of childhood" and a "demystification of the bourgeois myth of the writer," did so from within the traditional Rousseauian model of authentic public self-revelation.* Even Foucault, who must be counted as foremost among those poststructuralist critics who have recently repudiated Rousseauian confession as the very embodiment of the coercive "ideology of the person," offered the public notorious glimpses of self-revelation in several coyly revealing interviews. In fact, Miller, citing Foucault's avowal, in one such exchange, that each of his books represents the "fragment of an autobiography," and in another, that "there is not a book I have written that does not grow, at least in part, out of a direct, personal experience," has read the philosopher's entire oeuvre as a veiled autobiography.[8]

Bergson alone, among the public prophets in question, left no explicitly autobiographical texts. Yet, as recently suggested by R. C. Grogin, even Bergson may be viewed as an "artist" who consciously constructed his own "Janus image" before the press and the public. Such an interpretation underscores the increasing participation since the nineteenth century of biographers, journalists, essayists, and historians in the fashioning of modern France's consecrated heretic; indeed, the biographical discourse would seem at times to have helped demarcate the very confines of a given intellectual's legend. Even those commentators who remain acutely aware of their subject's mythic persona would appear unable to escape its cultural field of gravity. Hence, Didier Eribon's biography of Foucault, for example, which seeks to evade the paradox of lionizing a subject who explicitly repudiated the modern discourse of "the subject"—and, periodically, to unmask the groundless myths associated with him—nonetheless abounds with such romanticized passages as the following depiction of the philosopher at his doctoral defense in 1961: "Foucault's voice rose: tense, nervous, unfolding in rhythmic, staccato sentences. Every statement was

---

*John Gerassi recounts that, as a young man, Sartre found himself "fascinated" by Rousseau, and even more so by Stendhal. "'Stendhal,' the existentialist reportedly recollected, 'was my favorite; I wanted to be a modern-day Stendhal'" (*Protestant or Protestor?* vol. 1 of *Jean-Paul Sartre: Hated Conscience of his Century* (Chicago: University of Chicago Press, 1989, 75).

as polished as a diamond." Similarly, while undertaking to debunk Sartre's myth as "the great philosopher-novelist-playwright-journalist
who made some mistakes but was a great man," John Gerassi nevertheless glorifies the existentialist in his own portrait as an "*adulte terrible,*
who never once betrayed the underdog, the banished, the outcast, the
doomed."[9]

What follows here attempts to discern what might be deemed the
"public biography" of modern France's consecrated heretic: the common narrative, that is, arising out of the self-portraits through which
the consecrated heretics have helped shape their own public personae,
and such popular secondary portraits as those cited above.* But the
myth of the heroic intellectual will be evoked here, first of all, through
the archetypal character and tale of Julien Sorel. For if the saga of
Rousseau represents the seminal fable of the radical intelligentsia in

---

*While I shall, wherever possible, give primacy to the firsthand self-characterizations
of my subjects over secondary accounts of their lives, Rousseau is the only one among,
them to have submitted a more or less complete self-portrait and, as noted above, the
likes of Robespierre, Bergson, and Foucault left no explicitly autobiographical texts at
all. In lieu, however, of surveying the entire biographical literature on the consecrated
heretics—an operation which would yield a book in itself—I will employ select secondary accounts according to the following criteria: (1) how recently they have been published, and therefore how comprehensively they survey earlier biographical literature; (2)
how attentive they are to the self-fabrication of their subject's public persona; and (3)
how uncritically panegyrical they are, and therefore arguably reflective of that persona.
Thus, on Robespierre, apart from his public speeches, which were habitually couched in
the idiom of Rousseauian self- revelation, I will be guided above all by David Jordan's
1985 work, *The Revolutionary Career of Maximilien Robespierre,* which, as previously
noted, treats the Jacobin's political career precisely as a self-constructed Rousseauian
myth and relies heavily, therefore, on its subject's own words. I will also consult Norman
Hampson's *The Life and Opinions of Maximilien Robespierre* (London: Duckworth,
1974) and George Rudé's *Robespierre, Portrait of a Revolutionary Democrat* (New
York: Viking Press, 1975), both of which comment explicitly on the historical construction of Robespierre's legend. On Michelet, aside from the posthumous confessionals
found in his *Écrits de jeunesse* as well as autobiographical musings in several of
his published works, I will rely on Roland Barthes's *Michelet* (trans. Richard Howard
[New York: Hill and Wang, 1987]), which is acutely sensitive to the historian's self-
mythologization, and on two more recent biographies: Stephen A. Kippur, *Jules Michelet*
(Albany: State University of New York Press, 1981), and Linda Orr, *Jules Michelet:
Nature, History, Language* (Ithaca: Cornell University Press, 1976). On Bergson I will
consult R. C. Grogin's previously cited work, which has the virtue, like Jordan's portrait
of Robespierre, of analyzing its subject in terms of his cultural legend. That legend,
which is faithfully—if perhaps unwittingly—mirrored by H. Stuart Hughes (*Consciousness and Society* [New York: Vintage Books, 1958]), was established at least in part by
a number of the philosopher's devoted and subsequently renowned disciples, including
Raissa Maritain, Georges Sorel, Jacques Chevalier, and Charles Péguy, whose testimonials will also be cited. Péguy's own autobiographical reflections were collected by his son

modern France, Stendhal's fictional allegory, encompassing both that fable and its revolutionary postscript, offers a synopsis of the master fiction as a whole—an archetype, in other words, of the hero and plot structure within which the myth of the heroic intellectual would seem to have been framed in modern France.

Julien Sorel must have appeared to the nineteenth-century French reader as nothing if not a postrevolutionary Jean-Jacques. The motherless son of a provincial peasant whom he detests, the youth is not only precociously literate—we initially encounter him indulging his "passion for reading"—but as we later find, despite a critical attitude toward their author, he has committed to memory passages from *La Nouvelle Héloïse* and *Les Confessions*. Having acquired from the latter work Rousseau's "horror of eating with servants," Julien is most often spurred to action by an even greater "horror of contempt"— a proud aversion, despite his humble social standing, to submission before his superiors. Thus, Stendhal portrays the youth as both exceptionally intelligent and, above all, "strong willed"; in short, as a "man of spirit," even a spiritual noble: pure of will and fiercely independent.[10]

The hero's saga is no less extraordinary than his persona. Inspired by the legendary example of another talented Rousseauian outsider, Napoleon, whose "Bulletins of the Grande Armée" and *Mémorial de Sainte-Hélène* "filled out his Koran," Julien seeks fame and fortune within a Restoration universe just as hierarchical and degenerate as that of prerevolutionary France. His rise in that world, accordingly, precipitates an ongoing inner struggle to maintain his psychic purity against the corruptions of society. But while ever grappling with his own self-centered ambition, Stendhal's hero ultimately prefers to risk social catastrophe than compromise the integrity of his will. Hence, it is reckless impetuosity rather than calculated self-interest that first earns Julien notoriety in the provincial world of Verrières where,

---

in a previously cited volume entitled *Souvenirs,* and his legend, again well reflected by Hughes, is also displayed in two romantic memorials written by former compatriots— Jean and Jérome Tharaud, *Notre cher Péguy* (Paris: Plon, 1927); and Daniel Halévy, *Péguy and the Cahiers de la Quinzaine,* trans. Ruth Bethel (New York: Longman's, Green, and Co., 1947)—as well as a similar testimonial by Romain Rolland. Finally, I will supplement the self-portrait provided by Sartre in *Les Mots* and in occasional public interviews with the previously cited works of Cohen-Solal, Hayman, and Gerassi; and Foucault's autobiographical interviews with the portraits of Eribon and Miller. These latter widely publicized biographies of Sartre and Foucault, I would argue, both attend to the self-mythologization of their subjects and at times mirror it unselfconsciously.

flouting the social hierarchy, he cuts a visibly bold figure in an elite honor guard on behalf of the visiting king. Despite the public outcry, reports Stendhal's narrator, Julien shortly thereafter becomes "the fashion; people excused his donning of the guard uniform, or rather that act of folly was the real cause of his success."[11]

In Paris, it is Julien's energetic independence of spirit that first attracts the aristocratic Marquis de La Mole, who finds him "an original" capable "of the unexpected," and then the marquis's daughter Mathilde, who ranks him above suitors of her own station as a man whose qualities of soul "might get him condemned to death." Again, it is not Julien's conventional ambition that compels Mathilde, but rather his willful refusal of personal dependence. "Never in this favored being," she muses, "the slightest idea of seeking support from other people! He despises other people, and that is why I don't despise him." And in conquering the proud, sophisticated, beautiful, and vain Mathilde, in whom he sees "the ideal of Paris," Julien symbolically masters the capital city itself.[12]

But even while, by virtue of superior energy and intellect, he becomes the darling of a social world that once held him in contempt, Julien manages to remain fundamentally uncorrupted by it and to become its unforgiving mirror and critic. Contemptuous, for example, of a careerist Catholic Church for which, in the narrator's words, "inward submission is all," Julien finds in Paris as well only "[v]anity, dry and arrogant, every conceivable variety of self-approval [amour-propre]." Thus, Stendhal's protagonist would appear to express the author's repugnance for an increasingly egoistic, bourgeois world in which both spiritual faith and "genuine passion" have been replaced by small-minded profit and advancement. Fearing that even "the great Danton" would have "sold out" in "this century of Valenods and Rênals," Julien yearns throughout the novel for the days of his hero Napoleon when "there was a sort of grandeur in everything that men did." Indeed, the narrator depicts Julien at the very pinnacle of his social success as a man with "the look of a criminal outlaw . . . at war with his whole society."[13]

Ultimately, defending his honor against the charge of his former lover, Madame de Rênal, that he has exploited her in order "to find a position and rise in the world," Julien fires at and wounds her; and through this violent act of transgression he sacrifices his ambition and severs his ties to society. Thereafter, Julien repudiates the civilized Parisian Mathilde, whom he finds overly conscious of "a public and *other people*" (Stendhal's emphasis), and along with her the capital city itself: "He never thought of his success in Paris," remarks the narrator; "he was bored by it." Instead Stendhal's hero finds himself again "madly in love" with Madame de Rênal, a country woman of instinctive generosity and passion.[14] In short, Julien symbolically disavows civilized society and its corruptions in favor of genuine love and primal integrity of will.

But impelled again by his "horror of contempt," the hero's final act before submitting to the guillotine is to confess his crimes before the public. Julien couches his confession, however, as an indictment by "a peasant in open revolt" against the "good society" of his accusers. Thus, while claiming to harbor "no illusions" about himself and acknowledging his crime as "atrocious" and "premeditated," he casts himself before the public as an isolated martyr. Posing as a bold spokesman for those "born to a lower social order," Julien angrily denounces his judges, among whom he finds not "a single rich peasant, only outraged bourgeois."[15] Stendhal, in short, by having his hero choose tragic isolation over ignoble compromise, presents him as an authentic culture-hero; and in this light, Julien's public self-revelation emerges not as personal confession so much as powerful social criticism.[16]

Stendhal's cultural fable, in sum, may be outlined as follows:

1. The youthful protagonist, marked as precociously intelligent and literate—indeed as someone whose ambitions are shaped by the words of Rousseau and Napoleon—is noteworthy as well for his social misanthropy and, above all, for his vigorous independence of will. As his father's rebellious son and a provincial member of the popular classes, he is well situated to enact the role of defiant outsider seeking entry into the hierarchical fortress of civilized society whose symbolic apex is Paris.

2. The hero's innate prowess, both intellectual and personal, allows him to penetrate that fortress, and his ascent within it—achieved largely through the seduction and support of adoring women—betrays a deep ambivalence; an inner struggle, that is, between his vital and untainted will and the corrupting influence of society. Paradoxically it is the former trait, his willful audacity, that ultimately transports him to the very summit of a social world that had once disdained him.

3. Even as he triumphs within the established order, the hero struggles continuously to remain at a distance from it; he styles himself, accordingly, as its relentless critic. Harshly mirroring the petty egoism and hypocrisy, the political corruption, the avarice, and the spiritual

slavishness of bourgeois Parisian civilization, he remains a model of unconventional and insubordinate behavior until he finally commits an act of transgression—not to say symbolic revolution—against the established order.

4. Thereafter, the tale ends in tragedy: martyred through his own refusal to compromise, the hero finds himself isolated, betrayed, and persecuted; and his final act is to offer himself through sincere self-revelation as "the people's" prophet, a public paragon of authenticity and unblemished liberty.

While the public life narratives of seven so disparate individuals as those under discussion here could not be expected literally to replicate the saga of Julien Sorel, that tale's essential structure—including the hero's character and origins; his rise to celebrity; his public critique of the established order and transgression against it; and his martyrdom and confession—would seem to embody a tacit cultural archetype within which the heroic legends of the consecrated heretics have been erected.[17] Rousseau's celebrated self-portrait, of course, inasmuch as it served largely as Stendhal's model for *Le Rouge et le noir*[18] remains that archetype's historical point of reference and faithful mirror; and so too, for the most part, does the public biography of Robespierre, who deliberately fashioned himself after the legend of Rousseau. For the heretics of later generations, on the other hand, this paradigmatic plot of the revolutionary era would appear to constitute the fixed mold within which their heroic legends have been cast. Accordingly, as shall be seen, where the actualities of a given intellectual's biography more or less corresponded to the myth, his public legend has tended to emphasize or exaggerate them; but those biographical "facts" that diverged from the model would seem often modified, de-emphasized, or marginalized.

II. THE HERETIC AND HIS ORIGINS

The consecrated heretic, according to the Stendhalian model, is an uncorrupted "man of the people" armed only with singular intelligence and an autonomous will. He is therefore identified from the outset both as a socially misanthropic stranger to the Parisian establishment—which requires, at least in theory, that he be either of provincial or foreign origins and a member of the popular classes—and precociously literate.

Rousseau, as might be expected, incarnates the ideal-type. As the rebellious son of a Swiss clockmaker, the author of *Les Confessions* represents himself throughout his autobiography, in terms of social class and nationality, as the ultimate outsider to the intricate hierarchy of Old Regime Paris. Asking rhetorically, for example, why he had encountered so few "good people" during his Parisian years as opposed to his youth in Geneva, he replies that among le peuple "natural feeling" is not "absolutely stifled" as it is in "the higher ranks." And identifying himself perpetually with the "the weaker party" and the "oppressed," he proclaims: "[A]s a foreigner living in France I found my position most favorable for truth-telling." [19]

Rousseau also reconstructs his childhood so as to set himself further apart from the civilized mainstream. Deprived of a mother in childbirth, he reports having been frequently at odds with his father; yet he also recollects having been "idolized" as a child "by everyone around . . . [him]" and shielded from contact with other children. What is more, this self-fashioned man of the people depicts the young Jean-Jacques as nothing if not an embryonic man of letters, having learned to read at an early age and then become a devourer of books: "I read till my head spun, I did nothing but read." Indeed, Rousseau apologizes to his readers for what he calls "setting myself up as a prodigy"; but he then challenges them to "find a child who is attracted by novels at six, who is interested and moved by them to the point of weeping hot tears." [20]

Proposing, moreover, in the celebrated opening paragraph of Les Confessions, to paint "a portrait in every way true to nature," Rousseau discovers in his own persona that "natural man" who, in previous works, he had embodied in such characters as the "noble savage," Émile, and Saint Preux. Endowed with an impulsive and "sensitive heart," Jean-Jacques concedes that while his behavior has at times been "culpable," his heart "was always pure." And he professes such a "loathing of untruth" as to behave "on all occasions with a sincerity verging upon rashness." Finally, Rousseau burdens his protagonist with an innate "love of solitude" bordering on the misanthropic, as well as "that proud and intractable spirit, that impatience with the yoke of servitude," which would "afflict" him throughout his life.[21] Expanding, then, on the narrative convention established by such eighteenth-century "masters of sensibilité" as Abbé Prévost in Manon Lescaut, the Genevan constructs his own persona as innately passionate but pure of heart and without guile; entirely sincere and authentic; at home more in solitude than society; and above all, willfully independent.[22] Thus, the author of Les Confessions, as would his disciple Stendhal, simultaneously highlights his hero's severe social disadvantages as a non-Parisian member of the popular classes, and endows him with the singularity of intellect and will necessary to overcome them.

While sketchy in its details and lacking any primary documentary underpinning, the public legend of Robespierre as a youth also emphasizes his intellectual precocity, his alien origins, and his social isolation. Indeed, whether portraying a monster or hero, Robespierre's biographers have characteristically depicted a solitary, impoverished boy from the provincial town of Arras who, rendered motherless at six and abandoned by his father two years later, nonetheless distinguished himself intellectually by winning a scholarship to study in Paris at the age of eleven.[23] Robespierre the student is conventionally portrayed as unpopular with his Parisian schoolmates and socially withdrawn. "A fair amount has been written," summarizes Norman Hampson, "about the humiliation of Robespierre, the scholarship boy, mixing—or refusing to mix—with wealthy boys who were a good deal less intelligent and hard-working than he was, but it's almost all conjecture." As for his character, the youth is reputed to have been inflexibly austere and self-disciplined, traits which of course portend his notorious revolutionary self-portrait as the "incorruptible" paragon of republican "virtue." Thus, the received account of Robespierre's youth marks him as the talented provincial outsider and "*homme du peuple*" destined to conquer Paris by virtue of his superior intellect and will.[24]

Where, as intimated above, the childhood of a future heretic more or less conformed to the mythic paradigm, it would seem emphasized or embellished in his public biography. Hence, Péguy, for example, helping to construct his own legend, makes much of his status as the only child of a widowed peasant from Orléans—whose poverty he in fact exaggerates.[25] Indeed "[o]ne can say in the most rigorous terms," he asserted in 1913, "that a child raised in a city like Orléans between 1873 and 1880 [the dates of his own childhood] literally touched Old France, the old people, that is: the people." And in the opening chapters of their own testimonials to Péguy, both Jean and Jérome Tharaud, and Daniel Halévy quote the same telling passage. Recollecting having been singled out as a prodigy—"an extraordinarily devoted and advanced child"—in his "provincial faubourg," Péguy recalls also that during his student days in Paris he was socially ostracized owing to his humble origins. Even while seeking to acquire "university elegance" at the École Normale Supérieure, he confesses to having been unable to rid himself of "*l'air peuple*." Indeed "one had only to look at me for a single instant," he recalls, "to know that . . . in me, around me, beneath me, without asking my permission, everything converged to make of me a peasant." The conventional account of Péguy at the École Normale, as summarized by H. Stuart Hughes, elaborates on the same theme. Viewed by his fellow students as "a misfit and an exotic," Hughes writes, they "could not help but respect him" nonetheless, even while finding him "a difficult man to live with." The "misfit's" early departure from the elite institution before entering the fight on behalf of Dreyfus also became part of his legend.[26]

Again, where "the facts" of origin conformed less conveniently to the mythic paradigm, they would appear glossed or modified in the heretic's public biography. Hence, the public legend of Bergson, for example, all but passes over his comfortable bourgeois childhood in Paris without comment and seems to begin only with his days as a student at the École Normale. There, however, the narrative rings familiar. Remarkable as a student, according to his disciple and biographer Jacques Chevalier, for his "intellectual superiority and reserve," Bergson was "little seen in public" and "was scarcely ever present in the company of his comrades, either in the École Normale or outside." By Chevalier's account, which is repeated by Hughes, the future prophet-renegade of French philosophy was once chastised by his classmates for having "no soul."[27]

Michelet, by the same token, who seeks quite directly in the preface of *Le Peuple* (1846) to fashion a public persona, dwells on his Parisian birth only long enough to note his father's Jacobin affiliations during the Revolution. He prefers instead to emphasize the humble social roots of his extended family. "[T]he two families from which I am descended," he writes, "one from Picardy and one from the Ardennes, were originally peasants who added a little industry to their agricultural pursuits."* The historian then goes on to detail the sacrifices made by both families in order to educate their sons, finally drawing the conclusion that he remains himself "still one of the people." The remainder of Michelet's parable of origins, moreover, conforms strikingly to the archetype. Like Rousseau, he reports having been "admired and celebrated" as a boy by all the adults around him, who were convinced that he would become "a great man." Bereaved by the early death of the only friend of his youth, he recounts a solitary childhood, which only worsened at his Parisian lycée. There, marked by his impov-

---

*One of Michelet's biographers, Stephen Kippur, suggests that insofar as his father's family was actually *petit bourgeois*, this tale fit only his mother's family (*Michelet*, 5).

erished background, he felt "alone against all" and "persecuted" by his bourgeois peers. "I fell into a misanthropic humor rare among children," he recollects in *Le Peuple*. "In the most deserted quarter of Paris . . . I sought the most deserted streets."[28]

Sartre, similarly, in fashioning his own public persona, finds himself forced to justify a pampered bourgeois upbringing; he does so, however, more through self-renunciation than denial. Hence, while recalling his provincial origins with affection in *Les Mots,* he reviles the "bourgeois optimism" of an unproblematic childhood during which he imagined himself the "champion of the established order." Even as he debunks his own myth, moreover, Sartre portrays himself as a youthful prodigy preparing for future greatness. Thus, he recalls having been "adored" by his mother after his father's death, and encouraged by his grandfather to make books his "sacred objects" and "to regard teaching as a priesthood and literature as a passion." With some irony, in fact, Sartre writes of having viewed his childhood as resembling "that of Jean-Jacques and Johann Sebastian." Once again, the social isolation of the heretic's early years emerges as a motif both in the writer's autobiography and in his biographical legend. Depicting himself at the age of eight, for instance, as "an only child without a friend," Sartre detects this same sense of solitude in the first fictional writings of his youth: "One against all, that was my rule."* His biographers add, citing autobiographical interviews, that after his family moved to La Rochelle the young Sartre—in what seems a striking reverse-image of the mythic narrative—became the bourgeois scapegoat for a gang of working-class youths. Sartre's public legend, finally, does not underscore his social interactions at school—for he was apparently quite popular with his schoolmates both at the lycée and the École Normale—but rather his iconoclastic relationship with authority: Sartre is charged—or rather credited—with masterminding a scandalous theatrical review that led to the resignation of Gustave Lanson, then president of the École and a symbol of the liberal Third Republic. "This image of a provoking, disrespectful, subversive Sartre," writes Annie Cohen-Solal, "recurs again and again, like a leitmotif, throughout his life."[29]

Foucault as well, in shaping his own public persona, felt constrained

---

*One of Sartre's biographers, Ronald Hayman (*Writing Against: A Biography of Sartre* [London: Weidenfeld and Nicolson, 1986], 27), notes that in portraying his childhood as "blanketingly negative," Sartre left out stories that clearly attest to his social success as a youth.

to distance himself from a childhood in Poitiers which, in a 1983 interview, he describes as *"petit bourgeois."* He recalls it with pronounced distaste: "[T]he obligation of speaking, of making conversation with visitors, was for me something both very strange and very boring." (It might be objected here that Foucault's childhood was even further removed from the heretical archetype than he intimates: the upper-middle-class home in which he was raised as the son of a highly respected surgeon was hardly *"petit bourgeois."*) What Foucault's notorious reticence about personal confession leaves blank, moreover, his biographers fill in with the conventional portrait of youthful alienation and intellectual precocity. "As one critic has summed up the evidence, which remains sketchy," writes Miller, "the young Paul-Michel seems to have 'suffered, like Zarathustra, in fierce if lofty isolation.'" And having described a school picture in which Foucault appears "utterly alone and utterly strange," Miller continues: "Aloof he may have been—but gifted as well." Eribon's characterization of Foucault at the École Normale, as "a solitary, unsociable boy" with "a pronounced tendency toward megalomania," which made him "almost universally detested," or Miller's image of the future prophet as "a very odd young man" whose violent "idiosyncrasies quickly set him apart," could almost as easily refer to Bergson, Péguy, or even Robespierre.[30]

The public biographies of these postrevolutionary heretics, then, not only portray them as provincial prodigies from the popular classes or, if necessary, recast their pedigrees so as better to fit the myth, but mark them as exceptionally autonomous youths—as "self-created," in the words of Sartre's biographer, Ronald Hayman.[31] Indeed, as sons who, for the most part, either lacked or openly contested their fathers— Péguy and Sartre were both deprived of theirs in infancy, Rousseau and Foucault quarreled turbulently with theirs, and Michelet viewed his as something of an ineffectual dreamer—the consecrated heretics tend to appear metaphorically, and sometimes literally, alienated from paternal authority. "The death of my father," writes Sartre for example, "was the great event of my life: it . . . gave me my freedom." Hence, "being nobody's son," he asserts in a celebrated phrase, "I was my own cause." Both of Foucault's biographers, by the same token, emphasize not only his hatred of his father but his refusal to emulate the surgeon's choice of a career; indeed, Miller goes so far as to suggest that the young Paul-Michel, haunted by the recurrent memory-nightmare of a "sadistic father" who had forced him "to witness an amputation," chose thereafter to become a lifelong critic of the latter's profession and its cultural potency.[32]

In light of such classic estrangement of sons from fathers, one need hardly be a Freudian to wonder if the paradigm of consecrated heresy in modern France might be traced to "oedipal hostility." It is surely significant, however, that the absence or repudiation of paternal authority in the childhood narratives of the heretics is plucked not from their "subconscious minds" but rather their own public self-representations; that it would seem to function within their biographical legends, in other words, not as a means of cataloging their psychological afflictions so much as establishing the willful independence and even misanthropy of their respective characters. Indeed, the budding heretic's social isolation, his misanthropy, and even his intellectual "megalomania" would seem to represent not "neuroses" or even character flaws within his public biography, so much as portents of future greatness. For insofar as the consecrated heretics ultimately attain renown for denouncing the established order even while succeeding within it, their childhood legends appear to highlight that which portends their future apostasy.

III. THE RISE TO CELEBRITY

According to the heretical archetype the hero's upward climb to social celebrity unfolds as a tale of the inner struggle between his primal purity of will and the self-interested ambition and vanity wrought by civilized society. But it is his very refusal to compromise the former, indeed his defiance of "society" in order to maintain it, that ironically transports him to the pinnacle of the social world that had once disdained him.

Once again, this heroic mold was first cast by Rousseau in *Les Confessions*. In recounting his rise to fame, Rousseau in fact recapitulates a psychological morality tale initiated in his earlier works. As had several of his previous protagonists, such as Émile and the "noble savage" (whose tales will be addressed in later chapters), the hero of *Les Confessions,* the young Jean-Jacques himself, undergoes an inner struggle between his "*amour de soi,*" or natural self-love, and his "*amour-propre,*" the vanity and egoistic self-interest that threaten to corrupt him in society. Hence, Rousseau portrays his youthful protagonist as having vacillated between a powerful ambition for celebrity, fortune, sexual conquest, and even political authority atop the Parisian hierarchy, and the ever-present determination to be independent of others. He recalls, for example, having sought to foment a "revolution" in the art of musical notation, hoping thereby "to attain celebrity which . . . is always accompanied in Paris by fortune." At another point, he describes his "heart swelling" at the thought of becoming a military officer. At yet another we find him imagining himself as a "young Intendant." Yet the reader also finds Rousseau's protagonist periodically bidding "farewell to the capital, to the court, to ambition, vanity, love, and the ladies," and resolving "never again to attach myself to anyone, but to maintain my independence by making use of my talents."[33]

It is of course the latter resolution that invariably wins out in Rousseau's self-portrayal. In fact, it is willful "*amour de soi*" that typically activates his protagonist, and often to his own self-professed detriment.

> My passions are extremely strong, and while I am under their sway nothing can equal my impetuosity. I am amenable to no restraint, respect, fear, or decorum. I am cynical, bold, violent, and daring. No shame can stop me, no fear of danger alarm me. . . . But all this lasts only a moment; and the next moment plunges me into complete annihilation.[34]

Similarly, Rousseau professes "the greatest contempt for money" as an object to be pursued. "I adore liberty," he explains. "I hate embarrassment, worry, and constraint. . . . Money in one's possession is the instrument of liberty; money one pursues is the symbol of servitude." Acutely sensitive to personal dependency of any sort, Rousseau recounts how time and again he risked his future ambitions rather than allow himself to be humiliated. "I was not much afraid of punishment," he explains, foreshadowing Julien Sorel's "horror of contempt," "I was only afraid of disgrace. But that I feared more than death." Rousseau reports—more than once—having "renounced forever all plans for fortune and advancement" in favor of "independence and poverty." Indeed, he ultimately identifies liberty itself with a will that is "superior to fortune and man's opinion, and independent of all external circumstances."[35]

By his own testimony, furthermore, egoistic self-interest—or *amour-propre*—seems to motivate not even the most "depraved" of Jean-Jacques's actions. Recounting the notorious abandonment of his illegitimate children to a foundling home, Rousseau admits having "neglected [his] duties" but denies any malice or "unnatural" feelings. Hence, while many of his tale's most dramatic passages address his protagonist's oscillation between "the depths of villainy" and "sublime heroism," it is always the latter that seems to prevail: he remains ever the natural man protecting the purity and integrity of his will against the corrupting influence of society. And paradoxically, of course, Jean-

Jacques finally achieves notoriety in Paris by virtue of an audacious critique of civilized society, *Le Discours sur les arts et les sciences* of 1750. His meteoric rise thereafter within the very social world he disdains constitutes the first ambivalent climax of Rousseau's tale. "The success of my first writings had made me fashionable," he laments in a phrase later mirrored by Stendhal: "People wanted to meet this odd man who sought no acquaintances and only wanted to pursue his freedom and happiness in his own way." Finally, as foreshadowed by his discomfiting celebrity in the female-dominated salon culture of Paris, the social success of which Jean-Jacques had dreamed in his youth proves unrewarding: "So long as I lived unknown to the public, I was loved by all who knew me. . . . But as soon as I had a name I ceased to have friends." As would Stendhal's, Rousseau's hero achieves prominence within the established order precisely because of his avowed refusal to sacrifice his noble independence on the altar of personal fortune and renown.[36]

Robespierre, modeling himself directly after Rousseau, lent a potent political significance to the heretical narrative of ascent from provincial obscurity to establishment notoriety. With his election to the National Assembly in 1789, the lawyer from Arras launched his self-construction as Rousseauian hero by establishing himself as a perpetual gadfly and spokesman for the radical opposition. Making enemies of the many who resented his arrogant posture of moral superiority and unwillingness to compromise, he gradually cultivated a following beyond the world of parliamentary politics. Indeed, speaking ever and always as "tribune" of "the people, that great multitude whose cause I plead," he invited the criticism of the revolutionary establishment. The people's true representative, he proclaimed, will "sometimes struggle alone, with [his] conscience, against the torrent of prejudices and factions." Ever conscious of appearances, both before his contemporaries and posterity, he fostered a conspicuously puritanical public image, spurning all civic offices save "representative of the people." And ultimately, evincing a Rousseauian disdain for monetary gain and egoistic self-interest of any sort, he made "virtue" a watchword of the Revolution and himself its unquestioned embodiment.[37]

By the spring of 1791, as Jordan notes, even Robespierre's enemies had come to acknowledge his "austere virtues" and "absolute dedication" to the Revolution. Indeed, both reflecting his skill at manufacturing his own revolutionary vogue and neatly encapsulating its meaning within the heretical narrative, he had acquired the legendary title of "*L'Incorruptible*." In short, in the eyes of his contemporaries and those of "posterity"—that is, of public legend—Robespierre's self-fabrication within the Rousseauian mold had been remarkably successful: like his Genevan idol he had ostensibly, through verbal prowess and singular force of will, overcome great obstacles to rise to the summit of revolutionary Paris; and like Rousseau, he had parlayed the role of virtuous and intransigent public dissenter—which had initially inspired the disdain of his more "civilized" contemporaries—into popular celebrity.[38]

While perhaps never again quite so politically consequential, the public saga of the heroic intellectual's paradoxical rise to fame within the established order would continue thereafter to conform to the same archetype. Péguy and Sartre, for example, each translated into popular renown a public persona almost perversely dedicated to opposition. The former, having fought heroically—at least according to legend—in the Dreyfusard camp, quickly abandoned it in its hour of triumph on the grounds that the Dreyfusards themselves had become an established party. From then on, he gained increasing notoriety by using his independent review, *Les Cahiers de la Quinzaine,* to assault the "anticlerical churches" of parliamentary socialism and the Sorbonne that had arisen out of the Dreyfusard victory. But it was only by publicly denouncing the new Dreyfusard establishment in his celebrated essay of 1910, *Notre jeunesse,* that Péguy effectively inaugurated his own popular myth. Through his much acclaimed dichotomy of "mystique" and "politique," he contrasted those "impenitent Dreyfusards," those "men of heart" who willingly "sacrificed all" and "compromised nothing," with the "traitors" who "believe in nothing . . . who sacrifice nothing" and hence fostered the nation's degradation. In a gesture all too reminiscent of Robespierre, he identified unabashedly with the camp of the pure and uncorrupted. "We were heroes," Péguy wrote of himself and his early Dreyfusard comrades. "We were . . . that handful of Frenchmen who, under a withering fire, effected a breach in the line." And Péguy, too, transformed his uncompromising defiance of the established order into public celebrity within that order. By 1912, the notorious Parisian newspaper survey, *Les Jeunes gens d'aujourd'hui,* had ranked him among the icons of a "new youth" in revolt against the bourgeois liberal establishment,* and an early death at the front in

---

*This survey, authored by two young right-leaning nationalists, has typically been cited by historians as evidence that France's prewar youth was politically reactionary if not monarchist. While both Péguy and Bergson are cited therein as icons of the "new youth," neither embraced such political views; indeed, on closer examination, the "new youth" itself would seem more to have opposed the liberal order of the Third Republic

1914 secured his legend as both an ardent patriot—indeed a national prophet—and, in the words of H. Stuart Hughes, a "totally pure character" who "demanded total integrity" from his countrymen.[39]

Sartre, by the same token, openly acknowledged in *Les Mots* his own calculated ascent to anti-establishment renown within the established order; in fact, he likened himself to Robespierre for having "lived posthumously"—for having imagined a heroic destiny before realizing it. As a youth, Sartre recalls, he dreamt that his first book "would create a public scandal" and make him "a public enemy," but then opinion would shift: "[A] hundred reporters would go looking for me and not find me." Although not according to his own schedule—*La Nausée*, while creating a mild scandal in 1939 for its assault on *les salauds* of the bourgeoisie, earned him only a modest following—Sartre did, of course, enact his Rousseauian fantasy with remarkable fidelity after World War II. Through the sudden vogue of such works as the Resistance drama *Les Mouches,* the 1944 play *Huis clos,* and the war trilogy *Les Chemins de la liberté,* his paradoxical vision of freedom both scandalized conventional morality and captivated the Parisian public. Faithfully echoing the heretical archetype, Annie Cohen-Solal writes that especially the youth became "[e]nthused by his radicalism, his permanent transgression of conventional models, his café life, his transparency, his marginality, so shocking to the bourgeois." By 1946, Sartre's public lectures had become celebrated events; indeed, he had become the most acclaimed anti-establishment figure in Paris. Moreover, perhaps in unwitting testimony to the power of the master fiction, popular legend quickly made a Resistance hero of this formerly anonymous lycée professor whose only—and by his own account unexceptional—wartime action had been taken with his pen. Indeed, as Cohen-Solal puts it, Sartre took his place at the head of the "new race of writer-heroes" that emerged out of postwar France.[40]

Such a premeditated self-fabrication of the archetypal heretic's ascent was not always necessary, however. In the cases of Michelet, Bergson, and Foucault, it was the educational establishment itself, as suggested above,[41] that colluded in re-enacting the archetypal myth. That is, the hero's appointment to the Collège de France—which, as an official seat of opposition within modern France's established anti-establishment, had come to incarnate "the holy of holies in the French

<hr />

than to have championed any particular political agenda of the left or right. See Paul Cohen, "Heroes and Dilettantes: The Action Française, Le Sillon, and the Generation of 1905–14," *French Historical Studies* 4 (Fall 1988): 673–87.

university system"[42]—would ultimately betoken in popular legend his apotheosis as national gadfly. Michelet, for instance, was only able to put into practice his longstanding belief in "the power of the word" to "mold the ideas and sentiments of Frenchmen" following his appointment to the Collège in 1838. By the 1840s, the historian's public lectures at the Collège had become a rallying point for opposition to the July Monarchy. These famously charismatic paeans to revolutionary freedom, delivered before overflowing lecture halls, became central to Michelet's legend, a saga whose dramatic climax must be counted as the suspension of his course by a "despotic" July Monarchy on the eve of the 1848 revolution. Indeed, that this symbolic clash with authority—along with its re-enactment in 1851 by the government of Napoleon III—came to represent the defining moment of Michelet's public biography is tacitly acknowledged by Roland Barthes, who cites the brief notice on Michelet from *Le Petit Larousse illustré* of 1906–34: "French historian, born in Paris. His liberal opinions twice caused his lectures at the Collège de France to be suspended. In his *Histoire de France* and his *Histoire de la révolution,* he managed to effect a veritable resurrection of our national life (1798–1874)."

Thus cast in the unlikely role of anti-establishment militant, this previously little-celebrated historian would seem to have adapted himself to the master narrative of the consecrated heretic and to have been adapted to it by the public. By virtue of his legendary eloquence on behalf of revolutionary liberty and his symbolic confrontation with the established order from within its most hallowed halls, Michelet, no less than Péguy or Sartre, was able to attain the heights of cultural celebrity.[43]

No more plausible an anti-establishment heretic was Bergson. A successful and irreproachably bourgeois philosophy professor within the French academic hierarchy, he had steered clear of the major controversies of his era—most notably the Dreyfus affair—until his appointment to the Collège de France in 1900. By 1907, however, such eminent members of the French intellectual establishment as the psychologist Alfred Binet were publicly lamenting the ominous dominion of Bergson's anti-scientific, anti-intellectual philosophy. In 1912, *Les Jeunes Gens d'aujourd'hui* certified the philosopher even more than his disciple Péguy as the chosen oracle of the "new youth." By World War I, Bergson's fame as "the prophet of metaphysical revolution," in R. C. Grogin's phrase, was established worldwide, and his stature as apostate-hero of Paris was unchallenged. Attended by such future intellectual luminaries as Péguy, Sorel, and Gabriel Marcel, as well as by the "fashionable women" of Paris, his public addresses at the Collège, like those of Michelet before him and Foucault after, became "major public events"—at least according to the popular legend recapitulated by Grogin and Hughes. Like Michelet, Bergson was reputed to have lectured charismatically "in the face of the establishment" before overflowing audiences. "[H]e spoke without a note," reports Hughes, citing the romantic portrait of Jacques Chevalier, "his forehead enormous, his bright eyes . . . like two lights under his thick eyebrows, and his features of a delicacy that emphasizes the power of his forehead and the immaterial radiance of his thought." Newspaper accounts appeared of the weekly skirmishes over limited seating at the Collège, and were subsequently repeated by Bergson's chroniclers. One foreign journalist, notes Grogin, likened Bergson's lectures to "lay masses" for an audience of "worshipers."

Once again like Michelet, Bergson addressed himself above all to the nature of true freedom; and indeed, the fables of his prophetic power as "liberator," be it in politics, religion, or the arts, abound in the testimonials of his pre–1914 disciples. The revolutionary syndicalist Sorel (whose testimony is again cited by Hughes), for example, credits Bergson with having encouraged members of the labor movement to adapt "their mode of thought to their revolutionary conditions of life." And recounting the philosopher's role in rekindling the religious faith of Péguy, Jacques Maritain, and Ernest Psichari, Raissa Maritain cites the "marvelously penetrating critique" through which his lectures discredited "pseudoscientific positivism and re-established the . . . essential liberty of the spirit." As a result, she concludes: "Winter had passed for us" and "spring was appearing." The public, summarizes Hughes, left Bergson's lectures "with a sense of 'liberation.'" Thus, Bergson, no less than Michelet, came to be celebrated for having scaled the heights of Paris's established order solely by virtue of his uncompromising intellectual opposition to it; indeed, abetted even by his enemies within the liberal intellectual establishment, popular legend made of him an improbable Julien Sorel, standing courageously both atop and against civilized society.[44]

Perhaps even more striking is the public apotheosis of Foucault who, notwithstanding his professed desire "to have no face," became "recognizable in a crowd of thousands"—in Eribon's words—following his appointment to the Collège de France in 1970. Foucault had achieved a measure of fame in 1966 with the unexpected notoriety of his difficult work, *Les Mots et les choses,* and its enigmatic—and vaguely iconoclastic—proclamation of "the disappearance of man." In

1969, as a faculty member at Vincennes, the philosopher had actually joined students and militants in occupying the campus administration building and battling the police. Miller cites "witnesses" who "recall that Foucault exulted in the moment, gleefully throwing stones," and he quotes the then student-radical, André Glucksmann, who fought alongside the rising luminary: "He was very courageous. . . . When the police came at night he wanted to be in the front ranks." Miller concludes his account, moreover, by all but explicitly citing the archetypal narrative of ascent: through "fulfilling the hallowed French role of the *engagé* intellectual," he writes, Foucault "began to command the respectful attention of a larger French public."* And recounting the philosopher's inaugural lecture at the Collège in 1970, Eribon lapses into that legend's familiar idiom: "Several hundred people had crammed into the large amphitheater" where "[i]t seemed that nothing had ever changed. . . . Then Foucault began to read his text under the fixed gaze of Bergson, whose bronze profile dominated the room." Subsequently, Eribon continues, Foucault's weekly lectures became "one of the events of Parisian intellectual life": speaking before "unfailingly large and avid crowds," he would begin at 9 A.M. "in a vain attempt to cut down" on their size. In setting the scene of a 1975 lecture, Miller echoes the same formula: "The great hall where Henri Bergson once lectured was packed. Auditors crowded the aisles and spilled onto the floor in front of the dais."[45]

Foucault, of course, like the radical prophets before him, had achieved such notoriety through a scathing assault on the very establishment—above all, in his case, the secular church of the human sciences—wherein he had previously labored semi-anonymously. He too, both in his lectures and such contemporaneous best-sellers as *Surveiller et punir,* posed as public liberator—this time from the "omnipresent surveillance" of the doctors, psychologists, criminologists, and sociologists. Ironically, then, in light of his assault on the very notion of the individual "subject," Foucault came to be constructed popularly as the intellectual heretic who had mastered Paris by virtue of his radical critique of its establishment. Indeed, no less revealing of the master narrative's potency than Sartre's somewhat exaggerated Resistance career is the stubborn legend that Foucault participated and even played a leading role in the Paris student uprising of May 1968. The philosopher was in fact out of the country at the time.[46]

---

*Didier Eribon nods to the myth as well: "In 1969," he writes, "Foucault began to embody the very figure of the militant intellectual" (*Michel Foucault,* trans. Betsy Wing [Cambridge, MA: Harvard University Press, 1991], 210).

As a final note here on the consecrated heretic's rise to fame, the aspiring hero, according to the myth, must not only ascend without subjecting himself to paternal authority, he must flagrantly flout it. His heroic standing, on the other hand, would seem entirely unviolated by personal dependency on women. The roles, for example, that Madame de Rênal and Mathilde de La Mole play in the social advancement of Stendhal's hero mirror those played by Madame de Warens and Madame d'Épinay, among others, in Rousseau's celebrated tale of ascent. ("Nothing," Rousseau writes contemptuously in *Les Confessions,* "is achieved in Paris except by help of the ladies.") The standard portrait of Robespierre, by the same token, finds him first supported and pampered by his sister Charlotte and then, at the height of the Revolution, by the women of the Duplay household. The revolutionary's daily life, summarizes Jordan, was "discreetly arranged and maintained by Mme. Duplay and her daughters—and Robespierre seems to have loved all this female attention." Similarly, Michelet's public biography includes an openly acknowledged debt to his mother—"I owe her much," he wrote in the preface to *Du Prêtre,* "I sense myself profoundly her son"—as well as to his "spiritual passion," Madame Dumesnil, and his second wife, Athénai, both of whom he cites as significant "inspirations." Péguy, who was raised, according to Halévy, "between his mother and grandmother," credits the former with having fostered his career in letters, and is said later in life to have found in Madame Favre—the granddaughter of Third Republican Jules Favre, and mother of Jacques Maritain—both intellectual guidance and maternal support. Sartre, too, in a Cartesian phrase, evokes the effects of his own mother's attentions: "I am adored, hence I am adorable." And no less legendary, of course, is the existentialist's career-long dependency, both emotional and intellectual, upon Simone de Beauvoir as well as a number of lesser female companions. Didier Eribon notes, finally, that Foucault "remained very attached to his mother" throughout his life, and he credits her with having championed the future philosophe's choice of career over his father's objections. Thus, far from disrupting his autonomy, the hero's dependency upon women would seem, within the logic of the master fiction, to nurture his intellectual rebellion against the established order and thereby to enhance his rise to celebrity within it.[47]

IV. PUBLIC CRITIQUE AND TRANSGRESSION

Regardless of his newfound fame, the consecrated heretic, according to the archetype, must refuse to compromise his integrity of will. Insisting not only on his own purity but that of others, he repudiates those he deems inauthentic or corrupt, maintains his independence from established churches and parties, and becomes a critical mirror at the very heart of the establishment reflecting its hypocrisy and corruption. First scandalizing the cultivated world with his unconventional behavior, he must ultimately transgress symbolically against the established order.

In Rousseau's seminal account, in fact, the tale's hero all but wills his own public isolation by proudly refusing to play according to the rules of civilized society. Contrasting his own "natural" sincerity to the hypocrisy of social convention, Jean-Jacques recounts the popular sensations caused by his open cohabitation with a serving girl, his several religious conversions, and above all his differences with other men of letters. Thus, after detailing his public schisms with the likes of Diderot, d'Alembert, and especially Voltaire, Rousseau writes scathingly of "Paris life among pretentious people," of "the cabals of men of letters, their shameful quarrels, the lack of honesty in their books, and the important airs they assumed." He despairs, finally, at having found "so little gentleness, openheartedness, or sincerity even in the company of my friends."[48]

Thus, *Les Confessions* would seem, at bottom, to recount precisely the metamorphosis of the Rousseauian persona from Genevan man of nature into Parisian public gadfly. Able to see "only foolishness and error in the doctrines of our sages, nothing but oppression and misery in our social order," Rousseau depicts his conversion in 1756 to "virtue":

> This intoxication had begun in my head, but it passed to my heart. The noblest pride sprang up there on the ruins of uprooted vanity. . . . This was the origin of my sudden eloquence, and of the truly celestial fire which burned in me and spread to my early books. . . . Bold, proud, and fearless, I now carried with me wherever I went a self-assurance. . . . The contempt which my deep reflections inspired in me for the customs, the principles, and the prejudices of my age made me insensible to the mockery of those who followed them. . . . All Paris repeated the sharp and biting sarcasms of that same man who two years before . . . could never find the right thing to say or the right word to use.[49]

Rousseau's protagonist had, in short, discovered his true vocation as social critic, his "talent for telling men useful but unwelcome truths with some vigor and courage."[50]

Indeed, Rousseau offers through his own self-portrait a veritable prototype of the man of letters as self-marginalized heretic. In order to break "the fetters of prejudice, courageously doing" what is "right," he asserts, the writer must be willing to "live in poverty and independence." Even while residing still at the very summit of Paris's social and political establishment—Rousseau details his own ongoing relationship, for example, with the king's minister Malesherbes—the man of letters must remain stubbornly unaffiliated with any party, church, or "cabal." He must write neither for money nor acclaim—Rousseau reports, for instance, that he *refused* election to the Académie Française—inasmuch as "[i]t is too difficult to think nobly when one thinks only for a living. If [the writer] is to have the strength and the courage to speak great truths [he] must not depend on [his] success." He must willingly "doom" himself "to be an example to all who, solely out of a love for justice and the public good, and strong in their innocence alone, might dare openly to speak the truth."[51]

And of course Rousseau's protagonist quite literally fulfills his own prophecy through an ultimate public sacrilege: having brazenly assaulted revealed religion in *Émile,* he finds himself indicted by an outraged government and forced to flee into exile to avoid arrest. Condemned by the state, the church, and even his fellow men of letters, Jean-Jacques is able to represent himself thereafter as reviled by a once adoring public and betrayed by his friends—indeed as "surrounded" even as he writes "by spies and by vigilant and malevolent observers." While his enemies continue to move "freely in the fashionable world," Rousseau laments, Jean-Jacques survives "[a]lone, a foreigner, isolated, without family or backing, holding nothing but my principles and my duties"; and yet, by virtue of his very isolation, he is able "fearlessly" to follow "the paths of uprightness, neither flattering nor favoring anyone at the expense of justice and truth."[52] For such isolation and independence constitutes, at bottom, the very essence of Jean-Jacques's self-fashioned heroism.

It is, without doubt, in his fidelity to this segment of the heretical drama that Robespierre earned his posthumous fame and infamy. At home in his chosen role of opposition maverick, he accepted government office only when elected to the Committee on Public Safety during the crisis-ridden summer of 1793—and he scarcely abandoned his posture of uncompromising virtue and "incorruptibility" thereafter. Indeed, as Jordan points out, Robespierre's domination of the Committee is attributable more to the moral authority which that posture accorded him than to any dictatorial coup or decree.[53] The Jacobin's vision of revolutionary government, in fact, reflects nothing if not his heroic self-construction as the perpetual Rousseauian heretic, the un-compromising champion of absolute virtue—his own as well as that of others—within a corrupt civilization. "It is the function of govern-ment," he characteristically proclaims in his speeches of 1793 and 1794, "to guide the moral and physical energies of the nation"; hence, it must never be allowed to fall into "the hands of impure or treacher-ous men." Accordingly, the Committee on Public Safety and even the Terror itself signified for Robespierre an endless process of moral puri-fication, a perpetual public "critique" both of the nation and the indi-vidual. Hence his fondness for purges whether of the Convention or the Jacobin Club; his horror of "factions" and refusal to identify true revolutionary virtue with parties, be they moderate or extremist; his violent breaks à la Rousseau with former friends and allies—Danton, Desmoulins, Hébert—who proved corrupt or impure; and his insis-tence that the Committee's ruthless emergency government be perpetu-ated even after crisis had passed: "Maintain," he pleaded in the winter of 1794, "the sacred power of republican government instead of letting it decline." Robespierre even modeled his own role on the Commit-tee after the Rousseauian persona: the revolutionary magistrate, he de-clares, "is obliged to sacrifice his interest to the interest of the people, and his pride in power to equality." In other words, even as de facto head of a dictatorial state, Robespierre constructed himself before the public as an autonomous and selfless national gadfly. Finally arrested and condemned for perpetuating his own institutionalized transgres-sion of civilized norms—that is, the Terror—the Incorruptible, as shall be discussed more fully below, depicted himself as the persecuted critic of a corrupt revolutionary establishment, as an isolated hero fighting fearlessly not on his own behalf but on that of the public good.[54]

Unencumbered by political power, such postrevolutionary intellectuals as Péguy, Sartre, and Foucault could reprise the same role more sym-bolically—and less ominously. Indeed, Péguy's entire career, which represents nothing if not a study in public iconoclasm, was marked by a series of celebrated rifts with former comrades whom he accused of "selling out" to the established order: with the socialist leader Jaurès, for betraying the "socialist mystique" by entering parliamentary poli-tics; with Daniel Halévy, for betraying the "Dreyfusard mystique"; with Georges Sorel over his anti-Semitism; and with fellow Catholic converts, Jacques Maritain and Ernest Psichari, for their abandonment of Bergson and subservience to church orthodoxy. In fact, the essayist's final published work of 1914 echoed Rousseau's sacrilege of a century and half earlier against the Catholic Church. "I have fought all my life on the frontiers," Péguy proclaimed after rebuking the Vatican for consigning Bergson's works to the "Index of Forbidden Books." Péguy's public assault on the church was particularly pointed in light of the 1907 declaration of faith whereby the celebrated Dreyfusard had first divorced himself publicly from the "secular church" of anticlericalism. Only his fortuitous, as it were, death at the front several months later spared Rome the embarrassment of having to condemn its prodigal convert. Thus, Péguy, summarizes Romain Rolland encapsulating the myth, "resolved to suffer all—all, but to save his independence." And by 1914, he had indeed made of himself in popular legend the isolated and autonomous "*homme mystique*" of his own self-description: every bit the latter-day Rousseau or Robespierre dedicated to purifying the nation of "politique."[55]

No less the proverbial public provacateur, and if anything even more inclined toward public transgression, was Sartre. Ever ready to outrage the established order and lend support to radical causes, from Algerian liberation and the Cuban Revolution to the student uprisings of May 1968, Sartre's refusal following his rise to fame to affiliate permanently with any political party or institution became integral to his legend. The radical philosopher, writes Gerassi, "joined no party, worked for no institution, supported no establishment." And Cohen-Solal cites Irving Howe on "the Sartrean image" of "the independent intellectual, outside all institutions, free of all determinism." Indeed, having declined election to the Legion of Honor after World War II as well as the Académie Française and even the Collège de France, Sartre reconfirmed his notoriety by refusing the Nobel Prize in 1964 on the grounds that the writer ought not make "an institution" of himself. Thereafter, writes Cohen-Solal, Sartre acquired "a mythic place outside France . . . as the prophet of modern times": he was "the man of scandal, man of wisdom, man of freedom, man of truth. He was the one who had refused the Nobel, a hero."[56]

As noted previously,[57] Sartre, too, engaged throughout his career in highly visible breaks with former friends and allies whom he deemed less than politically pure. In Camus, Merleau-Ponty, Arthur Koestler, and Raymond Aron he found his own versions of Danton, Jaurès, Maritain, and of course, Voltaire. No less celebrated, moreover, were the writer's public transgressions: his open support, for example, of such modern-day Julien Sorels as the writer-felon Jean Genet and the

West Indian writer-terrorist Frantz Fanon, both of whom he embraced as alter-egos.* But Sartre's most notorious crime against the established order, the public sin for which he remains symbolically exiled from the Western intelligentsia to the present day, was his open support during the mid–1950s for communist Russia against the "bourgeois West" and his refusal at that time to criticize the tyrannical excesses of Stalinism.[58] Yet the writer's equally public refusal to join the Communist Party, as well as his ultimate condemnations both of the Gulags and of the invasions of Hungary and Czechoslovakia, not only won him no friends in the West but earned him the contempt of the communist establishment as well. Hence, by the mid–1960s Sartre had become both a mythic public figure and an entirely isolated one—indeed, in Gerassi's phrase, "the hated conscience of his century." [59]

According to Gerassi, Sartre had "said over and over," that "the job of the intellectual . . . is to criticize, to oppose, to denounce." And Sartre had indeed publicly maintained as early as 1947 that the writer's office is to give "society a guilty conscience." Echoing that thought in 1972, he wrote that it is the intellectual's role "to contest the whole of received truths." Receiving "a mandate from no one," the celebrated radical continued, he is nonetheless "in solidarity with the masses and the have-nots"; "but banished by the privileged classes [and] mistrusted by the disadvantaged classes . . . solitude is his fate." The heroic visage of the condemned Julien Sorel and the exiled Rousseau— "alone, a foreigner, isolated" and yet willing to tell men "useful but unwelcome truths" out of "a love for justice and the public good"— could hardly be more discernable; nor could Sartre's success have been greater at shaping his public legend to fit the master narrative. Even de Gaulle, having famously refused in 1960 to imprison the writer for his subversive activities on the grounds that "one does not arrest Voltaire," acknowledged Sartre's mythic stature in modern France. Placing him alongside the likes of Villon, Rousseau, and Romain Rolland—that is, "canonizing" him, in the words of Cohen-Solal—the president of the Republic insisted that while such "people caused great trouble in their time . . . it is essential that we continue to respect their freedom of thought and expression insofar as it is compatible with the laws of the state and national unity." [60]

Foucault also, notwithstanding his own well publicized—not to say

---

*Genet, writes Cohen-Solal, embodied "the Sartrean hero par excellence" (*Sartre: A Life,* ed. Norman Macafee, trans. Anna Cancogni [New York: Pantheon Books, 1987], 314).

prophet-like—repudiation of the traditional "prophetic" functions of the intellectual, came to embody the mythic archetype no less fully than Sartre. Indeed, in his resolve to differentiate his own public posture from that of the Sartrean "universal intellectual," he personified the role all the more compellingly. Both of Foucault's biographers suggest, in fact, that Sartre, whose work the younger philosophe disparaged in 1966 as the "magnificent and pathetic attempt of a nineteenth-century man to conceive of the twentieth century," represented for him almost an oedipal father-figure to be exorcized so as to establish his own public persona. "When I was a young man," Foucault is reported to have said after Sartre's funeral, "he was the one—along with everything he represented . . . from whom I wanted to free myself." And ultimately, Foucault did accumulate his own proverbial list of public ruptures with former comrades and confederates who proved unworthy—including Jacques Derrida, Gilles Deleuze, François Mitterand, and, of course, Sartre himself—not to mention his own legend as a radical liberationist of homosexuals, hospital patients, and prisoners. He even found in the person of Pierre Rivière, a nineteenth-century youth who had brutally murdered his family and then become a "case-study" for psychiatric "experts," his own Jean Genet—or Julien Sorel. Moreover, outspokenly denying membership in any philosophical sect such as structuralism, and explicitly assaulting such "established churches" as Marxism and psychoanalysis, Foucault actively cultivated his public persona as the uncategorizable intellectual. Hence, he boasted in an interview, for example, of having been classified at one time or another "as anarchist, leftist, ostentatious or disguised Marxist, nihilist, explicit or secret anti-Marxist, technocrat in service of Gaullism, new liberal, etc." Taken together, he declared, these characterizations "mean something. And I must admit that I rather like what they mean. It is true that I prefer not to identify myself and that I'm amused by the diversity of the ways I've been judged and classified.'[61]

No less notoriously than Sartre did Foucault gravitate toward public transgression. Emphasizing his personal search for the "'pure violence' of forbidden pleasures," Miller frames Foucault's entire biography as a quest for "limit-experiences," both private and public. But most legendary are the philosopher's political infractions: for example, his public celebration in 1972 of the French Revolution's September Massacres as an instance of "popular justice," his participation later the same year in a demonstration during which—to use Miller's description—"the great professor at the Collège de France" received blows from the police alongside his French Maoist comrades, and his fleeting support in 1979 for the Iranian Revolution, in which Foucault beheld the "rapture" of pure revolutionary action, "literally a light that lit in all [Iranians], that bathed all of them at the same time."[62]

Finally, while forbidding him the role of "mouthpiece for the masses" or the right "to tell others what they have to do," Foucault assigned to what he called "the specific intellectual"—as opposed to the Sartrean "universal intellectual"—the duty to "produce names" and "point the finger of accusation" on behalf of the "marginalized" and against "existing forms of power." This "elusive guerrilla warrior," as Miller labels him, must "disturb people's mental habits," "dissipate what is familiar and accepted," and "re-examine rules and institutions on the basis of this reproblematization." In a 1981 interview, Foucault envisioned carrying out "the work of deep transformation" in "a free atmosphere, one constantly agitated by a permanent criticism." Thus, far from failing to shape himself to the heroic mold of public prophet and iconoclast, Foucault echoed not only his erstwhile rival Sartre, but a more distant Jacobin precursor as well.[63]

Not all would-be heretics of the postrevolutionary era fulfilled the role so compellingly, however; and for those who did not, such as Michelet and Bergson, the structure of the master fiction would appear again to have fixed the boundaries of their public legends. The former, offered a position in the Republic of 1848, refused in favor of the Rousseauian role of perpetual critic. "I want to reserve the right to blame what is wrong," he explained, "even in those who are my friends." And the succession in 1851 of Napoleon III, who promptly suspended Michelet's course at the Collège de France for a second time, allowed him to preserve a public image of heroic independence. Indeed as noted above, the two governmental interventions of 1848 and 1851—moments of symbolic transgression more thrust upon the historian than initiated by him—contributed greatly to Michelet's posthumous vogue under the Third Republic. More academic essayist than revolutionary radical, however, the historian was ill fitted to enact the insubordinate and subversive behavior required by the narrative, and after his departure from Paris in 1852, "the spotlight of the ages dimmed," as Linda Orr has put it, "and he was abandoned." By the same token, Bergson's official legend would appear to close for the most part with his final public lecture at the Collège de France in 1914 and his symbolic reception the same year, through election to the Académie Française, into the most sacred corridors of the French establishment. Until his celebrated public posture under the Occupation in 1941, which will be discussed shortly, the philosopher's post–1914 biography is highlighted no more in popular myth than his bourgeois Parisian childhood.[64]

V. MARTYRDOM AND CONFESSION

Having through willful transgression and self-isolation fashioned his own tale as tragedy, the heretic's final act is to cast himself as a martyr to the public good; and ultimately, by confessing his innermost soul to "the people," he simultaneously renounces the established order as base and corrupt and authenticates his own status as consecrated heretic before the public.

Once again, Rousseau's *Les Confessions* set the standard both for the heretic's public martyrdom, as outlined above, and his equally public self-examination. Jean-Jacques's obsessive—even masochistic—self-scrutiny, his need "to reveal myself absolutely to the public," "to make my soul transparent to the reader's eye . . . to contrive that none of its movements shall escape his notice," constitutes the core of the Genevan's biographical legend.[65] Such self-revelation, Rousseau emphasizes, must be of the most painful and inward sort: an account of the writer's most private feelings, a "history of my soul" in "all situations good and bad." For if Jean-Jacques offers himself as a model of perpetual self-criticism and purification, the public will never have reason to "accuse [him] of refusing to tell the whole truth" and his self-construction as public hero will be deemed genuine.[66]

It is not surprising, in this light, to find Robespierre recasting his own imminent demise of 1794 in the mold of public martyrdom and self-revelation. Jordan notes that even in his early "literary" self-presentations, the revolutionary imagined a "violent end presented in stylized and even tragic form." When compared by his enemies to the Gracchi of ancient Rome, for example, Robespierre mused as early as 1791: "[W]hat there will, perhaps, be in common between us will be a tragic end." And in his final speech before the Convention in 1794, he seemed deliberately to set the stage for such a dire *denouement*. Professing to be surrounded by "the chiefs of factions," "conspirators," and "tyrants who pursue me," Robespierre represented himself in plainly Rousseauian terms as the very incarnation of "oppressed innocence." Indeed, he proclaimed himself already "a living martyr of the Republic," and vowed that if his life would satisfy his enemies, he would "abandon it to them without regret. . . . What friend of humanity can wish to survive the moment he is no longer permitted to serve it or his country and defend oppressed innocence!"[67]

While penning no Rousseauian autobiography, Robespierre did

adapt that "vigorous literary genre to the purposes of the Revolution"—to cite Jordan's formulation—by making his political life a perpetual public confession. At home in "the autobiographical mode," he spoke continually of his own revolutionary sincerity as a means of inciting—or indicting—that of others. The Jacobin's final speech before the Convention represents his purest and most dramatic moment of self-revelation. Proposing, like his revered Rousseau, to present his listeners not with "flattering pictures" but "useful truths," he claims to defend their "violated liberty" even as he defends himself. Indeed, professing to prefer his "status as representative of the people to that of member of the Committee on Public Safety" and his "status as *man* and *French citizen* before all" (Robespierre's emphasis), Robespierre offers to "open and unburden [his] heart" before the nation; he embraces, that is, the posture of public self-scrutiny. And having established his ongoing and uncompromising commitment to "uproot the system of corruption and disorder" implanted by the Revolution's enemies, he vows: "[I]f I must dissemble these truths, bring me the hemlock." Thus, as would Stendhal's fictional hero in his own final speech, Robespierre links confession to social criticism, authentic self-revelation to his own legitimate standing as culture-hero.[68]

This archetypal finale can be detected in the myths of subsequent heretics as well, regardless of their biographical circumstances. Hence, Michelet, for example, who would actually die in relative obscurity in 1874, had already been represented in popular mythology during the crises of 1848 and 1851 as a living martyr to the Republic. Furthermore, his posthumous legend emerged largely out of the public self-portrait that he etched in his writings; for the Rousseauian formula of public confession and self-sacrifice came as easily to Michelet as to Robespierre. He fashioned his posthumous *Mémorial* explicitly after its illustrious eighteenth-century precursor, insisting above all on the text's fidelity to his innermost self. "Rousseau," Michelet pledges in its opening passage, "will not be the only man who is known. . . . I am creating less the history of my actions . . . than that of my feelings and thoughts." And one of the historian's most celebrated works, *Le Peuple,* is framed by a Rousseauian avowal of self-sacrifice. "This book," he writes in its opening sentence, "is more than a book; it is myself. . . . I have made this book out of myself, out of my life, out of my heart." Offering himself ultimately as a virtual exemplar of that "virtue of sacrifice" which above all characterizes "the people," he depicts the volume's very publication as a renunciation of the "tranquil life that conforms completely to my tastes." Michelet's ongoing self-construction as national martyr is further underscored, moreover, in the astute portrait by Roland Barthes. "Michelet," writes Barthes, "afflicts himself with the most terrible historical diseases"; he "renews in himself the death of the People-as-god, of History-as-god. . . . for it is this death which constitutes Michelet as a historian, makes him into a pontiff who absorbs, sacrifices, bears witness, fulfills, glorifies."[69]

Bergson's public biography as well, reviving in 1941 from its post–1914 slumber, features a dramatic final display of martyrdom and symbolic self-revelation. Having flirted throughout his public life with religious conversion, the celebrated philosopher is alleged to have professed his Catholic faith on his deathbed but declined confession and last rites. His last will, made public following the liberation of Paris in 1944, revealed that only the "formidable wave of anti-Semitism" which had arisen during that era had postponed his conversion. "I want to remain among those," he wrote in 1937, "who tomorrow will be the persecuted." Under the Occupation, the eminent philosopher refused to accept a special exemption from Vichy's anti-Jewish laws, choosing instead to register formally as a Jew. "Wishing to stand with his brethren in their most tragic hour," summarizes Grogin, "Bergson resigned all his positions of honour including his chair at the Collège de France." Such a symbolic renunciation could only be constructed in retrospect as both a martyrdom on behalf of the Jews, and as a courageous defiance of the Nazi established order on behalf of martyred France.[70] With this final public-spirited act of self-sacrifice—not to mention a religious nonconfession, which, ironically, evoked the cultural mythos of heroic self-revelation far more compellingly than could any religious rite—Bergson's public legend was complete.

Péguy's death at the front in 1914, by the same token, was duly exploited by his memorialists as an archetypal instance of public martyrdom. Daniel Halévy, for example, having reconstructed his subject's final days of life in melodramatic detail—"'Come on friends,'" says Lieutenant Péguy to his exhausted troops at one point, "'this is no time to stop; I promise you we shall get there all right'"—finds in his death a "striking realization" of Péguy's own "lyrical vision" of a year earlier: "Blessed are those who die in great battles, / Lying upon the ground in the sight of God." Surmising that he was killed while charging forward in a lost battle, the Tharauds find it symbolically fitting that Péguy "was associated until the end with evil times." Indeed, "after his death in battle," writes Hughes, again faithfully echoing the myth, "Péguy became a symbol of the unity of the French people." And yet, Hughes continues, it was only "the Second World War which completed his apotheosis. In the Occupation and Resistance of 1940 to 1944 Péguy spoke with the voice of a martyred people."[71]

Péguy frequently contemplated the writing of his own confessions and even conceived their title: "Mémoirs d'un homme mystique." His son Pierre, in introducing a posthumous volume of his father's *Souvenirs*, portrays the latter's entire oeuvre as "one long memoir." Ceaselessly evoking his own "past, his childhood, the milieu from which he came, . . . the impoverished life which he freely chose," Péguy's *Cahiers*, asserts Pierre, "are laced with morsels of confession." And to be sure, the tone of Old Testament jeremiad that pervades Péguy's work is also one of nostalgic self-revelation. For example, in a 1913 passage he refers explicitly to Rousseau's autobiography in lamenting "innocences that cannot be recovered," and he does so again in writing of his student days when "everything was young." But by the age of forty, the essayist muses elsewhere, "one can hide nothing from oneself." Nevertheless, he concludes, while "the Sorbonne, the École Normale, and the political parties were able to strip [him] of [his] youth," they could not deprive him of "his heart." Echoing the tones of Rousseau no less than Robespierre and Stendhal, Péguy was able both to denounce the corruptions of his day and affirm his own status as national prophet through an ongoing public memoir.[72]

Sartre, similarly, in his own celebrated public confession, *Les Mots*, identifies heroic self-renunciation as one of the central motifs of his life. Having assigned himself the role in childhood fantasies of "inexorable martyr," he reports thereafter having made heroism "the sole object of my passion." Indeed, Sartre admits in his youth to having endowed "the writer" with "the sacred powers of the hero," to having "talked to myself constantly about men of letters, about the risks they ran." But notwithstanding a lifelong flirtation with disaster—including his capture by the Nazis in 1940 and confinement as a prisoner of war, his aborted Resistance career, the bombing of his Paris apartment twice during the 1960s, and his notorious penchant for bodily self-deprivation and even abuse—heroic martyrdom in fact eluded the acclaimed writer.* And for lack of "terrible dangers" against which to struggle, he ultimately chose to make of his own psyche a perpetual obstacle to overcome; to pride himself, that is, on "measuring the obvious truth of an idea by the displeasure it caused me." Sartre claims, in

---

*This does not prevent Cohen-Solal from portraying Sartre at his funeral as a Rousseauian martyr: "The lonely little man, isolated, anarchist, the childless father entered that day the realm of legend" (*Sartre*, 524).

a celebrated phrase, to have written always "against myself, which means against everybody." [73]

Here again the theme of martyrdom overlaps that of critical self-revelation as the heretic's means of offering his credentials to the public, which Sartre does quite directly and even self-consciously in *Les Mots*. Nothing if not a modern update of Rousseau's pledge to reveal himself, warts and all, "absolutely to the public"—a recasting of romantic "transparency" as existential "authenticity" [74]—the work consists of an ongoing and merciless self-critique. Sartre judges himself "an imposter" and a "liar" whose "sole concern has been to save [himself]," to justify his own "superfluous existence" through writing. He further castigates himself as "an *ersatz* of the Christian I was unable to be" whose "only purpose" has been to "merit posthumous bliss by enduring ordeals in worthy fashion." Hence, "[f]ake to the marrow of my bones and self-deceived, I joyfully wrote about our unhappy state. . . . I regarded anxiety as the guarantee of my security." And yet, implicit in such flights of anguished self-revelation remains the perpetually redeeming compulsion to re-invent himself, to purify himself ruthlessly of inner cowardice and bad faith. Thus, even while renouncing his youthful illusions of "predestination" as well as "the charms of the 'elite,'" Sartre offers his unflattering self-disclosures as figurative stigmata—the very tokens of his public status as consecrated heretic. [75]

Most paradoxical of all would seem the case of Foucault, whose entire oeuvre might be described as an extended public critique both of personal publicity and of public confession. For having proclaimed "the disappearance of man" and explicitly repudiated the very concept of the individual as a "subject," the philosopher famously denounced "the truthful confession" in 1976 as perhaps the most subtly subjugating of modern discourses: "One confesses one's crimes, one's sins, one's thoughts and desires, one's illnesses and troubles; . . . One confesses in public and in private, to one's parents, one's educators, one's doctor, to those one loves; . . . One confesses—or is forced to confess." Among the most notorious passages from Foucault's body of work, moreover, is his personal—but nonetheless public—refusal of public transparency: "I am no doubt not the only one who writes in order to have no face. Do not ask who I am and do not ask me to remain the same: leave it to our bureaucrats and our police to see that our papers are in order." [76]

Nevertheless, neither of the poststructuralist's biographers hesitates to cast the philosopher's untimely death in the mold of public self-sacrifice. Eribon, for example, portraying Foucault's entire work as "a revolt against the powers of 'normalization,'" castigates those who sought to conceal the philosopher's death by AIDS, and implicitly compares his protagonist's passing to the martyrdom of Socrates, which Foucault addressed in one of his final lectures at the Collège de France in order "to show how the practice of truth-telling . . . can lead us to the truth of ourselves." Miller, too, finds the philosopher's death by the plague of the marginalized to be of symbolic public import. But rather than likening Foucault to Socrates, he seizes on his subject's marked esteem during the final year of his life for the Greek Cynic Diogenes, whom the philosopher described as "'*le roi anti-roi*'—an antisovereign sovereign, a ruler at war with rules." For like Foucault himself, Miller asserts, Diogenes regarded philosophy "as a field of limit-experience. . . . Putting truth to the test, he mocked, shocked, and provoked." And "[a]bove all," both the ancient Greek philosopher and his modern French counterpart "issued a radical challenge to the society he criticized and rejected" by "living a life of bodily freedom." But in the latter case, according to Miller's unerringly archetypal portrait, the prophetic mission was to end in tragic self-sacrifice.[77]

Even more striking is Miller's previously noted contention that "*all* of Foucault's books, from the first to the last, comprise a kind of involuntary memoir, an implicit confession" (Miller's emphasis). Yet Foucault's own public words and deeds surely invite such an interpretation. Apart from the now notorious description of his own works as "a few fragments of autobiography," which is highlighted by both Eribon and Miller, the philosopher treated public interviews and television appearances as one of the obligations of his role. Confronted in 1983 over a personal interview that he gave to *Time* magazine, Foucault responded: "When newsmen ask me for information about my work I consider that I have to accept." For the Collège de France "obliges its members to make public lectures, open to anyone who wants to attend. . . . We are both researchers and people who have to explain publicly our research."[78]

Foucault, in truth, would seem to have made his public refusal to "have a face"—to "remain the same"—the very essence of his public persona. Miller, who notes that "Foucault never prohibited photographs, never shied away from interviews or even television appearances," recounts a celebrated appearance by the philosopher on the popular French television show *Apostrophes,* in which the eminent poststructuralist parodied the role of author before a national audience by refusing to discuss his most recent book. But Foucault's version of self-revelation achieved perhaps its most ironically "revealing" moment when he agreed to be interviewed for *Le Monde*'s 1980 series on leading European intellectuals only if allowed literally to have no face—that is, to remain anonymous. Solely through such public anonymity, explained the now notoriously "masked philosopher," would he have "some chance to be heard." And fittingly, in the same interview Foucault defined philosophy itself as "[t]he movement by which . . . one detaches oneself from what is accepted and seeks other rules"— as "a way of interrogating ourselves." Indeed, "what can the ethics of an intellectual be," he reiterated in 1984, "if not this: to make oneself permanently capable of detaching oneself from oneself?"[79] In other words, no less than Sartre or Robespierre did Foucault consider the willingness to engage in public self-scrutiny and purification a defining characteristic of his chosen status. Indeed Foucault's ongoing public anticonfessional served the same function as the public self-revelations of other would-be consecrated heretics from Rousseau through Sartre: by virtue of disclosing before the nation and the world his desire "to have no face"—of confessing publicly his refusal to confess—he fulfilled the last act prescribed by the heretical narrative and thereby asserted his right, as authentic culture-hero, to contest the established order.

If, in sum, the heretical narrative that seems to frame the public biographies of modern France's consecrated heretics may indeed be compared to Joseph Campbell's archetypal hero of the premodern world, what is its cultural meaning? Having emerged—at least symbolically— from "the world of common day," ascended the wondrous heights of Parisian civilization, and then braved various trials of the psyche no less dauntlessly than had his traditional counterpart braved physical ordeals, what "powers" does the heroic intellectual of modern France purport "to bestow on his fellow man"?

As a secular commoner who succeeds not by virtue of his birth or physical prowess but rather his unique powers of spirit—his intellect and will—this paragon of the revolutionary era represents a manifestly modern hero; indeed, he stands as a perpetual historical indictment of the corporate hierarchy of premodern France. Yet the heroic intellectual is by no means a nineteenth-century liberal individualist of the Samuel Smiles variety; a paragon that is, of the Protestant Ethic seeking private prosperity through methodical labor, personal thrift, and capitalist ingenuity. On the contrary, what appears most striking about this archetypal French hero from the perspective of the aforementioned Anglo-American school of liberty—including, of course, its French adherents—is that he not only disdains private gain but esteems public iconoclasm and even misanthropy.[80] He prospers, in fact, not by cultivating his personal self-interest so much as his purity of will; not by playing according to the rules of civilized society so much as publicly defying them. Accordingly, the hero's final deeds of public transgression, martyrdom, and confession neatly summarize the fable's moral: through sinning against the very established order that has consecrated him he symbolically renounces his own private ambition and self-interest on behalf of "the people"; and through engaging in a public ritual of self-purification, he both reconfirms his link to the common man and reminds him that genuine salvation lies in willful independence from the powers that be—indeed even in revolution against them.

At bottom, the myth of the consecrated heretic in modern France is about the true meaning of freedom. Not only, as shall shortly become apparent, do the received legends of the consecrated heretics define and embody that cardinal cultural virtue, but their most celebrated texts revisit it time and again through recapitulating the central motifs of the heroic myth: the horror of personal dependency and subjugation; the critique, on behalf of "the people," of civilized society and its corruption of the psyche; and finally, the recurrent gravitation toward transgressive outbursts against established authority—toward revolutionary moments of pure and willful liberty. These are the themes, accordingly, which will be explored in the chapters that follow.

THREE

HELL AND OTHER PEOPLE

I

If freedom constitutes the "moral" of the heroic intellectual's tale it amounts not to the hero's pursuit of self-interest in the open marketplace of material and spiritual goods—not, that is, to his exercise of the "negative liberty" so central to classical liberalism. On the contrary, the heroic intellectual tends to identify the pursuit of private gain with the psychic humiliation of personal dependency. Indeed, he both defines and incarnates liberty as that purity of will that may subsist only when one is not psychologically dependent on other people. "I could no longer see any greatness or beauty," recollects Rousseau in one of several such passages in *Les Confessions*, "except in being free and virtuous, superior to fortune and man's opinion, and independent of all external circumstances."[1] Marked from the outset by his singular personal autonomy, the hero must maintain it against the perpetual threat of psychic invasion by others. Hence, he rises to celebrity, it will be recalled, not by virtue of his social ambition or personal vanity, but rather his refusal to compromise his independence of will. And ultimately, he chooses public isolation and martyrdom over personal dependence of any sort.

It is hardly surprising, in this light, to find the avoidance of personal dependency—not to say the vigilant surveillance over its emergence in the psyche—pervading not only the biographical legends of the consecrated heretics but their oeuvres as well.[2] Stendhal's *Le Rouge et le noir* offers an exemplary point of departure here, inasmuch as the horror of personal dependency quite literally frames the novel: its narrator decries "the tyranny of public opinion" in the opening chapter, and following the novel's ostensible close the same voice informs us that "the author" was forced to invent the fictional town of Verrières in order to protect "private life" from "the reign of public opinion." Furthermore, while Stendhal invites harsh judgment of such characters as Monsieur de Rênal, the mayor of Verrières, who is depicted as conforming "to the program that *public opinion* prescribes," and the sophisticated Parisienne Mathilde de La Mole, "whose lofty soul had always to be conscious of a public and *other people*," his hero is virtually defined by his hatred of personal dependency on others—again displaying his obsessive "horror of contempt" (Stendhal's emphasis).[3]

At the crux of Stendhal's narrative is the perpetual tension between Julien's willful autonomy and the ever-looming menace of "other people." We first encounter the protagonist chafing under his father's yoke; and then, having accepted a salaried post under Monsieur de Rênal, Julien consciously mimics Rousseau—as noted above[4]—by proudly refusing to eat with the servants. Indeed, Stendhal portrays his hero as more Rousseauian than Jean-Jacques himself: Julien openly disdains his Genevan forbear for having behaved slavishly toward his social superiors. "Even as he preaches republicanism and the overthrow of royal titles," the youth exclaims at one point, "this upstart is drunk with delight if a duke changes the direction of his after-dinner walk in order to keep company with one of his friends."[5]

Not unexpectedly, Julien identifies his own freedom with detachment from civilized society. At one juncture early in the novel he is pictured as transfixed by "a solitary eagle" as it circles the sky. "Its calm, powerful movements struck him; he envied this power, this isolation." Shortly thereafter, Julien literally sequesters himself in a cave: "Here, said he—his eyes shining with pleasure—here people will never be able to misuse me." Feeling "happier than he had ever been in his life," Julien exults inwardly: "*I am free!*"[6] (Stendhal's emphasis). Even, in fact, while in avid pursuit of fame and fortune in high society, Stendhal's protagonist proves unwilling to conform to its demands. For example, his bid to rise socially through a career in the church is frustrated by his growing reputation within the seminary as "a *free-thinker*": "instead of blindly following *authority* and precedent," Stendhal's narrator informs us, "he *judged for himself*" (Stendhal's emphasis). And while seriously tempted by the prospect of riches, Julien evinces contempt for "an easy retreat to the world of commerce," inasmuch as it might rob him "of the sublime energy that goes into the doing of extraordinary deeds." At one point, he chastises himself at the very thought of "giving my soul to" the rich "in exchange for their money," determining instead to show "that my heart is a thousand leagues from their insolence, and in too lofty a sphere to be touched by their petty marks of favor or disdain."[7]

In the very midst, then, of Parisian high society, Stendhal's hero continues to stand in sharp contrast to the likes of the wealthy Comte Thaler who, lacking "most conspicuously" the "faculty of will," continually takes "the advice of everyone" but does not "have the courage to follow any opinion to the end." Indeed, it is precisely Julien's willful autonomy within civilization itself, as previously underscored, that wins him the admiration both of the aristocratic Mathilde de La Mole—"My little Julien," she muses, "prefers to act alone. Never in this favored being the slightest idea of being supported by other people!"—as well as that of her father. "[T]he usual seminarian," the marquis reflects, "is impatient only when he lacks pleasure and money"; but Julien, while lacking "connections with any set or any coterie," cannot "endure contempt at any price."[8]

Ultimately, of course, Stendhal's hero proves the marquis quite literally correct. Faced with the choice between a guaranteed income from Monsieur de La Mole and defending his honor, Julien does not hesitate to choose the latter course of action. Paradoxically enough, it is only by favoring psychic autonomy over life itself that Julien finds himself truly delivered from *les autres*. "What do *other people* matter?" he asks himself in prison. "My relations with *other people* are going to be severed abruptly" (Stendhal's emphasis). And musing, finally, on the significance of his own saga, Stendhal's hero draws a Rousseauian moral: "You may become learned, you may become shrewd, but the heart! . . . the heart can't be trained."[9] Even the corrupting invasion of civilization, in other words, cannot eradicate authentic freedom.

Thus, even—and especially—while in prison and en route to the scaffold, Julien surfaces, within the narrative logic of *Le Rouge et le noir,* as its freest character. Having emerged psychologically unscathed from conventional society's labyrinth of personal dependency and corruption, he has achieved a self-conscious independence that transcends his bodily imprisonment. Julien's is a liberty defined not by his external circumstances but rather his independence from them, not by his worldly success but his psychic purity, not by his material ambitions but his conscious autonomy of will. In short, within the fictional universe of *Le Rouge et le noir,* Julien has entirely emancipated himself from psychic dependency on other people—and thereby from the Stendhalian hell of "public opinion."

It will be argued below that Rousseau, too, as well as the consecrated heretics who succeeded him, executed corresponding—and equally celebrated—variations on the theme of personal dependency; indeed, that each, within the shared framework of a secular Genesis narrative, depicts (1) the impending fall of primal liberty into the hell of dependency on others, a psychic calamity, which they invariably link, as does Stendhal, to the pursuit of utilitarian self-interest; and (2) the prospect of liberty's salvation, which they inevitably equate with the achievement of self-conscious autonomy within civil society itself.

II

The abhorrence of dependence on others would seem at the very least a strikingly pronounced theme of Rousseau's entire oeuvre, if not the central one.[10] Indeed, taken together, four of Rousseau's principal works between 1750 and 1762—the first two discourses, *Émile,* and *Du Contrat social*—delineate an unfolding narrative about personal liberty, its threatened disruption by other people, and its imagined redemption. As previously noted,[11] Rousseau initially galvanized the attention of the reading public in eighteenth-century France by deliberately defying received opinion in his *Discours sur les sciences et les arts* of 1750. Explicitly setting himself against "all that is nowadays most admired among men" and distinguishing himself from "those who are subjugated by the opinions of society," he notoriously maintains that civilization has corrupted man's "original liberty" instead of nurturing it. Ancient politicians, Rousseau laments, "were always talking of morals and virtue," while "ours speak of nothing but commerce and money." The "indolence and vanity" resulting from such social debasement, moreover, begets subservience "to those who would tyrannize" over the artist's "liberty" on behalf of fashionable opinion. In short, true freedom must not be associated for Rousseau with the pursuit of material advantage or social acclaim. Indeed, his text stands as an indictment of those who would sacrifice "true felicity," which he equates with virtue and independence of mind, so as to please society and enjoy its applause. "Why," Rousseau asks finally, "should we build our happiness on the opinion of others, when we can find it in our own hearts?"[12]

If the renunciation of personal dependency was an important secondary theme of this first widely acclaimed work, it became the central fixation of Rousseau's even more notorious *Discours sur l'origine et les fondements de l'inégalité parmi les hommes* of 1754. His celebrated—and avowedly "hypothetical"—reconstruction of the "natural man" in this crypto-Christian myth of origins[13] prefigures his argument; for liberty and independence, according to Rousseau's anthropology, are imbedded in man's primeval essence. The ill-defined "original liberty" that civilization had corrupted in his first discourse, Rousseau now identifies as "the noblest faculty of man," the consciousness of which constitutes the very "spirituality of his soul." Indeed, it is not reason but will, Rousseau maintains, that distinguishes man from beast. "In the power of willing or rather of choosing, and in the feeling of this power, nothing is to be found but acts which are purely spiritual and wholly inexplicable by the laws of mechanism."[14]

Such pure and unencumbered freedom of will was incarnated for Rousseau in the "man of nature," whom he depicts as inhabiting a moral Eden predating good and evil. "Robust and strong," Rousseau's uncorrupted Adam wanders "up and down the forests . . . an equal stranger to war and all ties, neither standing in need of his fellow creature nor having any desire to hurt them." Only when man is as "dependent on others as he is when he is feeble," Rousseau maintains, does the desire to inflict harm arise. "But," he continues, "that man in the state of nature is both strong and dependent involves two contrary suppositions." In short, the natural man has no need to be socially rapacious because he has no need for society at all.[15]

In nature, then, man remained free of those "bonds of servitude" which are formed "merely by the mutual dependence of men on one another." For "it is impossible to make any man a slave unless he first be reduced to a situation in which he cannot do without the help of others." Even in his innate sympathy for his fellow beings, as well as his periodic sexual attractions to them, the man of nature is motivated not by abiding psychological attachments so much as *amour de soi*, or instinctive self-love, "which leads every animal to look to its own preservation." Thus "self-sufficient and subject to so few passions," he is bounded only by nature itself and his own inborn capacities.[16] In Rousseau's primitive paradise lost, in sum, the human psyche remains entirely uninvaded by the wills of other people.

But Rousseau's Eden of psychic autonomy is of course ultimately disrupted by the serpent of personal dependency, which emerges with society. "[F]rom the moment one man began to stand in the need of the help of another," he laments, "equality disappeared," and man—at least in Rousseau's foreboding biblical imagery—was evicted from the garden: "vast forests became smiling fields which man had to water with the sweat of his brow, and where slavery and misery were seen to germinate and grow up with the crops." With the advent of personal dependency, came the original social sin of *amour-propre*, or personal egoism, which Rousseau distinguishes radically from the natural man's inherent self-love. A "purely relative and factious feeling which arises in the state of society," *amour-propre* "leads each individual to make more of himself than any other" and "causes all the mutual damage men inflict on one another." It is, in short, the root of those self-interested vices—the "unbridled passions" for wealth, property, rank, and acclaim—that corrupt the individual and cause social inequality. Rousseau insists, in fact, that "in the true state of nature vanity [*amour-propre*] did not exist; for as each man regarded himself as the only observer of his actions . . . and the sole judge of his deserts," he remained free of any "feeling arising from comparisons"; hence, "he could know neither hatred nor desire for revenge." Thus, solely the man of nature is truly free in Rousseau's secular myth of origins, for he alone "lives within himself, while the social man lives constantly outside himself, and only knows how to live in the opinion of others."[17] Within the cosmos of his second discourse, Rousseauian hell is all but literally other people.[18]

It would be no exaggeration to suggest that Rousseau's two classic works of 1762, *Émile* and *Du Contrat social*, represent his attempt imaginatively to resolve the biblical melodrama that he had sketched in his first two discourses; that is, to redeem man's original liberty from the perdition of personal dependency and reconcile it with civil society. The man of nature is again the starting point—not to say the real protagonist—of both works. "The natural man lives for himself," writes Rousseau in *Émile;* "he is the unit, the whole, dependent only on himself." Such psychic independence leaves his will pure and unimpeded: "he is tied to no one place, he has no prescribed task, no superior to obey, he knows no law but his own will." Only such a man, who "gets his own way," who "desires what he is able to perform, and does what he desires," is "truly free"; and "freedom, not power, is the greatest good."[19]

Émile advances a system of education meant explicitly to cultivate such liberty, or, in Rousseau's words, "to preserve the supremacy of natural feelings in social life" and hence allow the individual "to be himself, to be always at one with himself." Portraying his imaginary pupil as a would-be man of nature, Rousseau recommends an upbringing of "well-regulated liberty"—one that will nurture the child's self-preserving *amour de soi,* which, as "the instrument of freedom," is "always good," but will avoid awakening the serpent of *amour-propre,* "which is always comparing self with others," and is hence "never satisfied and never can be."[20]

Accordingly, Émile is to be raised apart from society and thereby quarantined from what renders men "really bad": "a multiplicity of needs and clinging to the opinions of other people." What is more, the child should be made to do nothing because "he is being watched or heard; in a word, nothing because of other people, but only what nature asks of him." Such a policy, Rousseau maintains, will not only enhance Émile's strength and independence of will, but will also yield desirable moral side-effects: "[T]he more I make his welfare independent both of the will and judgment of others, the less is it to his interest to lie." Indeed, the child must be discouraged above all from depending on his tutor, who should exclude "the very words *command* and *obey* . . . from [Émile's] vocabulary" (Rousseau's emphasis).[21]

As to how Émile's tutor might accomplish this feat while continuing to guide his pupil's moral growth, Rousseau returns to a distinction he made in his second discourse between submission to the impersonal inequalities of nature, and the moral inequalities of society. Whereas "dependence on men gives rise to every kind of vice," he reiterates in *Émile,* "dependence on things," as "the work of nature," does "no injury to liberty and begets no vices." For, Rousseau later adds, "it is in man's nature to bear patiently with the nature of things, but not with the ill-will of another." The child is to be kept "dependent on things only"; his "unreasonable wishes" should be met "with physical obstacles" rather than personal commands from his tutor. Thus, while remaining himself "really master," Émile's tutor must let the child "always think he is master." Educated thereby through the impersonal "force of things," Émile will learn never to "rebel" against "necessity" and yet will never feel his own will personally invaded. Indeed, promises Rousseau, "[w]hen children only experience resistance in things

and never in the will of man, they do not become rebellious or passionate, and their health is better."²²

Ultimately, then, raised only with limitations as objective as those of
nature itself, Émile is prepared to enter society, and Rousseau describes
the character of a young man so molded: "[H]is heart as pure as his
body, he has no more knowledge of pretense than of vice; reproach
and scorn have not made a coward of him; base fears have never taught
him the art of concealment. He has all the indiscretion of innocence;
he is naively outspoken." But most critical for Rousseau, if the importance of an idea may be measured by its repetition, is that Émile cares
"little for the opinions of other people." Always ready to state "his
opinion without arguing with others because he loves liberty above all
things," his manner of address is "both natural and true," and he "is
just the same among a group of people as he is when he is alone."
While desiring to be loved, and possessed of a "tender and sensitive"
heart, Émile "cares nothing for the weight of popular opinion" or the
"arbitrary values" and "prejudices" of "the conventional world [le
monde]." How, Rousseau asks, could Émile "be dependent on anyone
when he is self-sufficing and free from prejudice? . . . He has been
brought up in complete liberty and servitude is the greatest ill he un-
derstands."²³ And so again Rousseau links liberty inexorably to psychic autonomy even and especially within civil society—that is, to
independence from the will and opinions of other people.

For Rousseau, however, the ultimate test of Émile's liberty is his willingness to transform his unselfconscious purity of will—his innate and
still unsullied *amour de soi*—into conscious self-mastery; that is, to
convert natural freedom into civic virtue. A virtuous man, Émile's tutor
asserts, is he "who can conquer his affections; for he follows his reason, his conscience. . . . he is his own master." Thus, if you want "real
freedom," he urges his pupil, "control your heart." And Émile, having
symbolically freed himself from his passions by voluntarily forsaking
his soul mate Sophie, finally pronounces his own declaration of independence:

> Rich or poor, I shall be free. I shall be free not merely in this coun-
> try or that; I shall be free in any part of the world. All the chains
> of prejudice are broken; as far as I am concerned I know only the
> bonds of necessity. . . . Were I without passions, I would be in my
> manhood as independent as God himself.²⁴

This passage does not end with Émile's words, however. Rather the
young man's tutor exhorts him to enter political society, carry out his

duty to "the public good," and undertake "the painful task of telling men the truth."[25] Rousseau, in other words, projects onto his imaginary protagonist both the willful autonomy and the self-sacrificing public virtue with which he would posthumously endow his own persona—not to say that of his historical heir, the consecrated heretic. But of greater import here is that Rousseau has envisioned in *Émile* a means to preserve the liberty of the natural man, even in the very midst of society, from the hell of other people.

The same would appear no less his goal in *Du Contrat social*. Promising in his very first sentence to take men "as they are," Rousseau begins once again in nature, where man is, in his renowned phrase, "born free." Indeed, even the "natural bond" of children to their father is "dissolved" in nature once they no longer need him; thereafter, they "return equally to independence," to that "common liberty" that "results from the nature of man." In fact, Rousseau proclaims that liberty—still man's "noblest faculty" and "greatest good," as it was in his second discourse and *Émile*—cannot be alienated; for "to renounce liberty is to renounce being a man . . . [and] to remove all moral significance" from one's acts. Hence, human slavery, as the abdication of one's free will in favor of another, is not merely a moral abomination but a contradiction in terms.[26]

Just as Rousseau had asked in *Émile* how an individual might be educated so as to sustain his natural liberty in society and thereby remain "always at one with himself," so too does he ask in *Du Contrat social* what kind of political system might accomplish the same end. What form of government, that is, might safeguard the natural man's inborn integrity of will from the corruptions and encroachments of civil society and thereby transform natural into civic liberty? Hence his celebrated aspiration "to find a form of association wherein each, while uniting himself with all, may still obey himself alone, and remain as free as before." Rousseau responds to his own challenge by conceiving the equivalent in politics of the impersonal and objective pedagogy he had recommended to Émile's tutor—not to say of the law of nature itself: to wit, his notorious "general will." For through the construction of an objective and impersonal social accord to which "each gives himself absolutely" he hopes again, as he had in *Émile,* to replace "dependence on men" with "dependence on things," and thereby to preserve in his imaginary polity the psychic autonomy of each citizen.[27]

Rousseau is quite explicit about this intention. In placing themselves "under the supreme direction of the general will," he emphasizes, all members of the original compact guarantee that each "in giving himself to all, gives himself to nobody." Indeed, there is no one over whom each member "does not acquire the same rights as he yields others over himself." Hence, even when a citizen, failing to obey the "general will," is "compelled to do so by the whole body," his freedom remains fully intact; in such a case, in fact, the individual is literally "forced to be free." For, as Rousseau explains immediately following that fateful phrase, "this is the condition which, by giving each citizen to his country, secures him against all personal dependence."[28]

In other words, to be compelled by "the whole body" is to be met with the same sort of objective "necessity," or "force of things," that Rousseau had enjoined the tutor to place in Émile's path in lieu of man's will. For, again, whereas dependence on men "gives rise to every kind of vice," dependence on things "does no injury to liberty" insofar as "it is in man's nature to bear with the nature of things, but not with the ill-will of another."[29] Thus, if constructed as a "thing," the "general will," even when compelling an individual to obey its pronouncements, will neither invade his psyche nor corrupt his will; that is, it will leave him personally autonomous, and hence "free as before."

But how might the will of "the body as a whole" remain always a "thing?" What, that is, must the "general will" be, so as never to submit the individual to the psychic emasculation of personal dependency? Rousseau's answer is again explicit and suggests that the "general will" as he conceives it is neither the mystical collective consciousness nor the blueprint for totalitarianism it is often reputed to be.[30] Rousseau requires, first of all, that the "general will" "come from all and apply to all," that it always be "general in its object as well as its essence." In other words, because "will either is, or is not, general," the "general will" must be formed with the direct participation of each member. And if it be truly "general," it must only consider "subjects en masse and actions in the abstract, and never a particular person or action." Thus, for example, while "the law may indeed decree that there shall be privileges," it "cannot confer them on anybody by name." Moreover, while reserving to itself the right to determine "what is important," the "general will" is meant to impose itself only upon those individual "powers, goods, and liberty" as are necessary "for the community to control." In the case of religion, for instance, Rousseau reminds his reader that subjects "owe the Sovereign an account of their opinions only to such an extent that they matter to the community," and he recommends therefore that "tolerance should be given to all religions that tolerate others, so long as their dogmas contain nothing contrary to the duties of citizenship."[31]

Rousseau also distinguishes the "general will," which "considers only the common interest," from "the will of all," which is "no more than a sum of particular wills." While the latter "takes private interest into account," he explains, the former is constituted by assembled citizens who, when they vote on a given law, decide not whether they personally approve of it, but "whether it is in conformity with the general will, which is their own." In other words, when establishing the law, which is nothing more than "the declaration of the general will," each citizen, strictly speaking, consults not his private desires but what he believes to be the common good. While the individual "may have a particular will contrary or dissimilar to the general will which he has as a citizen," he will have a powerful stake in "voting for all," Rousseau argues, insofar as he has agreed to submit himself "to the conditions he imposes on others."[32]

Here we meet the political counterpart of Émile's conversion from natural liberty to civic virtue—his capacity to "conquer his affections" and become his own master. For in relinquishing "natural liberty, which is bounded only by the strength of the individual" in favor of "civil liberty, which is limited by the general will"—that is, in consciously choosing the common good over his personal desires—Rousseau's citizen achieves that "moral liberty, which alone makes him truly master of himself; for the mere impulse of appetite is slavery, while obedience to a law which we prescribe to ourselves is liberty."[33]

But Rousseau is not content to rely upon the general achievement of "moral liberty" in his polity. Fearing that the "general will" might become sullied by "intrigues" and "partial associations," he insists on yet another provision: that the "general will" be formed only when the members of the aspiring polity, "being furnished with adequate information," hold their deliberations with "no communication one with the other." In short, the devil of personal dependence must be exorcized not only from the "general will" itself, but from the very public gathering at which it is fashioned. What is more, while recommending that the polity solicit the counsel of a "lawmaker" in formulating the "general will," Rousseau explicitly prohibits his would-be Solons or Calvins either from legislating or executing the laws; indeed, he no less explicitly divorces the formulation of the "general will" from its execution: "the depositories of the executive power," he asserts, "are not the people's masters, but its officers," and accordingly "the instant the government usurps the Sovereignty, the social compact is broken, and all private citizens recover by right their natural liberty."[34]

In sum, Rousseau's "general will" must not only be limited to mat-

ters of general import and reflect the direct will of every citizen, each
of whom must vote not according to his private passions but his perception of the public interest; it must also be formulated in circumstances whereby each citizen may exercise his will without the corrupting interference of others. Those who help design and carry it out,
moreover, must never be its creators—who must always be the people
as a whole—but rather appointed functionaries who may be dismissed
at will. Thus, speaking strictly of its design rather than its conceivable
flaws, *Du Contrat social* would seem to propose not an all-powerful
totalitarian state poised to invade the lives of its citizens, but rather an
impersonal, objective, and universal set of rules emanating from the
citizenry as a whole and applying equally to all; a political paradise of
personal autonomy in which individuals would submit "to the laws of
the State as to those of nature"[35] because those laws would never disrupt the integrity of their wills. Presumably, then, Rousseau's would be
a republic of Émiles: citizens who are socially authentic and unpreten-
tious, ingenuously outspoken, civically virtuous, and incapable of deceit; citizens who remain ever active in political decision making insofar as they must continually elevate the public good over private
interest; citizens, in other words, whose wills are wholly free and autonomous—entirely untainted by dependence on other people—even
as they participate in civil society.[36]

Rousseau's two classic works of 1762, then, completed the cultural
parable that his discourses of the 1750s had initiated. Setting out from
a psychological Eden situated either in human prehistory or childhood,
his perpetual protagonist, the natural man, is marked above all by his
innate liberty: that integrity of will, or inner spiritual "oneness," that
constitutes his "noblest faculty." Faced, however, with the inevitability
of entering society, he is confronted by the omnipresent societal serpent of personal dependency that threatens to corrupt his will, render
him vain and self-interested, and hence enslave him both to the whims
of others and his own passions. In Rousseau's narrative, that is, the
hell of other people and the pursuit of private utility are inextricably
bound. Only by meticulously restructuring the educational and political institutions that shape his social character might the hero's purity
of will be sustained against the invasion of others; only thereby might
his original freedom be salvaged and even transformed into a higher
civic and "moral liberty"—into conscious self-mastery.

The question of how directly Rousseau's works, and especially *Du
Contrat social,* influenced the revolutionary generation remains open

to debate. However, that Rousseau's great political treatise was among the least read of his works in the eighteenth century seems beyond question; and that even his most fervent disciples, such as Robespierre and Saint-Just, abandoned its more impracticable axioms—most notably, his prohibition of political representation—is a matter of historical record. Yet the tension between freedom and personal dependency that pervades Rousseau's oeuvre—his potent narrative of natural liberty, its impending corruption by others, and its projected regeneration in society—would seem to underlie the Revolution's radical phase at the very least. The Jacobins, writes David Jordan, considered "independence and self-sufficiency" the "mundane and necessary dimension of freedom." Hence, it is not surprising to find them emphasizing, as another historian has put it, "the autonomy of the self, preoccupied with its own purity." [37]

Robespierre, in fact, as early as his assault on the revolutionary Constitution of 1791 for dividing the populace into voting, or "active," citizens as opposed to nonvoting, or "passive," ones, embraced an explicitly Rousseauian definition of liberty: "it is freedom to obey laws of which one is oneself the maker, but it is slavery to be compelled to submit to the will of another." Moreover, both mirroring Rousseau's emphasis on unity of will and anticipating the illiberalism of later Jacobin discourse, Robespierre goes on to warn the Convention: "[I]f you do not do everything for liberty you will have done nothing." For "[t]here are not two ways of being free: one must be so entirely or one becomes once more a slave." This same Rousseauian formulation resurfaces unmistakably two years later in Robespierre's proposed redrafting of the "Declaration of the Rights of Man and Citizen": "Liberty," he asserts, "is the power which appertains to man to exercise all his faculties at will; it has justice for rule, the rights of others for limits, nature for principle, and the law for a safeguard." And while the people may choose representatives, "[e]ach and every section of the assembled sovereign must enjoy the right to express its will with entire liberty." [38]

Thus, individual freedom for Robespierre entails both the absence of all personal dependence on others and an absolute integrity of the will within civil society. Moreover, "[t]rue independence," he asserted in 1792, "is relative not to one's fortune, but . . . to the passions of men." Consequently, members of the popular classes, who are "not burdened by . . . ruinous passions," remain for Robespierre more free than the rich. Indeed, for the Jacobin leader, as for Rousseau, liberty is never to be mistaken for the unrestricted pursuit of personal gain.

"Unlimited freedom" would be possible, Robespierre argued in a 1792 speech favoring economic price controls, only "if all men were just and virtuous, if greed were never tempted to plunder the substance of the people." But such laissez-faire liberty, in light of its inevitable exploitation by the privileged classes, would give free reign to "self-interest over the public interest," to "the pride and passions of powerful men" over "the rights and needs of the weak." For Robespierre, in sum, true freedom—unimpeded psychic autonomy—is not only the province of "the people," but inherently inimical to the open-ended pursuit of private gain.[39]

In fact, Robespierre characteristically associates private self-interest with "ambition, pride, cupidity, and the most extravagant fantasies, passions harmful to society"; that is, with a Rousseauian *amour-propre,* which poses a greater threat within Robespierre's revolutionary vision than it did even to Rousseau. In his notorious address of 1794 "On the Principles of Political Morality," the Jacobin goes so far as to proclaim that in order to secure the "peaceful enjoyment of liberty and equality," we must "seek an order of things in which all the base and cruel passions are enchained," for "when the people is corrupt, liberty is already lost." He enjoins "the representative body," accordingly, to begin "by submitting all private passions within it to the general passion for the public welfare."[40]

Owing especially to the revolutionary crisis, Robespierre argues, the people's will must remain unsullied by *amour-propre* and focused entirely on the public good. Hence, he famously identifies revolutionary freedom with "virtue," which he defines as "nothing other than the love of the nation and its laws." Indeed, "[l]iberty and virtue," Robespierre had proclaimed earlier in 1794, "spring together from the breast of the same divinity; neither can live among men without the other." Consequently, he urges the establishment of laws that tend "to excite love of country, to purify morals, to elevate souls, to direct the passions of the human heart toward the public good" while curbing "selfishness" and the "enjoyment of petty things."[41] In this way, Robespierre both borrows the Rousseauian concept of "moral liberty"—the individual's voluntary mastery of his private passions on behalf of the public good—and extends it radically, on behalf of the Revolution, to the complete banishment of private self-interest from the wills of politically engaged citizens.

Such absolute and unsullied "liberty," finally, requires an unremitting vigilance over the psyche not to say its perpetual purification. "Mistrust," Robespierre had avowed as early as 1791, "is to the love of liberty what jealousy is to passion." Thus, while the people "are naturally upright," and indeed while "virtue," as he put it in 1794, "is natural to the people," the threat of inner corruption remains forever at hand. Looming ever large over the revolutionary citizen's freedom remains the perpetual shadow of the revolutionary enemy. Whether "tyrant," "conspirator," or "traitor," whether "within" the Republic or "without," the "enemy of liberty" stands ready to cast "the people" out of their new and fragile heaven of revolutionary liberty and back into the hell of personal dependency.[42]

Robespierre, as had Rousseau before him, increasingly cast his world in stark moral antitheses: "There are only two parties in France," he characteristically exclaimed, "the people and its enemies . . . that of corrupt men and that of virtuous men." The people's enemies, he contends, are guilty of all "the vices which destroy public liberty." Waging an ongoing "war of deceit and corruption . . . against the Republic," they are "supported by wealth" and "armed with every device to lure the voluptuary and ensnare the weak." It is in order "to defeat" these "enemies of . . . freedom" that Robespierre increasingly proclaims the need for a vigilant and ruthless revolutionary government. Defining the Revolution itself in 1793 as "the war of liberty against its enemies," he reassured the Convention's members that they would always "be right" to "subdue liberty's enemies by terror."[43]

Clearly discernable, then, in Robespierre's portrayal of the Revolution is the dramatic Rousseauian contest between authentic social liberty and that psychic contagion which ceaselessly imperils it. Defining the free man as he who obeys himself and is not "compelled to submit to the will of another," he finds in "the people" the equivalent of Rousseau's natural liberty: that autonomy of will which arises out of independence from the "burdensome passions" of self-interest. Moreover, suggests Robespierre, under the drastic pressure of Revolution the people's natural independence must of necessity be transmuted into a Rousseauian "moral liberty" or "civic virtue"—into a selfless love of the nation and its welfare. But such purity of will, necessary to the survival of both the Revolution and of liberty itself, is perpetually menaced by an omnipresent enemy, a revolutionary Other, onto whom Robespierre has projected Rousseau's original sin of *amour-propre,* along with its attendant vices of ambition, greed, envy, and egoism. Again like Rousseau, that is, Robespierre represents submission to the Other not only as the occasion for our literal servitude but, more insidiously, for subservience to our own internal devils. In the final analysis, then, Robespierre is able to justify the Terror as necessary to the ongoing purification of the people's will; for he has constructed the Revolution itself as a death struggle to rescue the integrity of the individual will—genuine liberty, both personal and political—from the corrupting invasion of *les autres*. Rousseau's abhorrence of personal dependence, his dread of psychic invasion by "other people," finds an unmistakable echo in Robespierre's demand that individual wills be continually purged of social vice and private self-interest.

A half-century later, and some fifteen years after Stendhal's postrevolutionary parable of Julien Sorel first appeared, Michelet framed a strikingly similar narrative in his back-to-back best-sellers of 1845, *Du Prêtre, de la femme, et de la famille* and *Le Peuple*. Neither of these works, of course, was literally fictional, and the two appear on their surface quite unrelated: the former comprises one of the classic texts of nineteenth-century French anticlericalism,[44] while the latter represents an archetypal statement of republican nationalism. Yet each outlined in dramatic fashion the impending threat of "other people" to individual liberty, and each emphasized the cultural urgency of sustaining the individual's purity of will against that threat.

Liberty, Michelet asserts in *Du Prêtre,* is "the internal God of man," and in *Le Peuple* he similarly finds "all human dignity" to reside in the word "free." Freedom constitutes again for Michelet an unsullied sovereignty of will innate to man's original nature. In *Le Peuple,* he identifies it with that inborn "instinct and action" which remains least impaired among children and the popular classes, who have retained their "simplicity of heart." He proclaims, in fact, in a conspicuously Rousseauian formulation, that "[m]an is born noble, and he dies noble. It takes the work of a lifetime to become coarse and ignoble and to produce inequality between men." In *Du Prêtre,* by the same token, Michelet speaks of "the sacred ingenuousness and freedom of character which are born" to each man and of "that which is most personally and individually his—the will." One's will, the historian elaborates, "attaches itself with perseverance to a person, and truly rules him, because it conforms him to its image."[45]

In both works, moreover, this original sovereignty of will is menaced by the familiar specter of personal dependency. Bearing the title "Of Bondage and Hate," the first part of *Le Peuple* compares the various personal dependencies foisted upon the peasant, the factory worker, the artisan, the manufacturer, the shopkeeper, the bureaucrat, and the bourgeois industrialist. "[T]he higher one goes toward the upper classes," Michelet concludes, "the less alive one becomes." For while factory workers, for example, are subject to "extreme physical dependence" and "outward bondage," they "still preserve a heart free from hatred." Indeed, the "most dependent workingman" is "a serf in body" but "free in soul" compared to the obsequious shopkeeper, who is forced "to enslave [his] soul and sacrifice [his] integrity," to "disguise [his] thoughts from morning to night," in order "*to please*," which, Michelet laments, epitomizes "the lowest form of serfdom" (Michelet's emphasis). Worse yet, however, is the "oblique, indirect dependence" of the bureaucrat, which "weighs heavily from high to low, penetrating, questioning, spying, and attempting to master even the soul." For even the shopkeeper, who must lie about matters concerning "his external interest," often "preserves his independence" in "what concerns the soul"; but the bureaucrat "is sometimes forced to lie about what concerns his religious and political faith." Finally, the worst bondage of all is the "personal interest" of the rich bourgeois. Trapped in "the pure egotism of the calculator," writes Michelet, his "soul is empty" as a result.[46] In short, Michelet offers in *Le Peuple* a Rousseauian (and Robespierrist) ranking of personal hells, which favors the "outward bondage" of nature or the factory—that is, of things—over the inner bondage of subjection to a foreign will. For, again, dependency on things, while perhaps entrapping the body, does not—as does dependency on other people, and worst of all, bondage to one's own *amour-propre*—violate the soul.

Michelet refers in *Le Peuple* to what he has "spoken of elsewhere" as "the bondage of the priest"; but the work to which he alludes, *Du Prêtre, de la femme, et de la famille,* does not address the clergy's own serfdom so much as its psychic enslavement of others. Michelet's text amounts in fact to an inflammatory account of the Catholic Church's attempt, since the seventeenth century, to invade the Frenchman's psyche through the spiritual seduction of his wife, and as such it offers a veritable pathology of personal dependency. Finding "the soft and feeble nature of women" more pliable than that of men, Michelet's archetypal priest employs the "great power" of confession to know "of this woman what the husband has never known." The priest also takes on the role of the wife's spiritual "director," regularly visiting her at home. "To the confessor," Michelet explains, women "told their sins, nothing more. To the director they tell everything." In fact, it is the priest's ambition "to reign over a soul," to "be the God of another." Accordingly, "he penetrates further" on the chance that her soul still conceals "a world of liberty which [he] cannot reach." Secretly, Michelet charges, "he wishes her as a lover—a lover of God; he deceives himself in deceiving her."[47]

Even worse than violating the "virginity of [a woman's] soul," or so Michelet argues, is the priest's intention "to undermine a rival authority; . . . that of the husband." Each day the wife repeats to her husband and son "the lesson she has learned," and it enters that "notable part of our activity" which "escapes . . . from the sphere of liberty to enter into that of habit." Through the wife's confidences, moreover, the priest gains access to her husband's "inmost thoughts"; hence, "[t]hat which he dreams on his pillow, he is astonished to hear the next day in the street."[48]

The church, in short, represents for Michelet the invading Other par excellence, a "revolutionary enemy" as dangerous to liberty in its own way as any denounced by Robespierre. Priests, he exclaims, even those who claim to support the Republic, are "*enemies of the modern mind, enemies of liberty,*" and "enemies of the Revolution" (Michelet's emphasis). For the church's ideal is "*annihilation,* the art of annihilating activity, the will, the personality" (Michelet's emphasis). *Du Prêtre,* then, portrays the insidious "penetration" of the "enemies of the Revolution" into the innermost psyches of free men, threatening all but literally to emasculate them, to violate that sovereignty of will which defines both their manhood and their freedom; it purports to disclose, that is, a veritable nightmare of personal dependency.[49]

But if French liberty is at risk for Michelet, be it from the psychic "bondage" of hierarchical dependency or the personal invasion of the church, it is not beyond redemption. And like Rousseau, Michelet suggests that at the very least man's natural liberty might be regenerated through education. Although Frenchmen have become "disfigured by their misfortune and corrupted by their progress," Michelet writes in *Le Peuple,* the "birth of genius"—of "the harmonious and creative man who manifests his inner excellence by a superabundance of love and strength"—is still possible. But, he asks, "[w]hat is the first part of public policy? . . . the second? . . . the third?" To each query his answer is "education." Only a public education that strives "to reunite men" in a love of the nation and the Revolution, bolsters "willpower and moral strength," and inculcates "the strength and generosity of sacrifice" will recapture that "freedom" that "is the possibility of virtue."[50]

In *Du Prêtre,* on the other hand, Michelet champions not so much public education as "education in the family," which, he asserts, is that of "liberty." And paradoxically enough, he advocates leaving young French sons at home to be educated by their mothers—presuming the latter, of course, to have divorced themselves from the church.[51] The apparent contradiction between Michelet's manifest contempt for "the soft and feeble nature of women," which leads to an unwitting betrayal of their husbands' liberty, and his willingness to place the budding freedom of French sons in their mothers' hands is perhaps less jarring than it might first appear. For the consecrated heretic, it will be recalled, while required to establish a pronounced independence from his father and from men in general, is not only permitted an emotional dependence on women—and especially his mother—but is often marked by such dependency for future greatness. Hence, for example, Madame Sartre's aforementioned "adoration" of her son and uncritical applause for his early writings, and Madame Foucault's defense, over her husband's protestations, of Paul-Michel's chosen career in letters.[52]

Michelet himself, as noted above, dedicated a second preface of *Du Prêtre* to his own mother. "How deeply am I indebted to her!" he exclaims; "I feel profoundly that I am the son of my mother."[53] And in the text he affirms somewhat immodestly: "It is a general rule to which I have hardly seen an exception that superior men are always the *sons of their mothers*" (Michelet's emphasis). For while it is a father's role to check his son's "natural impulse," he argues, it is the mother's instinct to nurture the boy's liberty. She becomes "a defender of his primal individuality," whose "dearest wish . . . is to sustain the moral force, the will" of he whom she loves. "The mother's ideal of education," in short, "is to make a hero; a man powerful in acts and fruitful in works." Asking if her child might "be a Bonaparte, a Voltaire, or a Newton," she makes certain that "he may receive strength and life, and breathe with a good heart the generous air of freedom!"[54]

Maternal dependency, then, not only poses no threat to a young boy's freedom for Michelet, but instead enhances it by bolstering his innate sovereignty of will. Indeed, somewhat ironically, it represents within the structure of Michelet's narrative one more means of inoculating the Frenchman's natural liberty against contamination by wills foreign to his own; another chance, alongside a patriotic public education, to rescue the integrity of his will from psychic bondage to other people and to his own "egotism of the calculator," and thereby to render him a self-consciously autonomous citizen.

At first glance, nothing could appear further removed from the jeremiads of Robespierre or Michelet than the abstract and cerebral prose of Henri Bergson's *Essai sur les données immédiates de la conscience* (1889) and *L'Évolution créatrice* (1907), which together encompass the framework of his celebrated fin-de-siècle philosophy. Yet, while seemingly unconcerned with social criticism or politics per se, Bergson would appear to recapitulate the now familiar heretical tale of freedom and personal dependency in the very structure of his metaphysics, which again evokes the potential subservience of natural liberty to a foreign tyrant. Indeed, Bergson's ever-expanding Parisian audience, as noted previously, had little trouble discerning from his lectures at the Collège de France a radical critique of the established order focusing on the theme of freedom;[55] nor did such disciples as Charles Péguy, as shall shortly be seen, have difficulty extracting political morals from the master's metaphysics.

The renowned dichotomies of Bergson's discourse—the "vital" versus the "geometrical" realms of nature, time versus space, pure "duration" versus the "ready-made" categories of language, human intuition versus intellect—prefigure the psychic drama to come. Bergson posits that there are, in effect, two human selves, each in contact with a different level of the real: the vital, "deep-seated self [*moi intérieure*]," which participates in *la durée,* the dynamic and uninterrupted flow of the real; and the mechanistic, empirical, social self, "a conscious automaton," which performs "the majority of our daily actions" through discerning what is immediately "*useful*" and driving "back into the unconscious" what is not (Bergson's emphasis). The one acts freely and spontaneously through its intuitive link to the dynamic indeterminacy of nature, while the other quantifies reality, calculates utilitarian self-interest, and remains within the fixed and predetermined categories of language.[56]

It is not difficult to detect in the former *moi intérieur* the Rousseauian motif of natural liberty. For Rousseau, it will be recalled, freedom constituted that "power of willing" which yields acts that "are purely spiritual and wholly inexplicable by the laws of mechanism."[57] Writing a century and a half later in *L'Évolution créatrice,* Bergson, too, finds that whereas for animals, conscious "invention . . . escapes automatism for only an instant, for just the time to create a new automatism," for man, on the other hand, "and man alone," it "sets itself free." Indeed, "[i]t is the whole soul," Bergson asserts in the *Essai,* "which gives rise to the free decision"; for "[w]e are free when our acts spring from our whole personality . . . when they have that indefinable resemblance to it which one sometimes finds between the artist and his work." Bergson, recalling both Rousseau and Michelet, finds such genuinely free acts to be "like a new childhood."[58] Thus, Bergsonian liberty amounts again to the uncorrupted integrity of one's primal will.

But alongside Bergson's "fundamental self" hovers the inevitable "parasitic self which continually encroaches upon the other" and thereby causes many a man to "die without having known true freedom." Indeed, "stronger than reason, stronger than immediate experience," this "mechanistic instinct of mind," which Bergson identifies with "the intellect," is characterized above all by "an insatiable desire to separate," to impose the fixed geometry of spatial categories upon not only inanimate matter, where its analytical gaze is accurate and appropriate, but also the temporal vitality of life—of *durée*—where it is not. It is above all the tool of human language that accomplishes this reductive violence. "[T]he brutal word," Bergson laments, "which stores up the stable, common and consequently impersonal element in the impressions of mankind, overwhelms . . . the delicate and fugitive impressions of our individual consciousness." Whereas, for example, "each of us has his own way of loving and hating," and "this love and hate reflects his whole personality," language "denotes these states by the same words in every case," thereby fixing only "the impersonal aspect of love, hate and the thousand emotions which stir the soul." In short, as Bergson proclaims in *L'Évolution créatrice*, "[t]he *intellect is* characterized by a natural inability to comprehend life" (Bergson's emphasis).[59]

Nevertheless, inasmuch as "social life is practically more important to us than our inner and individual existence," we typically submit our freedom to this mechanistic "shadow of the self," which "is much better adapted to the requirements of social life in general and language in particular" than the *moi intérieur*. But in so doing—in solidifying "our impressions in order to express them in language"—we begin to find "reflex action" and "automatism" supplanting our liberty. Our consciousness becomes "more and more lifeless, more and more impersonal"; and to the degree that "our life unfolds in space rather than time," we begin to "live for the external world rather than ourselves." Ultimately, instead of maintaining "an inner life" that "cannot be expressed in the fixed terms of language," we fabricate "a self which can be artificially reconstructed." The utilitarian intellect, by "invading the series of our psychic states" and "introducing space into our perception of duration . . . corrupts at its very source, our feeling of outer and inner change, of movement, and of freedom."[60]

In other words, Bergson reconstitutes the heretical narrative as a metaphysical drama unfolding entirely within the human psyche. Our innately free *moi intérieur*—autonomous, pure, and at one with the dynamic temporal flux of nature itself—is forever menaced, according to the philosopher, by the corrupting invasion of its own "parasitic" shadow, the mechanizing intellect. While in principle nonpolitical, this internal enemy is strikingly reminiscent of those dreaded by the likes of Robespierre, Michelet, Rousseau, and Stendhal: like Robespierre's revolutionary enemy and Michelet's priest, it is a self-serving egoist empty of soul; like Rousseau's civilized Parisian and Stendhal's rich bourgeois, it threatens to impose a regime of civilized mediocrity, mindless habit, and self-interested calculation—of personal dependence and *amour-propre*—upon the autonomous will, thereby sapping it of purity, vitality, and freedom. In fact, Bergson's metaphysical Other is all the more insidious for residing in the eternal Trojan horse of human language. For Bergson, that is, the hell of other people is forever internalized in man's dependency on discourse, which ceaselessly threatens to ensnare his innate liberty and spontaneity in the web of social utility.

But again, there remains the possibility of salvation. In order to restore "duration" to "its original purity," Bergson contends, our "ego" must cease "separating its present state from its former states" and "let itself live." Yet carrying out such an operation is exceedingly difficult; for our ordinary consciousness, which "is pre-eminently intellect," must be abandoned in favor of "intuition," which "goes in the very direction of life." Thus, "pure duration" as such may be recovered only through a great and deliberate effort of "deep introspection, which leads us to grasp our inner states as living things, constantly becoming, as states not amenable to measure."[61] Within Bergson's philosophical narrative, then, no less than the manifestly sociopolitical liberation sagas of a Robespierre or Michelet, lingers the prospect that the integrity of man's will may yet elude and overcome the psychic vampire forever poised to invade its realm.

Through his celebrated Bergsonian dichotomy of "mystique" and "politique," Charles Péguy immediately recast his mentor's philosophical drama in the mold of political and social criticism. Again, "mystique," for Péguy, represents all that is vital and free in the human soul, its intuitive link to Bergsonian *durée*, while "politique" describes that in us which is predetermined and sterile. "Everything begins in mystique and ends in politique," reads the most often cited sentence of Péguy's celebrated 1910 essay, *Notre jeunesse*. In the very title of that essay, he evokes the deep nostalgia for primal purity of soul that would

pervade his writings until his death four years later. In 1911, for instance, the essayist recalled his own school days when "everything"—
including socialism and Christianity—"was pure" and "everything
was young"; and in 1913 he glorified his generation's "[h]appy childhood," when "we loved the Church and the Republic together, with
the same heart, and that was the heart of a child."[62]

Péguy's universe of "mystique," then, evokes the Rousseauian paradise of the natural man as well as that "simplicity of heart" attributed
to "the people" by Michelet, whom the essayist cites approvingly on
occasion. For implicit in "mystique" is that original unity and independence of will which Péguy, too, identifies with freedom. "I love nothing
so much as liberty," he wrote in 1913, which amounts to "believ-
ing what one believes and living it." Defending Bergson in his final
work, Péguy associated the master's teachings with that "counterhabit
[contra-habitude]" of mind which preserves "the heart of liberty" from
the "ready-made [tout fait]." Bergson's philosophy, he contends, is "essentially liberating and libertarian [libertaire] . . . at its heart." Indeed,
"French liberty" itself is nothing more than "Bergsonian liberty."[63]

If freedom, for Péguy, constitutes a primal purity and autonomy of
will, it is besieged on every side—this time by the corrupting force of
"politique," which is Péguy's catchall term for the omnipresent enemy.
The traitor, he proclaims in Notre jeunesse, is he "who sells his faith,
who sells his soul, who sells his very being . . . who betrays his mystique in order to join the corresponding politique." And Péguy found
the personification of such inner debasement in the figure of Jean
Jaurès. Having fought alongside him during the Dreyfus affair, Péguy
denounces the socialist's exploitation of the "Dreyfusard mystique" to
further his political program of anticlericalism and internationalism.
Through such abuse of "our mystique," Péguy proclaims, Jaurès "not
only betrays us . . . he dishonors us." In 1905, Péguy had eulogized
at length the "Jaurès of the open air and of autumnal woods," the
"poetical Jaurès," who was "ruined" by his own capacity "to explain
by discursive, eloquent, conclusive reasons." Evoking their final meet-
ing, which Péguy characterizes as "sinister," he describes "an entirely
different man," one who "was tired, bowed, wasted," who had "abandoned the free life, the honest life, the open-air life of the simple citizen; forever and irrevocably he was to plunge . . . into politique. . . .
He was the spectator of his own decay." By 1913, Péguy was accusing
his former ally of having betrayed socialism to "bourgeois parties,"
Dreyfusism to "the State," and even France itself to "the German
party."[64]

Jaurès, however, represented only the tip of the iceberg for Péguy. Sounding every bit the latter-day Robespierre, he charges in *Notre jeunesse* that while "[f]ounders come first, profiteers come after." Indeed, "the modern world" itself comprises by its very nature, for Péguy, "the world of those who believe in nothing, not even atheism, who sacrifice themselves to nothing." It entails "a profound movement of *demystification*" and "sterility" (Péguy's emphasis). Never, Péguy elaborates in 1913, have "selfishness in particular and the preoccupations of self-interest . . . fallen to a like degree of baseness." And depicting the enemy in unmistakably Bergsonian imagery, he decries "the economic strangulation of today, that scientific, cold, rectangular, regular . . . strangulation." Indeed, in his 1914 defense of Bergson, Péguy mourns every "dead soul" that "has succumbed to the accumulation of its own red tape, its own bureaucracy."[65] Having capitulated, that is, to his own inner demon of egoistical "politique," the modern Frenchman, charges Péguy, has both imperiled the nation and sacrificed his own authentic liberty.

But all was not lost in Péguy's national melodrama. *Notre jeunesse* celebrated above all the stubborn integrity of will demonstrated by those who defended Dreyfus, proving that "a man of heart" may yet "remain loyal to a mystique." And evoking the "Dreyfusard mystique," Péguy exclaimed in his rhythmically repetitive prose that "we were heroes" who had devoted our "whole life," our "whole career," our "whole health," our "whole body," our "whole soul," our "whole life of the heart, in short, everything" to the Affair. Indeed, "our Dreyfusard mystique" aimed at nothing less than "THE ETERNAL SALVATION OF FRANCE" (Péguy's capitalization). Moreover, Péguy found a heroic counterpart to Jaurès in the Jewish journalist Bernard-Lazare, "a prophet" who virtually embodied the "Dreyfusard mystique." "I have never seen a man believe so deeply, have so deep a conviction, that a man's conscience was an absolute, an invincibility, an eternity, a freedom." In fact, "Dreyfusism" itself, Péguy would conclude in 1913, was nothing more than "a system of absolute liberty, absolute justice."[66]

Thus, foreshadowed already in the title of his most acclaimed essay is a plot structure that Péguy's readers might surely have recognized from Rousseau or Stendhal: the tale of "our youth," an Eden of unsullied freedom; its invasion and debasement by the eternal enemy of egoistic self-interest; and its ever-possible regeneration into civic virtue. Discernable in his much celebrated term "mystique" is the spiritual purity of Rousseauian *liberté,* and in his "politique," the corrupting power of Bergson's calculating, utilitarian intellect. The latter foe would seem, in fact, to embody for Péguy the perpetual threat to each individual both of literal enslavement to others and of subservience to one's own inner serpent of egoism. Indeed, whether indicting the self-serving treachery of Jaurès or the "cold, rectangular strangulation" of the modern world, Péguy evokes perhaps nothing more strikingly than the revolutionary hell of Robespierre: a steadily contracting universe in which the enemy, both within and without, forever conspires to disrupt the free citizen's will.

No modern writer has portrayed the hell of other people more vividly than Jean-Paul Sartre, who of course coined the phrase in his celebrated 1943 play, *Huis clos,* and explored its meaning exhaustively in his philosophical tome of the same year, *L'Etre et le néant.* In *Huis clos,* Sartre concocted a vicious triangle of bourgeois Parisians trapped together in a hell defined literally by their inability to escape each other's gaze. Deprived of nighttime, eyelids, and mirrors, each is condemned to see him-or herself only in the eyes of the other two—truly to face the others for eternity, as one of them puts it, "with one's eyes open all the time." Each, moreover, harbors a secret sin, which he or she is forced ultimately to disclose both inwardly and to the other two. Able to view themselves only through the eyes of the others, they must seek their psychic salvation entirely therein. Garçin, for example, a Spanish journalist captured and then executed for fleeing military service during the Civil War, hopes to redeem himself in the judgment of Inez, a sadistic lesbian postal clerk, from the accusation of cowardice. "You who hate me," he implores, "if you have faith in me I'm saved." And Inez, by the same token, serves literally as a mirror to the vain *femme fatale,* Estelle, who has murdered her child: "You know the way they catch larks—with a mirror? I'm your lark-mirror, my dear, and you cannot escape me." The other two, finally, serve no less as inescapable self-reflections for Inez. "Why, you've even stolen my face," she laments; "you know it and I don't." Thus, each remains for the other two "a gaze observing you, a formless thought that thinks you," thereby preserving in hell "an economy of manpower" inasmuch as each acts "as torturer of the other two." Hence the play's all-too-notorious catchphrase: "L'enfer, c'est les Autres" (Hell is other people).[67]

Almost equally familiar is Sartre's phenomenology of shame in *L'Etre et le néant.* Sartre imagines himself, "moved by jealousy, curiosity, or vice," peering through a keyhole, where he is initially without any awareness of himself as a limited being. "I am my acts . . . a pure mode of losing myself in the world." In truth, he cannot even define himself "as truly in the process of listening at doors. I escape this provisional definition of myself by means of all my transcendence. . . . I am absolutely nothing." But suddenly the scene changes dramatically. "I hear footsteps in the hall. Someone is looking at me!" And at this moment, Sartre concludes: "I see myself because someone sees me." What is more, he also recognizes that he is "indeed that object which the Other is looking at and judging," that "I am in a world which the Other has made alien to me, for the Other's look embraces my being."[68]

For Sartre, in other words, "the existence of the Other" constitutes an "original fall." Indeed "original sin," he asserts, "is my upsurge in a world where there are others." For "the Other's existence brings a factual limit to my freedom"; his "watchful look" is "a gun pointed at me," the "death of my possibilities." Accordingly, all human relationships are fraught with an underlying and inescapable tension. Rejecting Heidegger's concept of an ontologically stable "being-with-others," or *Mitsein,* which, he insists, "cannot be primary," Sartre maintains that "[t]he essence of the relations between consciousnesses . . . is conflict." Even as "I attempt to free myself from the hold of the Other, the Other is trying to free himself from mine; while I seek to enslave the Other he is seeking to enslave me." Indeed, we may "consider ourselves as 'slaves' insofar as we appear to the Other"; for "I am a slave to the degree that my being is dependent at its center upon a freedom that is not mine and which is the condition of my being."[69] In short, both in *Huis clos* and *L'Etre et le néant* Sartre depicts a recognizably Rousseauian hell of personal dependency in which the judgmental gaze of the Other—who has earned an upper-case initial not merely by way of Hegel and Heidegger—literally eclipses our freedom.*

At first glance, however, Sartre's ontology would appear to abandon the classic Rousseauian (and Stendhalian) plot of natural liberty lost. Explicitly repudiating that romantic nostalgia for primitive beginnings still evident in the likes of Péguy—"[t]here is no such thing as an 'innocent' child," Sartre asserts in *L'Etre et le néant*—the philosopher is no less explicit in discarding Bergson's "*moi intérieur*" as a fiction: "the for-itself"—or human consciousness—"is wholly selfless and cannot

---

*As shall be discussed more fully in subsequent chapters, Sartre would ultimately, during the 1950s and 1960s, reframe the same narrative in the language of neo-Marxist materialism. In the context of material "scarcity" and human "need," he writes, the Other becomes for each man "the material possibility of his own annihilation." See Jean-Paul Sartre, *Critique de la raison dialectique* (Paris: Gallimard, 1960), 205.

have a 'deep-seated self.'"[70] Nevertheless, and perhaps despite himself, Sartre recapitulates in the very structure and language of his ontology the familiar heretical narrative.

Human existence, for Sartre, amounts first and foremost to a *"lack of being,"* a "nothingness" acutely conscious of itself as such and yearning for self-completion or "being" (Sartre's emphasis). Yet, while we may never become a "being-in-itself"—that is, as self-complete as a chair or a tree—neither does human existence consist solely of a lack of being; for in choosing or acting we create our own essence or "facticity." Hence, for Sartre, the human being is "at once a *facticity* and a *transcendence*" (Sartre's emphasis). But it is the latter faculty, stemming from our lack of being, that constitutes the freedom to which we are, in Sartre's notorious phrase, "condemned": "the for-itself" "chooses because it is a lack; freedom is really synonymous with lack." Unlike a self-complete being, we must perpetually transcend our previous "facticity," reconstituting ourselves with our every choice. Thus, having "no essence" itself, our freedom both precedes and de-termines what we become, creating our "being" or "essence" at each moment. Human existence, in short, "perpetually makes itself" and "refuses to be confined in a definition."[71]

In this context, the role of the Other takes on new significance inas-much as it is the Other who provides us with the occasion of our self-definition—or rather, with "the death of our possibilities." Before the appearance of the Other, it will be recalled, Sartre's hypothetical spy at the keyhole had experienced himself as "purely nothing," having escaped any "provisional self-definition" by virtue of his "transcen-dence." Similarly, before being permanently fixed by the gaze of their fellow prisoners, the characters in *Huis Clos* felt able to flee their past lives. Estelle, for example, yearningly recalls the regard of a beguiled former lover for whom she had remained "clean and bright and crystal clear as running water." But the Other's accusing gaze forces the indi-viduals to confront their "facticity," to acknowledge what their actions have made them, whether it be voyeur, coward, or murderer. "Thus," Sartre summarizes, "for the Other I have stripped myself of my tran-scendence."[72]

The Other, then, not only encroaches upon our freedom—which en-tails, Sartre contends, "nothing but the *existence* of our will"—but introduces us to our own "bad faith," to the lies we have told ourselves in order to maintain at least the illusion of an unblemished self and open-ended liberty (Sartre's emphasis). In fact, *Huis clos* and Sartre's celebrated example of the keyhole are at bottom tales of inner corruption. Garçin and Estelle seek to flee their respective "facticities" as coward and murderer, the essential selves they have created through their actions, no less than the imagined interloper at the keyhole flees his own "facticity" as spy. The character of Estelle, furthermore, embodies for Sartre the "bad faith" of vanity, which amounts to one's attempt, as he puts it *L'Etre et le néant*, to constitute the Other "as an object in order . . . to discover there my own object-state." The vain individual, in other words, seeks to deny not his "facticity" but rather his "transcendence": he enlists the Other's admiring regard so as to constitute himself as a self-complete "object" and thereby escape his own inevitable lack of being. For Sartre, the attempt to construct oneself as a permanent entity, to play, for example, "*at being* a waiter in a café" in the same way "that an inkwell is an inkwell" (to cite another of his well known images), is no less an instance of bad faith—of inner duplicity—than the denial of one's "facticity" (Sartre's emphasis).[73]

Ironically, then, despite his heroic effort to disavow the romantic—and biblical—tragedy of primal human purity and its corruption in society, Sartre ends up reframing it instead. Human liberty for Sartre can be neither "natural" nor ontologically "essential" inasmuch as it has no essence. Yet it amounts for him no less than for Rousseau to a transcendent and unsullied will that constructs the very meaning and definition of our existence. Indeed, while our "transcendence" may be ontologically tainted from the outset by bad faith, our *experience* of it, as meticulously re-enacted by Sartre, mimics precisely the familiar tale of primal freedom under assault: the transcending self undergoes the invading look of the Other as an "original fall" and feels his existence in a world of Others to be "the original sin." The Other, moreover, not only threatens directly to enslave our liberty, to "strip" us of our "transcendence," but forces us to confront our submission to our own inner corruption. In fact, the daunting catalogue of vices that Sartre diagnoses in *L'Etre et le néant* as instances of bad faith—self-deception, vanity, greed, jealousy, hatred, and sadism, to name a few—recalls nothing more than the Rousseauian sins of *amour-propre*.

Despite the legendary pessimism embodied in the very title "No Exit"—not to mention Sartre's notorious definition of man in *L'Etre et le néant* as "a useless passion"—Sartre again offers the possibility that human freedom may be redeemed. Like Bergson, he envisions freedom as a profound self-realization requiring that we break our ordinary habits of mind, which in Sartre's case means discarding our bad faith. Thus, "authenticity," or true freedom, requires that we face our ontological situation without self-delusion, that we embrace both our "transcendence" and our "facticity"—both our free choice of our-selves and our self-entrapment by those choices—as the eternal di-lemma of being human. Our consciousness of authentic freedom, accordingly, consists of "*anguish*," which is "precisely [our] conscious-ness of being [our] own future," a "constantly renewed obligation to remake the *Self*" (Sartre's emphasis). In other words, if we are to be genuinely free, we must embrace "without excuse" our "absolute responsibility" for what we make of ourselves. Hence, Orestes, for example, the hero of Sartre's Resistance drama *Les Mouches* (1944), ultimately repudiates "the airy lightness that was mine"—the open-ended, liberal freedom of a man who had once felt it "unnecessary to commit oneself"—in favor of that "crushing freedom" embraced by he who takes action "without excuse, beyond remedy, except what remedy I find within myself."[74]

A "real life" instance for Sartre of freedom's regeneration emerges in his existential biography of the radical playwright, Jean Genet. In a scene plainly reminiscent of the notorious keyhole vignette, he recon-structs Genet's experience of being "*caught in the act*" of stealing at the age of ten: "Someone has entered and is watching him. Beneath this gaze the child comes to himself." Then, "a voice declares publicly: 'You're a thief.'" Having thus learned "what he *is objectively*," the young Genet is "trapped like a rat" (Sartre's emphasis). Yet Sartre's protagonist refuses to flee this "nature" fixed for him by the Other's gaze, and instead embraces it as that "essence" which his own deed has created. At first mired in his "facticity" as thief, he identifies with his judges and indulges in self-loathing. But then, demonstrating a "pure courage," a "mad confidence within despair," Genet discards his bad faith and "wills himself" to be a thief. Deciding, in other words, "to accept responsibility" for his self-definition, he makes it his own and thereby recaptures his freedom. And ultimately, through the trans-gressive power of his art, Genet turns "the formidable objectifying power" of the society that had "made a thief of him" back onto itself. Genet, Sartre concludes, has come to employ his "creative freedom" to make the Other "experience with loathing his own wickedness." Indeed, he "wins on all counts: he escapes from poverty, from prison, from horror; the decent people support him in style, seek him out, admire him."[75]

With this conspicuously Rousseauian tale of anti-establishment tri-umph and celebrity, Sartre's own tale of freedom and dependency would appear complete as well. Not only does Sartre reproduce in his ontology the familiar narrative of original liberty lost, but also, like his

Enlightenment forebear, he ultimately promises a freedom not merely recovered but improved: it is not difficult to discern in the anguished self-mastery of Sartre's "authentic freedom" the ghost of Rousseau's "moral liberty," which required that the hypothetical citizen achieve conscious mastery of his own passions.* Thus, for Sartre true freedom, once again identified with psychic autonomy, may rise even within the most daunting of societal hells, but only if the individual exorcizes from his consciousness both the Other's invading gaze and his own inner corruption.

Like Sartre, Foucault sought explicitly to divorce himself from any romantic nostalgia for a primordial self endowed with natural liberty. Refusing even to offer definitions of freedom or the will, notwithstanding his acknowledged debts to Heidegger and Nietzsche, Foucault, it will be recalled,[76] first came to the attention of a broad French public by repudiating in *Les mots et les choses* Sartre's "modern cogito"—his phenomenology of the human self—and heralding "the disappearance of man." The individual, Foucault insisted thereafter, "is not to be conceived as a sort of elementary nucleus, a primitive atom, a multiple and inert material on which power comes to fasten or against which it happens to strike."[77]

Yet if "man" as a free individual subject is nowhere to be found in Foucault's pivotal works of the 1970s, *Surveiller et punir* and *La Volonté de savoir,* subjection pervades them; and its most notorious image is once again the ubiquitous, invading gaze of the Other as embodied quite literally in Jeremy Bentham's late-eighteenth-century "Panopticon," his design for a prison in which all cells would be visible to an unseen observer. The Panopticon is for Foucault a "cruel, ingenious cage" in which the individual "is seen, but he does not see; he is the object of information, never a subject in communication." Its explicit purpose is "to induce in the inmate a state of consciousness and permanent visibility that assures the automatic functioning of power." Foucault notes, moreover, that Bentham offered his architectural "Columbus's egg" as a design not only for prisons, but for schools, hospitals, and factories as well.[78]

Yet this hypothetical Benthamite realm of the all-seeing eye is only emblematic for Foucault of its all-too-real counterpart in the modern

---

*The evolution of this Sartrean ideal of conscious personal autonomy into the ideal of a community of comrades participating freely and consciously together in a political uprising will be treated at length in chapter 5.

West, which he famously dubs "panopticism." Such new social scientific "disciplines" of the modern age as "clinical medicine, psychiatry, child psychology, [and] educational psychology," Foucault argues, have come to embody a "generalized" as well as a "permanent, exhaustive, [and] omnipresent surveillance, capable of making all visible, as long as it could itself remain invisible." This "normalizing gaze"—indeed "network of gazes"—is incarnated in the scientific "observations," objective "examinations," and impersonal "investigations" of the disciplines, and requires that power be "exercised through its invisibility." At the same time, "it imposes on those whom it subjects a principle of compulsory visibility." Indeed, the disciplines "characterize, classify, specialize; they distribute along a scale, around a norm, hierarchize individuals in relation to one another and, if necessary, disqualify and invalidate." Through them "we are judged, condemned, classified, determined in our undertakings." Hence Foucault's celebrated denunciation of the modern "disciplinary society" which is our own—that "*society of normalization*" (Foucault's emphasis), whose ideal punishment would be "an interrogation without end, an investigation that would be extended without limit to a meticulous and ever more analytical observation." [79]

This nightmarish image of inquisitorial personal invasion certainly calls to mind Michelet, who, it will be recalled, endowed his psychologically voracious priest with the power to "penetrate" his victim's "inmost thoughts" and thereby accomplish the very "extinguishment of the soul." [80] But Foucault in fact goes further. His normalizing gaze is no mere malevolent cleric who subjects the individual soul, or Sartrean Other who arrests its "transcendence"; rather the soul, for Foucault, is itself "born" of discipline. "Discipline 'makes' individuals" through "the establishment of truth." For the very concepts of "psyche, subjectivity, personality, consciousness" by which we define ourselves have themselves arisen out of "scientific techniques and discourses." Thus, the individual subject is itself "one of the prime effects" of a "power" which "circulates" through a "net-like organization" of "true discourses" and institutional "micro-mechanisms." And since such power "never ceases its interrogation, its inquisition, its registration of truth," we are quite literally "subjected to truth." We are, that is, not merely regulated by Foucault's omnipresent Other, by the linguistic and institutional gaze of the disciplines; our very "subjectivity"—our conscious experience of individuality—is produced by it. [81]

In *La Volonté de savoir*, Foucault uncovers beneath the "discourse of sexuality" a variation on the same harsh allegory of radical invasion and "subjectivization." Beginning all but literally where Michelet had left off in *Du Prêtre,* he detects in the generalized "pastoral power" of the seventeenth century Catholic confessional the culmination of a much older "scheme for transforming sex into discourse." Christianity, as Foucault later elaborated in a 1981 lecture, had conceived pastorship as a relationship "of individual and complete dependence" which required "personal submission" to one's spiritual "shepherd." The latter "must know what goes on in the soul," the "secret sins" of each individual under his care. By the same token, Foucault charges, modern medicine and psychiatry focused their "gaze" first upon "the 'nervous disorders'" and "mental illness" and then "annexed the whole of the sexual perversions as its own province." Thus, in "[t]he medical examination, the psychiatric investigation, the pedagogical report" he finds again a "power that questions, watches, spies, searches out, palpates, brings to light." Moreover, in a diagnosis again strikingly reminiscent of Michelet, Foucault charges the new discourse of sexuality with violating even the private realm of the family, first through children and then through women: "it was in the 'bourgeois' or 'aristocratic' family," he recounts, "that the sexuality of children and adolescents was first problematized, and feminine sexuality medicalized"; accordingly, "parents and relatives became the chief agents of a deployment of sexuality which drew its outside support from doctors, educators, and later psychiatrists." [82]

Once again, in *La Volonté de savoir,* Foucault emphasizes that "power's hold on sex is maintained through language, or rather through that act of discourse that creates . . . a rule of law." Reemphasizing, moreover, the "omnipresence" of such discursive power, he argues that sexuality is only one instance of its more general application. Insofar as such power "to qualify, measure, appraise, and hierarchize . . . operates more and more as a norm," we find ourselves once again within the Foucaultian hell of the "normalizing society." Indeed, if the darkest vision of subjection in *Surveiller et punir* consists of an "interrogation without end," in *La Volonté de savoir* it consists of an interminable confession. While originating, again, in those "Christian techniques of examination, confession, guidance, [and] obedience" that aimed at "a renunciation of this world and of oneself," Foucault now, in one of his most celebrated passages, situates his perdition of personal invasion at the very core of modern society:

> We have become a singularly confessing society. The confession
> has spread far and wide. It plays a part in justice, medicine, educa-

tion, family relationships and love relations. . . . one confesses one's crimes, one's sins, one's thoughts and desires, one's illnesses, one's troubles; one goes about telling, with the greatest precision, what is most difficult to tell. One confesses in public and in private, to one's parents, one's educators, one's doctor. . . . One confesses—or is forced to confess.[83]

The discourse of sexuality, then, takes Foucault—as Mark Poster has put it—"a step further" in "defining . . . the discourse/practices through which the individual is constituted as the subject of truth." For this discursive Other, Foucault claims, does not stop merely at extracting "a revelation of what one is"; it literally *defines* what we are through the "true" categories of the human sciences. Hence, Foucault points out, for example, that only late in the nineteenth century was "the psychological, psychiatric, medical category of homosexuality . . . constituted." While "[t]he sodomite had been a temporary aberration," he asserts, "the homosexual" was not only "a personage, a past, a case-history," but "a species." Indeed, like the madman, the patient, and the criminal of Foucault's earlier works—not to say the human subject itself—the homosexual is for Foucault a veritable invention of disciplinary discourse and born to live within its cage. In fact, the omnipresent disciplines and their "technolog[ies] of power and knowledge" would appear to function for Foucault as nothing less than a Sartrean Other writ large: they collectively "fix" individuals with no less profound a rigidity than that singular adult gaze which branded Jean Genet "thief." But Foucault's diagnoses both of modern "discipline" and sexuality unearth a degree of personal dependency—of unfreedom—heretofore unimagined even by Sartre. For like Robespierre's revolutionary enemy, Foucault's normalizing Other is socially ubiquitous; but like Bergson's geometric enemy within, it also conceals itself in the very fabric of analytical language, a language which for Foucault tells us literally what and who we are. Hence, the Foucaultian "individual" is not merely dominated by the insidious gaze of *les autres,* he owes it his very existence as an individual.[84]

As to why, finally, the individual is so produced and subjected in the modern age, Foucault, both in *Surveiller et punir* and *La Volonté de savoir,* offers a now familiar hypothesis. The Panopticon, he reminds us in the first work, was envisioned as a means "to increase production, develop the economy, spread education, raise the level of public morality." And the disciplines, by the same token, must be viewed as a means employed by bourgeois society "to increase the possible utility of individuals" not to say "the docility and the utility of all the elements of the system." For with disciplinary surveillance, Foucault elaborated in an interview, "[t]here is no need for arms, physical violence, material constraints. Just a gaze. An inspecting gaze, a gaze which each individual under its weight will end up interiorizing to the point that he is his own overseer." Similarly, in *La Volonté de savoir*, Foucault maintains that in the nineteenth century sex was "inserted into systems of utility" and "regulated for the greater good of all." It became one pole of "a bio-politics of the population" to be policed by "the disciplines." Such "bio-power," itself "an indispensable element in the development of capitalism," required "the administration of bodies and the calculated management of life."[85]

In other words, behind Foucault's ominous portrait of panoptic surveillance lurks once again the sterile, malevolent spirit of profit and utilitarian efficiency—an "economy of manpower" parallel to the Sartrean hell of *Huis clos,* but in chilling macrocosm. Like Robespierre's revolutionary enemy, Bergson's geometric intellect, or Péguy's "politique," Foucault's normalizing Other provokes the self-sacrifice of freedom on the altar of utility: panopticism first fabricates the individuals through its regime of political and economic "normalization" and then induces them to enslave themselves to its demands. Once again Foucault links personal dependency indissolubly to the corrupting passion for power and gain.

But if Foucault's hell vividly mirrors that horror of personal violation and corruption which may be traced back to Stendhal and Rousseau, what of the narrative of original liberty lost and redeemed? As noted above, Foucault directly repudiates any notion of "natural" freedom. And yet several of his best-known works, by virtue of their explicitly Nietzschean format as historical "genealogies," seem to gravitate back toward more or less "primordial" origins. Both *Surveiller et punir* and his earlier *Folie et déraison* (1961), for example, open with notorious images of corporeal punishment and savagery, which are relatively foreign to modern "humanitarian" sensibilities: the execution of the regicide Damiens in 1757, which Foucault depicts in infamous detail and contrasts with the "economy of punishment" soon to follow; and Hieronymus Bosch's sixteenth-century painting *The Ship of Fools* through which Foucault claims to evoke a "zero point" at which "madness was an undifferentiated experience" of "dark freedom" and "primitive savagery" before being confined within medical hospitals and discourse. Questioned by Bernard-Henry Lévy in 1977 about the "diffuse naturalism" that had "haunt[ed]" his previous works, Foucault concedes having implied that one might recover "things themselves in their primitive vivacity": hence, "behind the asylum walls," he acknowledges, one seems to find "the spontaneity of madness; through the penal system, the generous fever of delinquency; under the sexual interdict, the freshness of desire." The poststructuralist even defends such "simplifications" and "dualism" as a "provisionally useful" means of promoting "new strategies" in the struggle against established power.[86]

Thus, while it would be mistaken to suggest that Foucault expressly or even unwittingly reverts to the Rousseauian ideal of a "natural" liberty unviolated by society—that he glorifies a savagely free, "prediscursive" past in favor of the "civilized society" of the present[87]—he would seem acutely aware of the political potency conveyed by that myth. For once again, notwithstanding even the omnipresent and enslaving surveillance of the disciplines, Foucault clearly envisions the possibility of liberation in modern society. Indeed, many of Foucault's most renowned formulations—the "disappearance of man," the aspiration "to have no face," the "re-emergence" of "marginalized" and "subjugated knowledges"—are nothing if not images of emancipation from the normalizing gaze of discourse. In 1983, echoing an earlier assertion that critical understanding must begin "from *a certain decisive will not to be governed*" (Foucault's emphasis), Foucault characterized his own critiques as means of opening up "the space of freedom . . . of possible transformation." This description surely fits *La Volonté de savoir*, which explicitly calls for "liberation" from "the austere monarchy of sex." In the same work, moreover, Foucault notes that the nineteenth-century profusion of "discourses on the species and subspecies of homosexuality" also "made possible the formation of a 're-verse' discourse" which allowed homosexuality "to speak in its own behalf."[88] In other words, just as Genet, for Sartre, was able to internalize the Other's label of "thief" and reaffirm it as his own freedom, so too has the homosexual, for Foucault, successfully employed the very discursive eye that entraps him on behalf of his own partial emancipation. Even in Foucault, then, the tale of freedom's impending fall into the hell of other people, as well as its ever-possible redemption, remains clearly discernable—if only, perhaps, as a politically indispensable myth.

III

If there indeed remains in Foucault the "provisionally useful" remnant of a Rousseauian narrative, it is certainly not by explicit design. In a 1977 interview, Foucault detected the hell of personal subjection lurking within the very social paradigm outlined by Rousseau. Cringing at "the Rousseauist dream" of a society in which the "opinion of all" would "reign over each," he charges that such a "reign of 'opinion,'" in which power would circulate through a "collective and anonymous gaze," would "refuse to tolerate areas of darkness."[89] In the vaunted universality, generality, and objectivity of Rousseau's "general will," in other words, Foucault recognizes the direct ancestor of disciplinary discourse—that universal and "objective" "general will" of "the experts" which signifies for him the very essence of unfreedom and psychic dependency. Such an impersonal "norm" offers Foucault not, as it did for Rousseau, a guarantee against personal invasion, but rather its very embodiment; and his legendary craving for self-effacement would appear nothing less than an authentic horror of personal subjection to that all-seeing normative eye.

Ironically, then, Foucault's account of hell and dependency would seem both opposite and equal to that of Rousseau. For if Foucault, as James Miller has suggested, does indeed find his own postmodern nightmare in Rousseau's Enlightenment dream,[90] he quarrels more with the latter's proposed solution than with his diagnosis of the problem. Foucault, that is, would surely agree with Rousseau that "the social man," inasmuch as he "only knows how to live in the opinions of others," is subject to the most profound of psychological prisons; and Rousseau would surely agree with his iconoclastic descendant that liberation must begin with "a decisive will not to be governed" by other people.

Thus, notwithstanding his revulsion for Rousseau's utopian vision, Foucault's postmodern fantasy of escape from the "normalizing gaze" would seem itself—like Julien Sorel's "horror of contempt," Robespierre's dread of the revolutionary enemy, Michelet's parable of the invading priest, Bergson's battle against the encroachment of intellect, Péguy's campaign against "politique," and Sartre's angst-filled confrontation with "the Other"—a variation on Rousseau's narrative of psychic dependency and liberation. And that narrative, notwithstanding its fluctuations in appearance, would seem to have shifted little in its meaning. Each of the consecrated heretics, that is, identifies subservience to the Other with the inner slavery of egoistic self-interest; and each associates liberation inescapably with willful independence both from les autres and the pursuit of utilitarian gain. In short, the heretical parable of freedom and psychic dependency comprises an ongoing condemnation of the classical liberal model of "negative liberty."

FOUR

THE CRITIQUE OF SOCIETY

If, within the heretical narrative, all personal dependency must be purged from the individual so as to set him free, the same may be said for society as a whole. Hence, it will be recalled that the heroic intellectual, having established his public celebrity and autonomy, proceeds ever thereafter to denounce the petty avarice, political corruption, and spiritual depravity of the established order. Indeed nothing emerges more prominently in the works of the consecrated heretics—or better defines their self-appropriated role of societal gadfly and liberator—than their unrelenting denunciation of conventional society. In what follows, accordingly, it will be suggested that the consecrated heretics have in fact generated an archetypal critique of modern France's "established order"; a common assault, that is, upon (1) high society and the bourgeoisie, (2) the Catholic Church and its secular equivalents, and (3) the centralized state and parliamentary politics. This critique, as shall be seen, discloses an entirely enervated social universe, a world in which the shadow of servility threatens perpetually to efface that autonomy of will which defines true freedom.

I. "HIGH SOCIETY" AND THE BOURGEOISIE

The French cultural ritual of ridiculing the bourgeoisie emanates at the very least from the time of Molière, when it entailed an aristocratic critique of the social *parvenu*.[1] *Le Rouge et le noir*, on the other hand, would seem to represent a classic—indeed classically heretical—post-revolutionary rendition of the ritual. Stendhal's novel is permeated with Julien Sorel's "hatred and horror" of what "the rich in their arrogance" refer to simply as "'la société.'" And the author discovers *la société* both in the petty "high society" of provincial Verrières and in the "new Babylon" of Paris, where Julien, as previously noted, finds "vanity, dry and arrogant, every conceivable variety of self-approval and nothing else." At the head of one chapter, for example, Stendhal places the lament of Julien's idol Napoleon that "thousands and millions" of Frenchmen "know nothing but their pleasures, their vanity"; and more particularly, he portrays the beautiful and refined Mathilde de La Mole, as an "arid soul" raised "amid the excess of civilization which Paris admires." The celebrated "mirror," then, which *Le Rouge et le noir* professes to hold up to the world of France in 1830 would seem above all to reflect the universally "unhappy effect of too much civilization."[2]

Dissecting *la société* in notorious detail, Stendhal focuses his critical lens most broadly on what one of his characters labels "the bourgeois aristocracy." Through such characters as Monsieur de Rênal, a factory owner and the mayor of Verrières, and Monsieur Valenod, the director of the town's poorhouse, he mercilessly satirizes this new social class. Rênal, explains the narrator, while proud of his ostensibly "ancient" and "established" family lineage and "always intent on copying court manners," is a man whose talents are "confined to exacting every penny owed to him, and to paying his own debts at the last possible moment." Valenod, by the same token, is said to embody, alongside other men of his ilk, a "coarseness and brutal indifference to anything that is not money, promotion, or a cross; a blind hatred for any sort of thought that [goes] against [his] interests." When Julien arrives at the Valenods' for dinner, accordingly, he is "told the price of each piece of furniture." Next, seated among an assortment of bourgeois notables—the local "tax collector, the assessor, the chief of police, and two or three public officials" as well as "a number of rich liberals"—Stendhal's protagonist finds himself afflicted with the thought that "on the other side of the dining room wall were the prisoners, whose portion of meat had been *chiseled* in order to purchase all this luxurious bad taste" (Stendhal's emphasis). Indeed for Julien "there was something ignoble" about the director's abode: it "stank of stolen money." [3]

In the new bourgeoisie, then, Stendhal unearths a veritable catalog of social vices, the most obvious of which is the love of money and its corollary, the base—and frequently dishonest—pursuit of material gain. "*Yield a return,*" remarks the narrator, "is the grand phrase" that "represents the habitual mind-set of three quarters of the townspeople" in Verrières. A related bourgeois foible, well represented by Valenod, is the callous handling of one's social inferiors: "I've had the beggars shut up!" the director of the poorhouse boasts at his party in reference to his destitute charges. A third bourgeois malady is embodied in Rênal's hypocritical aping of the aristocracy and disavowal of his links to commerce. In Paris, Julien encounters a foreign countess whose "entire life seemed to have no other goal than to make people forget she was the daughter of *a man in trade.*" Reflected, finally, in such social hypocrisy is what would seem the ultimate bourgeois vice for Stendhal: a mindless subservience to social convention. "Never suppose," the adulterous Madame de Rênal assures Julien, "that my husband won't conform, in every detail concerning you, to the program that *public opinion* will prescribe for him" (Stendhal's emphasis). And the intelligent and aristocratic Mathilde de La Mole, it will be recalled, is for Stendhal no less a creature of the "public and other people"— no less figuratively "bourgeois"—than the mayor of Verrières.[4]

Stendhal, in sum, delineates a social order increasingly overrun by the bourgeois vices of greed, self-interested ambition, hypocrisy, and above all servility. The works of the consecrated heretics yield essentially the same portrait of civilized society, complete with the aforesaid bourgeois blemishes as well as the ominous specter of subjugation.

The seminal critique of society in modern France is again that of Rousseau, who successfully transformed the Enlightenment critique of the Old Regime into an all-encompassing assault upon the established order—including the Republic of Letters itself. Indeed, through his celebrated denunciation of civilization during the 1750s, and his subsequent attack on his fellow philosophes, the Genevan antiphilosophe condemned not only France's Old Order but the emerging "bourgeois aristocracy" of Paris as well.

The social evils of material greed and inequity, which appear as the vices of *la société* in Stendhal, surface no less conspicuously in the familiar portrait of "civilization" which Rousseau renders in his first two discourses. Civilization, he contends in the *Discours sur les sciences et les arts* has "corrupted our morals" and "defiled the purity of our taste." More specifically, it has introduced a universal taste for "luxury," not to say a desire "to enrich ourselves at any cost." This lust for material wealth, continues Rousseau in his second discourse, has produced an unjust social universe in which "the extreme idleness" of "the wealthy," who are able to "excite and gratify" their "sensual appetites" to unhealthy excess, stands in stark contrast to the "excessive labor" of the poor, who must "voraciously" ingest their "unwholesome" and "insufficient" food when "the opportunity arises."[5]

Rousseau reiterates fundamentally the same charges in such later works as his *Lettre à d'Alembert* (1758) and *La Nouvelle Héloïse* (1761), but now levels them more specifically at the new "enlightened" social order of which he has himself become a part. Thus, in the former work he denounces "the big city," and Paris in particular, for its "scheming, idle people . . . whose imagination, depraved by sloth, inactivity, the love of pleasure, and great needs, engenders only monsters and crime." And *La Nouvelle Héloïse*, which, Rousseau promises, will surely displease "high society [*le monde*]," "people of taste," and "the philosophes," is replete as well with condemnations of Paris, that city of "the world's most unequal fortunes, where the most sumptuous opulence reigns side by side with the most deplorable misery."[6]

But beneath the corrupt materialism of civilized society lurk maladies of the spirit, which, for Rousseau no less than for Stendhal, are still more ominous: namely, the lust for social advancement and the hypocrisy of appearances. As would Stendhal after him, Rousseau conceives of society as "an assembly of artificial men and divisive passions"; a universe "of ubiquitous competition and rivalry, or rather enmity, among men," in which all are equally "inflamed" by the "universal desire for reputation, honors, and advancement." Saint Preux, Rousseau's famous alter-ego in *La Nouvelle Héloïse*, alleges that every Parisian "seeks his own interest and no one seeks the common good." Insofar, moreover, as "particular interests are always opposed," one finds oneself in a universe of perpetual "intrigues and cabals."[7]

For Rousseau, the fall of man from his primitive paradise of psychic autonomy takes place when each individual begins "to consider [*regarder*] the others, and to wish to be considered in return"; that is, when our social vanity or *amour-propre* begins to eclipse our natural self-regard, or *amour de soi*.[8] It is precisely this "petulant" and increasingly pervasive "activity of our vanity [*amour-propre*]" that shapes the Rousseauian portrait of human society fully evolved. "Behold then all human faculties developed," he proclaims in the second discourse, "memory and imagination in play, *amour-propre* engaged, reason active, and the mind at almost its highest point of perfection." Yet at this very pinnacle of human progress "the rank and condition of each man" has become dependent upon his "share of property and power to serve or injure others," and above all, upon "his wit, beauty, personal charisma, skills, and talents." Inasmuch as these qualities "are the only ones capable of commanding respect, it soon became necessary either to possess or affect them"; it came to be "in the interest of men," in short, "to appear other than what they were. Being and seeming became two entirely different things."[9]

The same image of social deceit and hypocrisy re-emerges in the *Lettre à d'Alembert* as an indictment of "Paris, where everything is judged by appearances"; and equally pointed is Saint Preux's condemnation of the capital city in *La Nouvelle Héloïse*. In Paris, laments Rousseau's protagonist, a man "never says what he thinks, but rather what is convenient to have others to think of him." Indeed, "the same people alter their maxims according to which coterie they are in," becoming "servile courtesans before a minister of state, mutinous rebels before a dissenter." The "society of philosophes" represents of course no exception for Rousseau. Among "savants and men of letters," contends Saint Preux, "the cause of lying is pleaded artfully" and "all morality is pure verbiage." In fact, "the apparent zeal for truth" among the Parisian intelligentsia "is only a mask for self-interest"; hence, in order to divine what they will say, "one need not know men's characters but only their interests."[10]

The most calamitous by-product of such social duplicity, for Rousseau as for Stendhal, would seem to be the increasing inclination of civilized men "to love authority more than independence, and submit to slavery, so they may in turn enslave others." Having denounced the "servile and deceptive conformity" of contemporary society in his first discourse, Rousseau concludes the second with a strident echo of that charge: "Civilized man . . . pays court to men in power, whom he hates, and to the wealthy, whom he despises; he stops at nothing to have the honor of serving them . . . and, proud of his slavery, he speaks disdainfully of those who have not the honor of sharing it." Yet another echo of this Rousseauian indictment may be detected in Saint Preux's ironic "first wise maxim" of Parisian high society: "*one must do like the others*" (Rousseau's emphasis). Fearing, in fact, that "a too long sojourn" in Paris "might corrupt my own will," Rousseau's hero wonders if "perhaps in about a year I will be nothing more than a bourgeois"; and if, accordingly, "I will no longer possess the soul of a free man and the mores of a citizen." Even the common people of France, he later suggests, who "always monkey and mimic the rich," might ultimately "become more foolish than those they imitate."[11]

Thus, Rousseau castigates the same social vices of greed, self-interested ambition, and hypocrisy as would Stendhal in *Le Rouge et le noir*; and he too would seem to reserve his most damning judgment for the conformity and servility that pervade civilized society. Finally, Rousseau's portrait of *le monde*, like Stendhal's of *la société*, features not a waning aristocratic social order so much as an emerging urban one—a new "bourgeois aristocracy" which threatens to engulf the nation in its expanding net of social corruption and servitude.

In 1793, echoing the famous first words of *Du Contrat social*, Robespierre proclaimed that while "man is born for happiness and liberty . . . society everywhere degrades and oppresses him." The Jacobin leader's recasting of the revolutionary social universe within the Rousseauian mold proved, of course, notoriously successful. Throughout the Revolution Robespierre denounced the "capitalists," the "profiteers," the "speculators," and the "aristocracy of wealth"—in sum, the new "bourgeois aristocracy" of revolutionary France. Arguing in 1791, for example, against the restriction of the suffrage, he declared that "social abuses are the handiwork and province of the rich" whose "particular interest" is opposed to the "general interest" of the people. And arguing in the following year on behalf of price controls, he railed against "the pitiless vampires" who "coldly calculate how many families must perish before supplies have been withheld long enough to satisfy their atrocious avarice."[12]

But even more than its cupidity and injustice, Robespierre deplored the escalating moral degeneration of revolutionary society. "Egoism," summarizes David Jordan, "became the most significant word in Robespierre's vocabulary of denunciation." And indeed, that term heads the list of social sins that the Jacobin leader promised to eradicate in his notorious "Report on the Principles of Political Morality" of 1794. The others, which include "insolence," "vanity," "wit," "glamour," "pettiness," and "sensuous boredom"—"all the vices and absurdities of the monarchy"—read like an inventory of the spiritual depravities that according to Rousseau emerge out of civilized *amour-propre*.[13]

The Jacobin leader, moreover, assigned himself the Rousseauian task of unveiling the social masks and hypocrisies that had arisen within the revolutionary social order. Hence, during the early days of the Revolution, for example, Robespierre charged Lafayette with disguising his "aristocratic prejudices" and "personal interests" behind a mask of revolutionary zeal. In the years that followed, he came increasingly to accuse his enemies of donning "the mask of patriotism in order to disfigure, by insolent parodies, the sublime drama of the revolution." Indeed, as noted above, Robespierre characteristically divided revolutionary society in two: on the one side, he declared in 1794, stands the "mass of citizens," which is "pure, simple, attached to justice, and a friend to liberty," while on the other has emerged a "factious and intriguing rabble; the prattling, artificial charlatans . . . the rascals, foreigners, and counterrevolutionary hypocrites." In characterizing this latter "sect" in his final speech before the National Convention, Robespierre calls to mind nothing more readily than Saint Preux's critique of Parisian society. Revolutionary France, he exclaims, has become a world of "intrigues," "mysterious coteries," and "nocturnal cabals"; of "traitors more or less adroit at concealing their hideous souls under a mask of virtue." Therefore, while "the majority is itself paralyzed and betrayed, intrigue and foreign influence triumph! There is concealment, there is dissimulation, there is deception"; and inevitably, he prophesies, the "traitors," who have remained "concealed under hypocritical outward appearances," will "accuse their accusers" and thereby "smother the voice of truth." [14]

Once again, in other words, the most perilous consequence for Robespierre of his society's increasing depravity and hypocrisy is the re-emergence of servility within the heart of the Revolution itself. Already in 1791, while unwilling to pronounce "the liberty of the people besotted and enslaved by despotism," Robespierre had expressed alarm at hearing "prating about universal freedom" from "servants of the Court" who have been "corrupted" by its "rottenness." Thereafter, he periodically cautioned his fellow citizens against any professed revolutionary who has been seen "clawing his way up at court or humiliating himself at the feet of a minister or a mistress," and most particularly against those moderates and intellectuals who, like the philosophes and "Encyclopedists" of Rousseau's day, have been "bold in their writings and servile in reception rooms." It comes as no surprise, then, to find Robespierre defending himself in 1794 as the champion of "the Conservative principles of liberty" within a "world peopled by dupes and knaves." What will the Revolution signify, he implores, "if we re-

cede before the vices which destroy public liberty, . . . if we are van-
quished by the vices which bring back tyranny?"[15] Robespierre, in
sum, stages an unyielding Rousseauian critique of "civilized" society,
even as it surfaces within the revolutionary social order itself. He too,
finally, in denouncing the avarice, ambition, and hypocrisy which have
come to flourish in the Revolution's emerging "bourgeois aristocracy,"
portrays a social universe in which true freedom is perpetually menaced with extinction.

It is ironic, but perhaps not surprising to find Michelet, in his *Histoire
de la révolution française*, detecting many of the bourgeois vices in
Robespierre which the latter had unearthed in revolutionary society.
Carefully "groomed, coiffed, and powdered," the Robespierre of Michelet's acrimonious portrait takes care never to jeopardize "the economy of his person" in the "harsh society" of popular uprisings. In
the Jacobin's "tedious personality," moreover, in "the inexhaustible
I which permeates his leaden speech," Michelet discerns a "visible
hypocrisy" (Michelet's emphasis).[16]
     In truth, however, Michelet's profile both of revolutionary society
and of his own social universe has much in common with that of his
Jacobin antagonist. No less sharply than Robespierre does the historian demarcate his Revolution's "one sole hero, the people" from the
"bourgeois aristocracy," that "true modern monarch," which, though
"not numerous," came ultimately to "dominate" the Revolution by
virtue of its ability "to read, to write, to count . . . to verbalize, to fill
out forms [*paperasser*]." And just as explicitly does Michelet dichoto-
mize the social universe of his own day: while "old France" he proclaims in *Le Peuple*, "had three classes; new France has only two—the
people and the bourgeoisie."[17]
     Whether denouncing "the businessmen" and "hidden speculators"
of 1793 or the greedy bankers and industrialists of 1846, Michelet
condemns "bourgeois materialism" as a matter of course. But he taxes
the bourgeoisie more for its sins of the spirit than of the body. Thus,
in the liberal revolutionary Mirabeau, for example, Michelet denounces not monetary greed so much as the "true corruption" of "a
heart filled with ambition and pride." In fact, the revolutionary bourgeoisie on the whole, the historian maintains, while initially "generous
and disinterested," became "corrupted by egoism and *fear*" as well as
by "hatred"—by, as he later calls it, "the great bourgeois principle:
'every man to himself, every man for himself'" (Michelet's emphasis).
Echoing in *Le Peuple* the satirical verdict of Stendhal, Michelet con-

tends that the bourgeois, while "liberal in principle," is "an egoist in practice" who invariably "places himself on the side of established power."[18]

Again for Michelet, then, the "bourgeois aristocracies" both of the Revolution and his own day embody the familiar vices of social ambition and hypocrisy. Those sins, moreover, yield equally familiar results. In the Parisian salons of 1793, for instance, Michelet rediscovers the dissolute urban cosmos of Rousseau and Robespierre. "Here was a squalid, infected, gloomy world" of "shameful pleasures" populated by counterrevolutionaries and men "without party"; by men who had become "disgusted, bored, crushed by events" and had "ceased to possess either heart or ideal." Here, Michelet summarizes, "we find ourselves plunged into the most debased egoism," and, he later remarks, however isolated such pockets of social corruption might appear within revolutionary France, they reflect only "the beginnings of the social divisions which, with the rise of industrialism," would become the "true obstacle" and "weakness" of "our own day." For "our" world, he proclaims in Le Peuple, has become entirely fragmented by "interests," "competition," and "rivalry." Led once again by the bourgeoisie, those "great egoists" who, bound by "habit and inertia," typically "cling to their initial gains which they are afraid of risking," the French people have become "disfigured by misfortune and their own progress."[19]

Finally, Michelet would seem to dread above all what he refers to in Le Peuple as "Machinism": the increasing tendency in modern society for the products and "social acts" of men to become "uniformly automatic." Identifying this phenomenon most immediately with the Industrial Revolution, Michelet notes that even while the "power and riches" of England's middle classes have "increased beyond calculation," a "certain sad uniformity has established itself among the 'gentlemen,' a universal similarity of men and things." Nor does he find this state of affairs limited to England. France's revolutionary bourgeoisie had itself, Michelet contends in his Histoire, "imbibed the English opium, complete with all its ingredients: egoism, well-being, comfort, liberty without sacrifice." And such "liberty" as that, he emphasizes, arises "from a mechanical equilibrium in which the soul plays no part."[20] It is no surprise, in this light, to find Michelet devoting the entire first part of Le Peuple—as previously noted[21]—to the varieties of social "bondage [servage]" that pervade France at mid-century; for like Robespierre, Rousseau, and Stendhal, he too depicts a French society in imminent danger of relinquishing its freedom.

Bergson, at first glace, would seem to offer an explicit critique neither of "society" nor the bourgeoisie. And yet inherent in the aforementioned dichotomies of his philosophy—the "vital" as opposed to
the "geometrical" realms of nature, the "intuitive" as opposed to the
"intellectual" realms of the mind[22]—would appear to be precisely such
a critique. For Bergson quite clearly identifies society and its requirements with the domain of "geometry" and the intellect. "Our outer
and, so to speak, social life," the philosopher claims in his *Essai sur les
données immédiates de la conscience*, "is more practically important
to us than our inner and individual existence." And insofar as our intellect, which characteristically superimposes its geometric grid over the
"pure duration" of reality, "is much better adapted to the requirements
of social life in general and language in particular," our conscious
self—or "superficial ego"—prefers it over our "fundamental self." In
fact, laments Bergson, echoing Michelet's critique of English "Machinism," our everyday existence lends credence to the psychological determinism of a John Stuart Mill inasmuch as it may be reduced to "clear-
cut distinctions" of "pain and pleasure." But should the "cleverly
woven curtain of our conventional ego" be torn off, Bergson asserts,
we would discover the "fundamental absurdity" of mistaking our utilitarian social masks for our authentic selves. For that in us which may
be analyzed and "translated into words" encompasses only "the common element, the impersonal residue, of the impressions felt in a given
case by the whole of society."[23]

Thus, for the sake of "society," Bergson seems to suggest, and "the
promotion of social relations," each and every one of us becomes a
bourgeois egoist. We routinely pursue our narrow interests and mundane ambitions, and we practice a sort of metaphysical hypocrisy by
obscuring our vital singularity behind the uniform logic of social utility. Again, moreover, the spiritual debasement and conformism toward
which our social selves gravitate yield still more ominous repercussions. In "the majority" of our "daily actions," Bergson laments, we
remain "conscious automaton[s]" because we "have everything to gain
by being so." But if we allow this "parasitic" social persona free reign
over our psyches, if "we live for the external world rather than ourselves," then gradually "automatism will cover over liberty." We will,
in short, become no more free than the animal who, Bergson contends
in *L'Évolution créatrice*, "escapes automatism . . . for just the time it
takes to create another automatism."[24] Imbedded, then, in the narrative framework of Bergson's philosophy, lies an implicit rebuke of the

universal bourgeois within us all, as well as an explicit condemnation of the social servility it begets.

Anything but implicit is the repeated denunciation by Bergson's disciple, Péguy, of bourgeois society. One can scarcely turn a page of Péguy's writings without encountering condemnations of "the bourgeois world," "bourgeoisism," "bourgeois sabotage," or "the bourgeois spirit." It is, moreover, "expressly the capitalist bourgeoisie and the big bourgeoisie" that Péguy accuses of introducing "all evil . . . all perversion, all crime" into the world. And for Péguy, like Stendhal, the most conspicuous offense of this bourgeois aristocracy is its "universal venality," a vice which it has managed to implant into modern society as whole. "Money is everything," he laments in *Notre jeunesse;* "it dominates the modern world." Indeed "only the modern world," he reiterates in a later work, "being a world of money, is a world of complete and absolute materiality." No less than Rousseau or Robespierre does Péguy deplore the radical "separation of the rich from the poor" which results from such material avarice; and no less does he repudiate "the monster of a . . . modern Paris in which the population is severed so entirely into two classes."[25]

But bourgeois "avarice and venality" betoken for Péguy more than social injustice alone. What he too labels the "egoism of the rich" or "bourgeois egoism"—thereby echoing the discourse of Robespierre or Stendhal—carries with it a now familiar array of spiritual vices. Like Michelet, for example, Péguy assaults that bourgeois "prudence" and "wisdom" which "calculates," "saves money," and "saves time." For "he who saves, who *economizes* . . . alienates his liberty and his fecundity, which are his truest possessions" (Péguy's emphasis). Like Rousseau, Péguy condemns above all his colleagues in the Republic of Letters for their self-serving careerism and hypocrisy. The "writers, the publicists, the social scientists [*sociologues*]," he maintains in *Notre jeunesse,* who are themselves "intellectuals and bourgeois," blame the workers rather than themselves for "the sabotage of the working world." And defending Bergson four years later against the intellectuals of the Sorbonne, Péguy charges that what the latter call "science" amounts in fact to:

> the tranquility of the savant and the orderly career of the expert. What they call scientific method is the method of their own establishment. What they call progress is the progress of their own ca-

reer. What they call security, fixedness, establishment, is the security, fixedness, and establishment of their own career. These are
placid, sedentary civil servants and they have an immobile philosophy, a philosophy suited to placid, sedentary civil servants.[26]

But worst of all, declares Péguy in a particularly Bergsonian flight
of prose, "this mechanicism, this economic automatism" of the bourgeoisie, "this scientific, cold, rectangular, regular, proper, clear . . .
strangulation," reflects "a materialism, a mechanicism, a determinism,
an associationism of the heart"; in short, a "principle . . . of universal
infertility" and "universal servitude." Indeed, Péguy attests, "it is always liberty" that ultimately "pays the price"; for "in order to have
peace tomorrow (and peace may only be purchased with money), one
. . . sells one's liberty today."[27]

For Péguy, then, just as for Robespierre, the spiritual depravity of
the bourgeoisie quite literally spells "the death of vitality and liberty."
His bourgeoisie, like that of Stendhal, Rousseau, and Michelet, would
seem both omnivorous and expanding. Péguy shudders in *Notre
jeunesse* at the "gradual bourgeoisification" of the proletariat, and in
his 1913 essay, *L'Argent,* he deplores the "infection" of Michelet's
"peuple" "precisely with the bourgeois, capitalist spirit." Indeed both
in *L'Argent* and its successor, *L'Argent suite,* Péguy repeatedly charges
that "everyone is bourgeois." In fact, "[t]he people," he proclaims, "no
longer exists," for the popular classes "possess only one idea: to become bourgeois." Even modern socialism consists of nothing more
than "an arousal of bourgeois instincts within the world of the worker,
an invitation to the workers to become, in their turn, dirty bourgeois."[28] In short, the entire social universe of prewar France stands
poised in Péguy's foreboding portrait to surrender its freedom.

The critique of society and the bourgeoisie assumes an all but axiomatic character in Sartre, whose works are notorious for their condemnations of "the bourgeois world" and its "right-thinking people,"
of "bourgeois humanism" and "false bourgeois universalism," of
"Science, Industry, and the Moral Code," of "the Social Machine"; in
short, of "the bastards [*les salauds*]" and the "monstrous" society they
have fashioned. As previously noted, the paragons of "bad faith"
in Sartre's *Huis Clos*—Garçin the journalist, Inez the postal clerk,
and Estelle the *femme fatale*—are conspicuously bourgeois, as are the
voyeurs, café waiters, and coquettes who haunt *L'Etre et le néant.* Indeed, the provincial "Bouville" of Sartre's career-launching novel, *La*

Nausée, offers a distant mirror-image of Stendhal's "Verrières." Blessed, explains Sartre's protagonist Roquentin, by "a first-class financial position," Bouville's city council and its local bishop had brokered a compromise in 1887 between "the nouveau-riche gentleman of the Boulevard Maritime" and "the upper bourgeoisie" in order to construct an ostentatious church—"a monstrous edifice"—at the price of "fourteen million francs." At present, in Roquentin's derisive summary, the town is populated by a "fat, pale crowd" of stockbrokers, commercial officials, small businessmen, and their ostentatious wives. Again recalling Stendhal—who is perhaps not coincidentally Roquentin's favorite writer—Sartre's protagonist remarks acidly that "no one will mistake" the new factory designer's wife "for a lady" inasmuch as "real ladies do not know the price of things." At another point in the novel, Roquentin catalogs "the distinguished faces" which peer out at him from the walls of the Bouville Museum:

> M. Bossoire, President of the Board of Trade; M. Faby President of the Board of Directors of the Autonomous Port of Bouville; M. Boulange, businessman, with his family; M. Rannequin, Mayor of Bouville ... M. Thiboust-Gouron, General President of the Trades Council; M. Bobot, principal administrator of the Inscription Maritime.[29]

Monsieur Boulange, Roquentin surmises sardonically, "was economical and patient," and Monsieur Thiboust-Gouron "was as hard on himself as on others." Then, bidding farewell to these "beautiful lilies, elegant in [their] painted little sanctuaries," Sartre's alter-ego takes a celebrated parting shot: "Adieu, Salauds."[30]

Thus, for Sartre no less than for Stendhal, the critique of bourgeois society would seem a fundamental point of departure—and bourgeois society, once again, would seem most easily recognized by its ubiquitous greed and materialism. In *L'Etre et le néant,* in fact, Sartre situates the phenomenon of avarice within human ontology itself.[31] For in "the project to possess," he explains, we seek symbolically to apprehend that fleeting ghost of "Being" which we are condemned forever to pursue. "In the primitive form of luxury," Sartre writes in a distant echo of Rousseau, "I possess an object which I *have had made* for myself by people who are mine (slaves, servants born in the house)" (Sartre's emphasis). In contemporary society, by the same token, he writes, it is "money" that, "through a continuous degradation," symbolizes "my magical bond with the object," not to say a universal "bond of appropriation" between the human subject "and the totality of objects in the world." And while it is in fact "impossible to realize the relationship symbolized by appropriation," I come nonetheless to view "the totality of my possessions as the totality of my being. I *am* what I have" (Sartre's emphasis).[32]

Such bourgeois materialism, however, represents merely an external manifestation of that sovereign Sartrean sin of "bad faith"—that is, of hypocrisy and self-deception. And in delineating the "bad faith" of the bourgeoisie, Sartre, in the tradition of Rousseau, Robespierre, and Péguy, would seem to reserve his most pointed disdain for the Republic of Letters. Through *La Nausée*'s renowned "Autodidact," for example, whose rote-memorized philosophy of "voluntary optimism" epitomizes "precisely the sort of lie" such men "tell themselves," Sartre scorns the self-serving "humanism" of the bourgeois intelligentsia which "melts all human attitudes into one." There is, recites Sartre's protagonist, "the radical humanist," who is "the particular friend of officials," and there is the "so-called 'Left' humanist" whose

> main worry is maintaining human values; he belongs to no party because he does not want to betray the human, but his sympathies lean toward the humble. . . . The Communist writer has been loving man since the second Five-Year Plan; he punishes because he loves. . . . [There is] the humanist who loves men as they are, the humanist who loves men as they ought to be, the one who wants to save them with their own consent, the one who will save them in spite of themselves. . . . They all hate each other: as individuals, of course, not as men.[33]

Nor does Sartre fail to point the finger of accusation at himself. Mathieu, the distinctly Sartrean protagonist of the postwar trilogy, *Les Chemins de la liberté,* is a self-confessed "bourgeois" who writes "for Left reviews" so as "to escape from [his] class." Dismissed by his communist friend Brunet as "a bourgeois, a dirty intellectual, a watchdog," he finds himself indicted as well by his brother Jacques, a wealthy lawyer, on the charge of hypocrisy. "You are trying," the latter accuses, "to evade the fact that you are bourgeois and ashamed of it." Indeed Jacques's final verdict recalls nothing more immediately than Péguy's indictment of the Sorbonne and its intellectual establishment:

> you have a delightful apartment, you get a competent salary at fixed intervals . . . and you like that sort of life—placid, orderly, the typical life of an official. . . . you condemn capitalist society, and yet you are an official of that society; . . . You despise the

bourgeois class, yet you are a bourgeois, son and brother of bourgeois, and you live like a bourgeois.[34]

The culmination of bourgeois bad faith for Sartre, just as for Stendhal, Bergson, or Michelet, is the degeneration of liberty into mechanical conformity. The "right-thinking man," Sartre proclaims in *Saint
Genet,* the "decent man," renders "himself deaf, dumb, and paralyzed." Defining himself "by obedience, by the automatism of Good,"
he repudiates that which is "wild, free, beyond the limits he has set for
himself." And thus, indeed, is how Sartre tends to portray bourgeois
society in general. The citizens of Bouville, remarks Roquentin, "come
out of their offices after their day of work" and "look at the houses
and the squares with satisfaction." For they know it to be "*their* city,
a good, solid bourgeois city," and "[t]hey have proof, a hundred times a
day, that everything happens mechanically, that the world obeys fixed,
unchangeable laws" (Sartre's emphasis). Mathieu, by the same token,
pronounces the occupied Paris of 1940 "already dead" and superseded
"by the austere and practical world of functional objects." And "Argos," the surrogate Paris of Sartre's Resistance drama, *Les Mouches,* is
similarly depicted as "a half-dead city, a carrion city"; for its citizens
remain entrapped within "Goodness," within that conventional, prefabricated moral code which produces sufficient "fear" and "remorse"
to keep them from rising up against their captors.[35] For Sartre, then,
bourgeois civilization would seem again to breed at best a moral automatism, and at worst a literal and universal servitude.[36]

The case of Foucault is a particularly telling one. The poststructuralist's
inaugural book, *Folie et déraison* (1961), advances nothing less than
a crypto-Rousseauian critique of civilization as a whole—of that
"botched society" which first invented and then nurtured "madness."
For "madness," Foucault summarized in a 1961 interview, "exists only
in society."[37] Secondly, while explicitly rejecting the Marxist proposition that "one group or class," as a self-constituted "subject," exercises
"homogeneous domination over others," Foucault refers as reflexively
as does Sartre to "bourgeois capitalist or industrial society"—to that
"bourgeoisie" which has emerged since the eighteenth century as "the
politically dominant class"; in short, to bourgeois "social hegemony"
in the modern age. In a 1977 interview Foucault acknowledges as one
of "the obscurities of my own discourse" the problem of social class.
But he hardly proceeds to resolve the difficulty. Instead, he reiterates
that while one cannot treat "the bourgeois class" as "a sort of at once

real and fictive subject" and then accuse it of "forcibly" imposing its interests on the working class, one can nevertheless "say that the strategy of moralizing the working class is that of the bourgeoisie," and that the very same strategy "allows the bourgeois class to be the bourgeois class and to exercise its domination."[38]

While refusing to reduce bourgeois domination to economic self-interest alone, Foucault—as suggested above[39]—evinces a visceral disdain for the capitalist profit motive. He contends in *Surveiller et punir*, for example, that modern "disciplinary power" has emerged with and served "the growth of a capitalist economy," and in *La Volonté de savoir*, that the "transformation of sex into discourse" in the modern age has aimed at constituting "a sexuality that is economically useful and politically conservative." Indeed, in the latter work he goes so far as to argue that "the proliferation of sexualities" has been "ensured and relayed" by the "countless economic interests" which are "mediated" by "medicine, psychiatry, prostitution, and pornography."[40]

But once again, the most alarming vice of bourgeois society rests for Foucault not in its material avarice so much as in its discursive hypocrisy, as it were; in the cloaking of its actual power structure behind the humanitarian drapery of enlightened law and social reform. Foucault maintains that the legal superstructure of modern society, its liberal and democratic theory of "collective sovereignty," comprises "a system of right" which successfully "conceal[s] its actual procedures, the element of domination inherent in its techniques." Indeed, the very emergence of bourgeois hegemony in the eighteenth century, as Foucault famously argues in *Surveiller et punir*, "was masked by the establishment of an explicit, coded, and formally egalitarian framework, made possible by the organization of a parliamentary representative regime." But the "dark side" of this superstructure consisted in such new and putatively benevolent disciplines as "clinical medicine, psychiatry, child psychology, [and] educational psychology." Thus, crime, for example, maintains Foucault, ultimately became the province "of experts in psychiatry, criminology, psychology, etc.," and sexuality, that of "doctors, educators, and . . . psychiatrists." Once again, in other words, bourgeois duplicity emerges above all for Foucault out of a "republic of letters" of sorts: namely, that of established social science. For the latter has provided modern society with those "tiny, everyday, physical mechanisms," those "systems of micropower," whereby social control could be established and maintained.[41]

In the final analysis, then, Foucault seeks—like Sartre, Bergson, and Stendhal before him—to disclose beneath the mechanistic facade of bourgeois convention an ever-increasing social subjugation. "The power of the bourgeoisie," he proclaims in a phrase that might have been lifted from Michelet or Péguy, "is self-amplifying." And "disciplinary power," he elaborates elsewhere, insofar as it "presupposes a tightly knit grid of material coercions," which both increases "the subjected forces" and improves "the force and efficiency of that which subjects them," represents "one of the great inventions of bourgeois society." Thus again, Foucault's previously outlined "society of normalization" and its suffocating web of "panopticism" would appear drastically to restrict—if not entirely foreclose—the possibility of generating liberty in society.[42]

II. THE CHURCH

The collective heretical portrait of civilized society, to recapitulate, features an ever-expanding "bourgeois aristocracy" whose characteristic vices of greed, egoism, hypocrisy, and above all servility threaten to overrun the entire social body and extinguish its liberty. Equally foreboding is the heretical depiction of the Catholic Church and its secular counterparts—which should come as no surprise insofar as anticlericalism represents at least as hallowed a tradition in modern French letters as denouncing the bourgeoisie.[43]

Thus, in Stendhal's archetypal epic, for example, "bourgeois" vices would scarcely seem confined to the bourgeoisie: just as greedy, hypocritical, and ignoble in *Le Rouge et le noir* is the Catholic Church. Hence, Julien finds his own worldly ambitions, both social and pecuniary, rekindled by the appearance at Verrières of an elegant young bishop: "The higher one rises in society, Julien thought to himself, the more one finds these charming manners. . . . And how much does it bring in? Two or three hundred thousand francs, perhaps." Much later, contemplating his now chosen vocation, Stendhal's protagonist muses: "[T]wenty years ago I would have worn a military uniform. . . . Nowadays, it is true, by donning the black coat, a man of forty can have a hundred thousand francs in salary." Julien's ecclesiastical careerism, moreover, is hardly unique in Stendhal's universe. Just as the unofficial motto of Verrières was "yield a return," that of the young peasants at Julien's seminary is "the sublime idea of *cash on the line*" (Stendhal's emphasis). And, counting upon similarly terrestrial motives—"the icy egotism," in the narrator's phrase, "of a priest already glutted on power and pleasure"—Mathilde de La Mole successfully secures the aid of a well-connected Jesuit by dangling before him the prospect of a "rapid road to the episcopacy." The priest, reports Stendhal's narrator, fell "almost at her feet, avid with ambition to the point of a nervous tremor."[44]

The secular aspirations of Stendhal's churchmen are not restricted to wealth and professional advancement. "How many cardinals born lower than I," Julien dreams, "have risen to power in the government!" And in their compromise with—and ardent pursuit of—political power, Stendhal's clergymen exhibit no less subservience to the established social hierarchy, both spiritual and secular, than do his Rênals and Valenods. "Render yourselves worthy of the Pope's bounty by your life, by your obedience," explains the Jesuit Abbé Castanède to the young acolytes of Julien's seminary, "and you will obtain a marvelous position where you will command from on high, free of all control; a post from which you cannot be dismissed, in which the government will pay one third of your salary, and the faithful, guided by your preachings, the other two thirds."[45]

Indeed, just as his most barbed criticisms of the bourgeoisie would seem aimed at its social servility, Stendhal's most severe condemnation of the church would seem directed at the slavish submission which it seeks to exact both from its own minions and the populace at large. Hence, the Abbé Castanède's exhortation to his flock finds an ominous echo during a conspiratorial political gathering called together by Monsieur de La Mole. A "lofty ecclesiastic," soon identified as a cardinal, reminds the group that, "the clergy, guided by Rome is the only body that speaks to the little man. Fifty thousand priests repeat the same words on the exact day appointed by their leaders, and the common people, who, after all, furnish the soldiers, will be more stirred by the voice of their priests than by all the little worms in the world."

Even Stendhal's upright Abbé Pirard, in warning his charges against the "*personal questioning*" that comes of "a too profound reading of the Scriptures," confirms the narrator's previously cited verdict that "in the eyes of the church inward submission is all" (Stendhal's emphasis). Ultimately this clerical dictum proves pivotal to Stendhal's tragic climax, when Madame de Rênal reveals that she has denounced Julien neither of her own will nor even in her own words. For her letter of incrimination, she informs her now condemned lover, was composed for her by "the young priest" who was her "spiritual director." "What a horrible thing religion has made me do," she exclaims.[46]

It is worthy of note, however, that Stendhal's novel indicts neither religious belief nor spirituality as such. Two of its clergymen, in fact— "the good curate" Chélan and the aforementioned Pirard—emerge as

honest and authentically devout souls. Julien finds himself "astonished," for example, at the genuine piety of Pirard's study circle, inasmuch as "the idea of religion was indissolubly linked, in his mind, with
hypocrisy and the hope making money." Moreover, upon hearing that
his attempt on the life of Madame de Rênal has failed, Stendhal's protagonist embraces "the truth and sublimity of the idea of God," which
he seeks to rescue from "the priestly hypocrites." Indeed, Julien goes
so far as to imagine a "true religion," which would represent not the
God of the Bible—"a petty despot, cruel and thirsting for revenge"—
but "the God of Voltaire, just, kind, infinite."[47] Thus, Stendhal's hero
comes himself to exemplify, within the social universe of *Le Rouge et
le noir,* an authentic spirituality of sorts.

Stendhal would therefore seem to vent his anticlerical spleen not
upon the faith of individual believers so much as the earthly institution
of the church itself, wherein he rediscovers the familiar vices of egoism,
hypocrisy, and social subservience. The anticlericalism of the consecrated heretics, by the same token, would appear characteristically
to manifest not a denial of the spirit so much as the championing
of a "true" spirituality—indeed a spiritual liberty—against all "established orders" of the spirit.

Rousseau displays his religious views most explicitly—and he-
retically*—through his celebrated "Savoyard vicar" who seeks to en-
lighten his earnest apprentice, Émile, concerning the truths of faith.
Let us not confuse "religion itself," cautions the defrocked priest,
"with the rites of religion." For God would hardly concern himself
with "the form of a priest's garments, . . . the gestures he makes before
the altar," or, for that matter, any "external aspects of worship." Dis-
sociating himself from "the jealous spirit" of all "factions" and
"sects," Rousseau's spokesman specifically repudiates the Catholic
Church's "fixed dogmas," which not only "debase" religious faith but
"render man haughty, intolerant, and cruel."[48]

In *La Nouvelle Héloïse,* Rousseau attributes a still more damning
condemnation of the established church to the cosmopolitan nobleman, Monsieur de Wolmar, for whom Catholicism is a religion "of
vain pretenses" whose primary "interest is that of its ministry." Claiming to have encountered only three priests who actually believed in
God, Wolmar accuses the clergy of mocking "in private what they

---

*It will be recalled the Rousseau was forced into exile owing to the religious views
he expressed in his *Émile.* See above, p. 45.

[teach] in public." In *Du Contrat social*, by the same token, Rousseau directly renounces the "antisocial code" and "theological intolerance" of "Roman Christianity, which may be called the religion of the Priest"; and in *Les Confessions*, he no less openly condemns "the host of petty forms" that obscure the essence of religion, as well as "the Jesuit party" whose "machinations," he believes, have led to his own present persecution.[49]

Thus, for Rousseau, like Stendhal, ambition and hypocrisy would seem to have defiled established religion—indeed, for both writers the Catholic Church reflects all too faithfully the degenerate social order of which it is part. For Rousseau, as well, the church's most egregious sin resides neither in its system of belief nor even its earthly depravity, but rather in its effort to "tyrannize" over the reason and will of the individual. "A Protestant," proclaims Rousseau in *Les Confessions*, must at least "learn to decide for himself," whereas "the Roman faith," he asserts in a proto-Stendhalian phrase, "demands submission." In fact "[t]rue Christians," Rousseau charges in *Du Contrat social*, "are made to be slaves" insofar as "Christianity preaches only servitude and dependence."[50]

But Rousseau's anticlericalism does not stop at organized religion. Having repudiated "a Church which decides everything and permits no doubt," the Savoyard vicar goes on to unleash his critical ire upon "the philosophers," whom he finds equally "proud, assertive, and dogmatic, even in their supposed skepticism." Is there a single philosophe, asks Rousseau's ex-priest, "who in the secret depths of his heart, has any other goal than making himself famous?" Willing, in exchange for personal glory, to "deceive the entire human race without hesitation," these self-proclaimed skeptics "seek imperiously to impose their peremptory decisions on us" in a manner "a hundred times more assertive and dogmatic" than their "religious adversaries." Likewise, in *Les Confessions*, Rousseau claims that his association with "the Encyclopedists" has not "shaken" his faith so much as "strengthened it." Indeed, among the entrenched "parties" opposing him he eventually includes not only "the Jesuits" and "the Jansenists" but "the Encyclopedists" and "the philosophes" as well.[51]

The Republic of letters, in short, incarnates for Rousseau not only an emerging bourgeois aristocracy but an intellectual church as well. Accordingly, he finds himself no more able than Stendhal to recommend philosophical skepticism or materialism. Indeed encouraging Émile to follow his own "inner light"—"the light of conscience and reason"—as opposed to "the authority of fathers and pastors," Rousseau's heretical vicar famously advances a "natural religion"; one emanating from that "inner voice" through which God has "presented everything to our eyes, our conscience, our judgment." Similarly, in *Du Contrat social*, Rousseau favors "a purely internal cult of the supreme God and the eternal obligations of morality," a "true theism" founded not upon "temples, altars, or rites" but rather "natural divine right or law." Even *Du Contrat social*'s notorious state religion represents for Rousseau a "purely civil profession of faith" which will address neither the private "opinions" of its citizens nor their lot "in the life to come." [52] Far, in sum, from repudiating faith altogether, Rousseau champions an autonomous—and hence inherently "free"—spirituality against all established churches, both secular and sacerdotal.

"Historians have" long recognized the impact of Rousseau's religious views, and especially the Savoyard Vicar's "profession of faith," both upon Robespierre and the revolutionary generation as a whole. [53] And indeed, from the Revolution's outset Robespierre espoused what represented, by the end of his century, a somewhat conventional anticlericalism. Maintaining in 1790, for example, that for the church to be "a landlord" is neither "good for religion, the state, nor for itself," he supported the Civil Constitution of the Clergy, which divested the church of its lands. By 1794, the Jacobin leader was proclaiming that "priests are to morality what charlatans are to medicine." Having created, Robespierre argues, a "jealous, capricious, greedy, cruel, and implacable" God "in their own image," the priests have "brought Him down to earth only to demand tithes, riches, honors, pleasure, and power for their own profit." Inasmuch, in fact, as the Catholic clergy incarnates the "baseness, pride, perfidy, debauchery, and falsehood" of the world, God could hardly have intended that it "harness us like beasts to the carriages of kings." [54] Robespierre, then, faithfully recapitulates Rousseau's indictment of the earthly avarice and hypocrisy of the Catholic Church, and especially its aspiration to place society under its own dominion.

By publicly renouncing the "fanaticism," on the other hand, of those revolutionary atheists who sought to establish a "cult of reason" in the fall of 1793, the Jacobin leader would seem also to echo his idol's critique of the philosophes and their secular orthodoxy. "By what right," he demands, do these purveyors of "truth, reason, and philosophy" attack "liberty of worship in the name of liberty?" In fact "atheism," Robespierre charged in the spring of 1794, is "bound up with a conspiracy against the Republic." In his final speech to the National Convention shortly thereafter, Robespierre again accused "the impure apostles of atheism and immorality" of seeking "to destroy the Republic."[55]

Robespierre's anticlericalism, then, like that of Rousseau before him and Stendhal after, constitutes anything but a repudiation of faith. The Jacobin's alternative to the cult of reason, however, would seem at first glance more akin to *Du Contrat social*'s state religion than the "natural religion" of the Savoyard vicar.[56] Robespierre's infamous cult of the Supreme Being, complete with its public articles of faith and manufactured national festivals, claims above all to establish the Revolution's "civil society" upon "the sole foundation" of "morality." Yet for Robespierre such a state-sponsored religion represents not the imposed orthodoxy of an established church, but rather the merging of "all sects"—"without compulsion, without persecution"—in "the universal religion of Nature." As long as "public order" remains undisturbed, vows the Jacobin, "liberty of worship" will be "respected." But more to the point, he insists, is that "liberty and virtue spring together from the breast of the same Divinity. One cannot reside among men without the other." While genuine freedom, in other words, may be reconciled neither with established religion nor Enlightenment materialism, it remains forever reconcilable with—if not identical to—the virtuous citizen's faith in "a superior being who watches over oppressed innocence and punishes triumphant crime." The cult of the Supreme Being, then, epitomizes for Robespierre that free and authentic spirituality which should—and indeed must—be embraced if the Revolution is to be delivered from the established churches of Catholicism and "Reason."[57]

For Michelet, of course, it was Robespierre himself, as the "high priest" and "Pope" of the Jacobins, who came to incarnate a clerical despotism of sorts. Having aspired "his entire life" to be "the dictator of souls," the historian asserts, Robespierre "possessed less the heart of a king than a priest." Hence, in the "violent machiavellianism" of his apostles, in "the inquisitorial spirit, the corporate spirit, *the priest-spirit*" of the Jacobins, "the true tyranny" of institutionalized religion resurfaced with a vengeance (Michelet's emphasis). For Michelet, in other words, the Jacobins and the Catholic clergy embodied within revolutionary France "two great corporations, two great powers"— that is, two equally oppressive churches.[58]

Michelet's assault on the more traditional of these institutions remains, as noted above,[59] legendary in its zeal. Catholic priests, he proclaims in *Du Prêtre de la femme et de la famille*, are *"our enemies,"* the *"enemies of the modern spirit,* of liberty," and hence "of the Revolution" itself (Michelet's emphasis). Even before that momentous event, Michelet maintains in his *Histoire de la révolution française,* "the body of the clergy, monstrously rich in comparison to the nation, was also, in itself, a monster of injustice and inequality." The ecclesiastical Palace of Avignon, for example, had survived for centuries as a "Babel of the Popes," a "Sodom of legates," a "Gomorrah of cardinals." Not surprisingly, therefore, once the Revolution erupted "the prelates" put up "a grand, heroic resistance": they defended "*their property* . . . as the early Christians had defended the faith!" Moreover, charges Michelet, while the clergy themselves "had no faith," they found "instruments in those who still possessed it." The Revolution, accordingly, was forced to contend with the ongoing "error and lie" of "the great Jesuit enterprise"—in short, with "the hypocrisy" of "the priest" (Michelet's emphasis).[60]

In his critique of the Catholic Church, then, Michelet rediscovers the familiar Stendhalian vices of greed, ambition, and hypocrisy. But only in detailing the subservience of the clergy, as well as its attempt to extinguish the liberty of the faithful, does his anticlericalism reach its greatest intensity. Echoing Rousseau, the historian characterizes "the Gospel" itself in his *Histoire* as "a book of resignation, submission, and obedience to authority." Accordingly, he laments, when forced to choose "between their ecclesiastical tyrants and the Revolution which offered to free them," the priests "reaffirmed their habitual obedience." What is more, Michelet recapitulates in the *Histoire* his previously cited thesis—which is itself strikingly mirrored in Stendhal's tale of Madame de Rênal and her "spiritual director"—that the church chronically subverts society's freedom through invading the all-too-permeable psyches of its female devotees. In a chapter titled "The Priest, the Wife, and the Vendée," the historian charges that the provincial "wife," owing to her "devotion to and dependence on priests," became the unwitting "champion of counterrevolution" in 1792.[61]

Thus, established churches for Michelet, whether of the Jacobin or Catholic variety, remain ever and always a grave menace to societal liberty. Yet no more than Rousseau or Robespierre does the historian advocate a skeptical materialism. Having imbibed not "a single religious idea" in his youth, recollects Michelet in *Le Peuple,* faith nonetheless became "very strong within me. It was something of my own, a free and living thing." Like Stendhal, moreover, Michelet draws a sharp distinction, even in the case of the clergy, between the institution of the church and genuine spirituality. Claiming that *Du Prêtre* was written not "in opposition" to "the priests," but rather to the "slavish state" into which "hypocritical authority" has "dragged" them, the historian concludes his anticlerical tract with the hope that it might "prepare" clergymen for an "epoch of deliverance, of personal and spiritual emancipation."[62]

Genuine freedom and spirituality, moreover, remain inescapably intertwined for Michelet with "faith in the Revolution." Hence, at the close of *Le Peuple,* the historian envisions a national program not far removed, ironically enough, from Robespierre's cult of the Supreme Being. All French children, he exhorts, should be educated to have faith first in a "God, revealed by the mother, in love and nature," and then in a "God, revealed by the father, in the living nation, its heroic history, and the sentiment of France." Let "the Fatherland," proclaims Michelet, "that God which is invisible in his supreme unity," become "your first gospel."[63] Michelet's condemnation of established religion, in other words, doesn't deter him from championing private spirituality or a public religion of *la Patrie.* For both, he contends, as opposed to any established church, would appear to sustain rather than suppress society's liberty.

Having flirted himself with Catholic conversion,[64] Bergson would seem an unlikely candidate for anticlerical iconoclasm, at least in any conventional sense. Yet through his acclaimed assault upon scientific—and especially social scientific—positivism, the philosopher promoted a figurative anticlericalism worthy of Michelet. "Positive science," contends Bergson in *L'Évolution créatrice,* represents the crowning achievement of the human "intellect"—of that facet of us all which, owing to its "latent geometricism," remains inherently unfit "to comprehend life." For the primary "object of science," asserts the philosopher in his *Essai sur les données immédiates de la conscience,* "is to forecast and measure," and therefore it is solely "practical utility," he reiterates in *L'Évolution,* "which science has in view." Moreover, in its utilitarian ambition "to furnish us with the best means of acting" on the material world, positive science not only fails "to show us the essence of things," it "makes the mistake of constantly" substituting for real "duration" the "artificial reconstruction of it" advanced by its own "determinism." Hence, the English Darwinist Herbert Spencer, for example, in attempting to reconstruct "evolution with fragments of the evolved," exhibits the chronic fallacy of biological positivism. Having "*imitated* the Whole" by fabricating a biological "mosaic" with his own intellect, Spencer "imagines" that he has described nature's true "design" and "genesis" (Bergson's emphasis).[65]

Bergson, in other words, first represents "positive science" as an established church—a secular cult of reason, as Robespierre might have it—and then accuses it of what amounts to metaphysical avarice and duplicity: not only, he suggests, does the positivist ministry reduce the real to the exploitable, it then veils its own materialist reductionism behind the false orthodoxy of scientific truth. But worst of all, the philosopher protests, is the aspiration of the social sciences to "isolate" and "artificially entrap" what is above all "a living being." In "doing away," that is, "with the qualitative element" in real human activity, and retaining "only the geometrical and impersonal element," the social scientist substitutes for the free human being "a phantom self, the shadow of the ego projecting itself into space."[66] No less, in short, does the positivist church threaten society's liberty in Bergson's narrative than does the Catholic Church in those of Rousseau, Michelet, and Stendhal.

Once more, however, it is not science per se that Bergson impugns but rather the imperial aspirations of its established order. Scientific analysis is at home, the philosopher allows, when measuring "the external world" of objects and "the homogenous medium" of space. But "it goes beyond its province" when imposing its geometrical grid upon real time (*la durée*) and above all, the "vital impetus [*élan vital*]" of life itself. It is in this latter realm, Bergson contends, that "the true function of philosophy" resides. For in grasping the "ascent" of "life and consciousness," in turning the human mind toward "the living principle from which it originates," the "philosopher must go further than the scientist." Philosophy, that is, "introduces us . . . into the spiritual life," and therefore it represents nothing less than "the true continuation of science."[67] And so Bergson's secular anticlericalism constitutes not a repudiation of scientific faith, as it were, so much as the affirmation of a true spiritual freedom against that orthodoxy of the spirit which would extinguish it.

Péguy, who publicly proclaimed his conversion to the Catholic faith in 1907, would seem even less plausible an anticlerical than Bergson. Yet in contesting, as Claude Nicolet has suggested, "all the churches" of fin-de-siècle France—including the Dreyfusard, the Socialist, and ultimately the Catholic as well—the maverick essayist ultimately styled himself the most thoroughgoing anticlerical of his day. Around the time of his conversion, in fact, Péguy had launched a Bergson-inspired assault on that combination of materialist philosophy, Durkheimian sociology, and Jaurèsian socialism which had mutated, in his view, into a new "Dreyfusard Church." Indeed, Péguy's critique of this secular liberal establishment would continue unabated until his death in 1914. In *Notre jeunesse,* for example, he rails against the increasingly powerful *"parti intellectuel"* which had hatched within "the four walls of the Sorbonne"; and in *L'Argent,* he denounces the "scientific sacraments"—those dogmas of "practical, empirical, experimental use and experience"—which serve the "economic automatism of the modern world."[68]

Furthermore, Péguy the reborn Catholic scarcely left his own church unscathed. The Catholicism of "today," he admonishes in *Notre jeunesse,* represents "a religion of the bourgeois, a religion of the rich." Echoing Rousseau's Monsieur de Wolmar, Péguy pronounces "the clerics . . . as well as the good bourgeois clericals," to be nothing more than "would-be Catholics" and "sham Christians" who have forgotten the "imprecations against the rich man, the foreboding denunciations of money, which all but saturate the Gospel." In truth, he concludes, notwithstanding its official separation from the state in 1905, "the Church" has "never ceased to function as the official religion of the bourgeoisie and the State"—that is, as "the formal religion of the rich."[69]

Nor does Péguy spare the contemporary Catholic intelligentsia, be they "modernist" or orthodox. For "the intellectuals and the clerics, the intellectual clerics and the clerical intellectuals" remain cut, for Péguy, from the same unholy cloth. The Catholic modernist, he professed in 1911, is he who "would sell his God in order not to be ridiculed" by the skeptics of the "intellectual party." And two years later he cautioned the young Catholics at the École Normale Supérieure— which was, of course, his own alma mater—against fraternizing with the reigning "politicians" of the Sorbonne. In "the obscene cuddling up with liberals," he scolds in an image reminiscent of Stendhal, "there lies true moral turpitude." But Péguy is equally contemptuous of those "young pillars of apologetics" who "wish to displace Bergson in favor of scholasticism." For Thomism is itself "materialistic, intellectualistic, associationistic, [and] mechanistic"; it too represents "a deterministic system."[70]

All established churches, then, whether secular or ecclesiastical, materialist or scholastic, remain for Péguy both morally corrupt and spiritually sterile—contaminated, that is, by avarice, ambition, and hypocrisy. But like Rousseau, Robespierre, and Michelet before him, Péguy also professes to defend the true faith. Genuine Christianity, he proclaimed in 1909, is "not in the least a public, superficial . . . historical operation," but rather "an event, a completely secret operation, internal, quite profound." Hence, "our Christianity," he wrote the following year, "will never be either a parliamentary Christianity or a Christianity of the rich parish." Defending Bergson, by the same token, against those "politicians of the spiritual life" who sought in 1914 to have him condemned, Péguy exalts the man who has reawakened "the heart of liberty." Jesus himself, Péguy reminds Bergson's ecclesiastical foes, was no philosophical "determinist," nor are the Gospels "at all of a logical-deductive, mathematical, physical, so-called scientific order." In truth it is Bergsonian liberty alone, he proclaims, that "guarantees that the Church will not succumb to its own mechanism."[71] Thus, Péguy's declared Catholic faith doesn't prevent him from combating the official church establishment or its secular counterparts on behalf of a genuinely emancipated spirituality.

Equally critical of spiritual orthodoxies, both religious and non, is Sartre; indeed, anticlericalism would appear as axiomatic for him as the critique of the bourgeoisie. It will be recalled, for example, that the Catholic Church, having helped erect the "monstrous edifice" to which the town's bourgeoisie flocks each Sunday, is deeply implicated in the avarice and ostentation of La Nausée's Bouville. And Roquentin goes on to detail the ritual hypocrisy of Bouville's Sunday routine: the "long and copious Sunday meal"; the visit "to the memorial cemetery or to your parents"; the frequenting of "fine shops" which remain open for "the passage of the elegant and the notable . . . every Sunday until noon," not to mention "Easter Monday" and "all Christmas night." Likewise, in Les Chemins de la liberté, Mathieu finds a fitting metaphor for wartime Paris in the "large white bulk" of "a new handsome church which served no purpose."[72]

Perhaps even more severe is Sartre's critique of orthodox humanism—or the "cult of humanity," as he branded it in 1945. Hence, La Nausée's self-deceived "Autodidact," while "never a believer," periodically attends Sunday Mass so as to merge in "the communion of souls." And Roquentin catalogs the spiritual sects—"anti-intellectualism, Manicheism, mysticism, pessimism, anarchy and egotism"—which the benighted humanist has "digested" in the process of melting "all human attitudes into one." Nor does Sartre exempt socialism and communism from his critique of lay religions, his own political leanings notwithstanding. The "Autodidact" proudly proclaims himself "a registered member of the Socialist Party," and Brunet, the more sympathetically portrayed communist of Les Chemins de la liberté, nonetheless plays the Stendhalian cleric in seeking to recruit Mathieu to the Party. "[R]enounce your own freedom," he implores, "and everything shall be rendered unto you." Mathieu laughs and responds: "You talk like a priest."[73]

In fact, much like Stendhal, Sartre would seem to reproach the Communist "church" above all for requiring its minions to submit entirely to its orthodoxy. "I put my trust in the Central Committee of the U.S.S.R.," Brunet sermonizes later in the trilogy to Schneider, a fellow prisoner of war.

> I know that history has its laws and that, by virtue of these laws, an identity of interest binds the country of the workers and the European proletariat. I give no more thought to these things than you do to the foundation of your house. . . . That certainty supports and shelters me.[74]

Schneider exclaims angrily in response: "[I]t's *you* who are the bastard! . . . It's easy to be superior when you've got a Party behind you, when you've been schooled in a political orthodoxy" (Sartre's emphasis).[75]

Thus, Sartre's anticlericalism would seem once again to comprise a defense of liberty against any and all episcopacies of the spirit. Perhaps paradoxically, moreover, the same assault upon institutionalized spirituality would appear to underlie the forthright atheism for which the existentialist is notorious. Inasmuch as what "religions call God," Sartre argues in *L'Etre et le néant*, refers to an eternal being who is both transcendent and self-caused, both self-complete and entirely free, and that freedom is by definition an ontological "nothingness" at the heart of "Being," then "the idea of God" must be "contradictory." But faced with the terrifying prospect of having to "choose our being," most of us flee into the "a priori Good" offered by religious faith—or again, as he puts it in *L'Existentialisme est un humanisme*, into that humanistic materialism "which would abolish God with the least possible consequence" and grant "certain values," such as honesty, integrity, and devotion to one's family, an "a priori existence."[76]

In this way, the belief in God or in any "cult of reason" constitutes for Sartre a species of "bad faith," or ontological hypocrisy, which threatens to degenerate into complete servility. Hence, in Sartre's allegorical drama, *Les Mouches,* the citizens of Argos "creep along the ground in the dark like smoke wraiths" before a Jupiter who, incarnating the self-complete "Goodness" of foreordained "justice," demands from his subjects "meek acceptance and abject humility." The play's hero, on the other hand, in declaring his independence from "the Good," successfully wrests himself from Jupiter's grasp. "Neither slave nor master," he informs the false god, "I *am* my freedom"; therefore, he concludes, "I am doomed to have no other law but my own" (Sartre's emphasis).[77] Even atheism, in other words, represents for Sartre not a disavowal of the spirit so much as an attempt to rescue spiritual autonomy—authentic freedom—from "God" and all other prefabricated programs of the soul.

The outline of Foucault's anticlerical critique, both secular and religious, has of course emerged already. It will be recalled, for example, that like Sartre, Foucault denounces such secular churches as Marxism and psychoanalysis for their "global, totalitarian theories." And it has been noted as well that, very much in the tradition of Michelet, the poststructuralist castigates those "Christian techniques of examination, confession, guidance, [and] obedience" which coerce "individuals to work at their own 'mortification.'" Hence, in *La Volonté de savoir*, for example, Foucault cites the oft-repeated commandment of the Counterreformation's "Catholic pastoral" that the sinner "'tell everything . . . not only consummated acts, but sensual touchings, all impure gazes, all obscene remarks.'" Such sexual injunctions as these, he suggests with savage irony, find their nineteenth-century counterpart in the Marquis de Sade, whose words often "seem to have been transcribed from the treatises of spiritual direction." Indeed, the very paradigm of Christian "pastorship," contends Foucault, presupposes a relationship between the "shepherd" and his "flock" of "complete dependence" and "personal submission." The priest "must know what goes on in the soul of each" parishioner, and above all "his secret sins." Recognizable, then, in Foucault's portrait of established religion is the familiar anticlerical condemnation of the church's corruption and hypocrisy; and reminiscent especially of Michelet and Stendhal would seem his account of the clergy's invasion of the soul—of that vampire-like penetration of the individual psyche which yields, as he puts it, "a kind of everyday death."[78]

Foucault famously submits, moreover, that secular modernity has produced an analogous clerical melodrama of sorts—one which, though virtually unnoticed, would seem infinitely more insidious: in place of the Catholic Church have emerged "the human sciences," which claim to embody a "whole new system of truth, . . . a corpus of knowledge, techniques, 'scientific' discourses"; and the Catholic clergy, by extension, has been supplanted by a "whole army" of "warders, doctors, chaplains, psychiatrists, psychologists, education-alists"—of scientific and technical "experts in psychiatry, criminology, psychology." As do Rousseau, Bergson, and Péguy, in other words, Foucault likens the modern bourgeois intelligentsia to a lay priesthood; and periodically he renders the parallel all but explicit. In a 1977 lecture, for example, Foucault suggests that those "networks of power" which formerly passed "'through the soul,'" have come now to "pass through health and the body." Hence, "the social body," he later elaborates, has become "a field for medical intervention," and "the doctor" both a "technician" of the "social body" and an intrusive representative of "public hygiene."[79]

This new social scientific clergy, moreover, would seem at the very least as two-faced as its Catholic precursor. In *La Volonté de savoir*, for instance, Foucault charges that the "onanism" of the child or the "hysteria" of the "nervous" or "idle" woman, while they may have been designated in the nineteenth century as evils "to be eliminated," represented in fact "not so much an enemy as a support." For just as Michelet's duplicitous "spiritual director" had discovered in the psychologically vulnerable "wife" a direct avenue into the family's intimate circle, the "entire medico-sexual regime" found in both child and woman "*lines of penetration*" into "the family milieu" (Foucault's emphasis). Indeed, Foucault concurs with his anticlerical forbear that such "power" entails a secret "pleasure": "[t]he pleasure" of a "power that questions, monitors, watches, spies, palpates, brings to light." Thus, those "sciences of man," Foucault summarizes in *Surveiller et punir*, "which have so delighted our 'humanity' for over a century," are characterized above all by "the petty, malicious minutiae" of "scientific" investigation, and "the terrible power" it incarnates.[80]

Ultimately, then, Foucault's anticlerical portrait underscores not only the hypocrisy of the priesthood, both Catholic and lay, but its ambition to place society under its yoke. And for Foucault it is again the confessional which provides the paradoxical link, first of all, between an "obligatory and exhaustive" Catholic ritual and "the *scientia sexualis* that emerged in nineteenth century"; and second, between that same rite of self-disclosure—both religious and scientific—and "men's subjection: their constitution as subjects in both senses of the word." While always "speaking to us of freedom," Foucault charges, the modern confessional—be it medical, criminal, or psychiatric—represents in fact "an extortion of confidential evidence according to the rules of scientific discourse." Thus the "confessional science" of psychiatry, for instance, justifying its "therapeutic or normalizing interventions" on the hallowed ground of "objective" scientific truth, appropriates "the power to forgive, console, and direct." Indeed just as "the public execution," charges Foucault in *Surveiller et punir,* is the logical extension of "a procedure governed by the [Catholic] Inquisition," so too is the "practice of placing individuals under 'observation'" the "natural extension" of those "disciplinary methods" developed by the church of social science.[81]

Yet no more than Bergson does Foucault ultimately disavow "the contents, methods, or concepts of . . . science," and no more than Michelet does he condemn modernity's scientific "priesthood" per se. For "power," Foucault insists, "is not to be taken to be a phenomenon of one individual's consolidated and homogenous domination over others, or that of one class or group over others." It emerges rather out of those scientific "discourses of truth" which exercise the institutional authority—through their ceaseless "interrogation," "inquisition," and "registration of truth"—to "diminish" or "disqualify" their "subjects." Thus, we "are opposed," Foucault summarizes, "to the institution and functioning of an organized scientific discourse within a society such as ours," to the public consecration of science, in other words, as modernity's secular church. Finally, no less than his anticlerical precursors, does Foucault nurture the hope of liberation from this new spiritual orthodoxy. But in place of Robespierre's critique of the cult of reason, for example, or Bergson's antipositivistic "philosophy," the poststructuralist offers "anti-sciences": those disciplinary "genealogies" epitomized by his own celebrated "anti-psychiatric discourses." These comprise for Foucault "not positivistic returns" to scientific "truth," but rather means of emancipating "local, discontinuous, disqualified, illegitimate knowledges"—that is, of rescuing authentic spiritual liberty once again from the modern secular church which has subjected it.[82]

III. THE STATE AND "LA POLITIQUE"

If "the Church," be it ecclesiastical or secular, represents but one more corrupt, hypocritical, and servile face of bourgeois society in the heretical narrative, so too does the realm of the state and parliamentary politics. Indeed, no less characteristic of modern French political culture than anticlericalism or the critique of the bourgeoisie would seem the critique of the centralized government and its "politique."[83]

It has already been noted—to begin again with the Stendhalian archetype—that political posts, patronage, and power represent objects of universal lust in the social cosmos of *Le Rouge et le noir.* Monsieur de Rênal, for example, priding himself on his eminence as a local governmental official, seeks to "immortalize] his administration" by constructing an absurdly unnecessary wall—a metaphorical bureaucracy—for which he must "make three special trips to Paris." He later participates in "various complicated intrigues" involving "the prefect of Besançon" so as to secure for a political ally the post of "first rather than second deputy to the mayor of Verrières." Valenod, by the same token, has "as much as said to the businessmen in town: 'give me your two biggest fools; to the lawyers, a pair of your stupidest; and to the medical men, your two biggest charlatans.'" And then, having "assembled the most shameless men in trade, he said to them, 'let us form a government.'" [84]

Such profiteering and influence peddling would appear a permanent fixture within Stendhal's political universe regardless of the status or party affiliation of those involved. "There will always be a king anxious to enlarge his prerogative," asserts Stendhal's world-weary philosophe, Saint Giraud:

> always the ambition to become deputy, and the memory of Mirabeau who gained glory along with several hundred thousand francs. . . . Always our ultras will be consumed by the passion to become peers or chamberlains. Aboard the ship of state everybody will want to stand at the helm because the job pays well. [85]

Even Bonaparte, Saint Giraud concludes, "was great only on the battlefield. . . . With his chamberlains, his ceremonies, his receptions at the Tuileries, he simply offered a new version of all the imbecilities of the monarchy." Julien himself echoes the same sentiment later in the novel, musing that "even the great Danton stole," that "Mirabeau sold out too," and that "Napoleon stole his millions in Italy." [86]

Once again, even more than by the institutionalized graft of government, Stendhal's satirical ire would seem inflamed by the hypocritical ambition and servility of parliamentary politics. Hence, he passes up no opportunity to tweak the so-called "liberals" of the Restoration—the ostensible parliamentary "opposition"—for their obsequiousness before established power. We discover, for instance, that "especially the liberals" of Verrières protest the inclusion of the lower-class Julien in an honor guard to meet the king. And among the aristocrats and legitimists gathered at the Parisian dinner table of the Marquis de La Mole, Stendhal places "Monsieur Sainclair, the great liberal." When one of Mathilde's suitors asks how a man of "such extreme ideas, so generous, so independent" will be received by the family, she replies: "Take a look . . . there's your independent man who's bowing to the floor before M. Descouliz"—a Stendhalian reactionary—"grasping his hand I almost thought he was going to carry it to his lips." A moment of equally barbed irony finds Julien in Paris face to face with Valenod, who has arrived "to thank the Minister for his barony." Now "the ministerial candidate" for the mayorship of Verrières, the former poorhouse director is to be opposed in the upcoming elections by his old nemesis Rênal, "who was being pushed by the liberals." Julien, reports the narrator, "was shaken with silent laughter" upon learning that "M. Rênal has been discovered to be a Jacobin." [87]

Thus, the established state, for Stendhal, would seem just as debased and entrenched as the established church; and electoral politics, far from comprising a constructive mechanism through which individual and societal liberty might be enhanced, would appear to reflect rather the self-serving ambition of its practitioners as well as their subservience before the powers that be. The same contempt for administrative degeneration and sterility surfaces conspicuously in the discourse of the consecrated heretics, as does a profound mistrust of parliamentary politics as a plausible route to social emancipation.

Nothing, of course, has earned Rousseau more enduring celebrity than his prerevolutionary critique of established government and its politics. Having invented "political institutions," Rousseau laments in his second discourse, in the "hope of securing their liberty," men instead "ran headlong into their chains." For by "eternally fix[ing] the law of property" and thereby converting "clever usurpation into unalterable right," this primordial government "bound new fetters on the poor, and gave new powers to the rich." Rousseau in fact traces "the progress of inequality" from the "establishment of laws and of the right of property," which first "authorized" the relationship "of rich and poor"; through "the institution of magistracy," which sanctioned the relationship "of powerful and weak"; to "the conversion of legitimate into arbitrary power," which established the relationship "of master and slave." [88]

Thus, in its very essence, Rousseau suggests, government embodies the institutionalization of material inequity and social oppression. Moreover, even while delineating in *Du Contrat social* that "form of association" which will protect and defend "each associate" and yet leave each "as free as before," Rousseau extends the same portrait of governmental ossification and corruption. The "executive power" of Rousseau's imagined state, it will be recalled, amounts to an appointed magistracy, which, representing "not the people's masters but its officers," may be deposed at any time by the "general will." For the government, Rousseau maintains, tends inherently to develop its own separate "personality," or "corporate will"; and that "implies assemblies, councils, . . . rights, titles, and privileges exclusive to the prince, all of which renders the office of magistrate the more honorable as it becomes more troublesome." What is more, Rousseau cautions, foreshadowing Stendhal, "those who rise to the top"—above all in a monarchy—"are often petty blunderers, petty swindlers, and petty intriguers, whose petty talents allow them to get into the highest positions at court." Indeed, in any governmental body, he summarizes, "the general will is always the weakest, the corporate will the second, and the individual will strongest of all"—which represents "exactly the reverse of what the social system requires." [89]

Nor of course does Rousseau place any faith in the give and take of parliamentary politics. Scorning "the idea of representation" as a remnant of that "iniquitous and absurd system" of "feudal government" which "degrades humanity," he champions the classical model of the polis that requires each citizen to participate directly in the shaping of the law. And fearing the emergence of "intrigues" and "partial associations" within the community, Rousseau insists that citizens attend political assemblies having had "no communication with one another," and that "each citizen," accordingly, "express only his own opinion" rather than that of "a partial association." For Rousseau, in fact, the emergence of "contradictory views and debates" reflects a debasement of the "general will." "When particular interests begin to make themselves felt," he writes, "and the smaller societies begin to exercise an influence over the larger, then the common interest changes and finds opponents." Such a "tendency to degenerate" represents for Rousseau "the unavoidable and inherent defect" of every "body politic": "the government," he contends, "continually exerts itself against the Sovereignty," and therefore, "sooner or later the prince must inevitably suppress the Sovereign and break the social treaty." [90] For Rousseau, in sum, just as for Stendhal, the state not only inclines invariably toward material corruption and bureaucratic intractability—and parliamentary politics toward private ambition and self-interest—but the body politic itself evolves naturally in the direction of its own subjugation.

Robespierre as well, even while guiding the Jacobins to the pinnacle of power, never ceased to declare himself the enemy of established gov-

ernment. While still in the parliamentary opposition, he regularly ex-
horted the revolutionary assembly to scrutinize the motives of "the
Court and the Ministry"; for, as he put the matter in 1791, "mistrust"
of government "is to liberty, what jealousy is to passion." Echoing its
Rousseauian inspiration, Robespierre's "Proposed Declaration of the
Rights of Man and Citizen" of 1793 decrees that "[t]he people is sovereign, the government is its property, [and] its functionaries are its
employees." Indeed "in every free state," the document proceeds, "the
law must, above all, defend public and individual liberty against the
abuse of authority by those who govern"; therefore, "every institution
which does not assume that the people are good and the magistrate
corruptible is vicious." Somewhat paradoxically, this disparaging view
of government would appear entirely unaltered by Robespierre's own
rise to power. Even the "revolutionary government," the Jacobin leader
proclaimed from his perch on the Committee on Public Safety, which
has been forced "to found" the Republic by waging a ruthless war of
"liberty against its enemies," must remain "trusting of the people
and severe to itself." Its magistrates must "sacrifice" their interests "to
the interest of the people" and their "pride in power to equality"; and
"if there exists a representative body," it is required "to inspect and
ceaselessly control all public functionaries."[91]

As the previous citation suggests, Robespierre, like most revolutionary politicians, explicitly parts ways with his Genevan forebear over
the issue of political representation. No less than Rousseau, however,
does he disdain the parliamentary "politics of transaction" in Anne
Sa'adah's apt formulation.[92] In his *Adresse au Français* of 1791—to
cite David Jordan's summary—Robespierre "bitterly opposed the politics of compromise and accommodation and self-interest pursued by
the majority of his colleagues." The Jacobin came ultimately, of course,
to portray his own party as the oracle of the people and any that opposed it—"the Girondin faction," for example, or the "party" of "*the
ultrarevolutionaries*"—as politically partisan and divisive (Robespierre's emphasis). His final speech before the Convention, as previously recounted, bristles with accusations against "the chiefs of factions and their agents" in the government, against those who would
"factionalize" the "National Representation," against the audacious
"parties" which ceaselessly "intrigue" against the Revolution. "I know
of only two parties," he proclaims, "that of *good*, and that of *bad*,
citizens. Patriotism is not an affair of parties, but an affair of the
heart"[93] (Robespierre's emphasis).

Robespierre would seem also, finally, to espouse a Rousseauian law
of political degeneration. "A nation is truly corrupt," he asserts in his

"Report on the Principles of Political Morality" of 1794, "when, having gradually lost its character and its liberty, it passes from democracy
to aristocracy or to monarchy; this represents the death of the body
politic through decrepitude." Hence, "according to the natural course
of things," the government tends eventually to forget "the interests of
the people" and "lapse into the hands of corrupt individuals." In this
light, it is no surprise to find Robespierre prophesying, on the eve of
his own demise, the imminent doom of the political nation. If the revolutionary government, he exhorts, "falls into perfidious hands, it will
become itself the instrument of the counterrevolution." And the counterrevolutionaries stand poised to reveal their traitorous dispositions,
hitherto "concealed under hypocritical outward appearances," by
instigating "violent discussions in the National Convention." Should
they fail, he continues, to "master the Convention," they "will divide
it into two parties; and thus a vast field will be opened to calumny and
intrigue." They will then seek to "sever the Convention from the
people," to "embroil the Republic in disorders," and finally, to "re-
establish the old tyranny!"[94] In short, for Robespierre, not only does
government deteriorate naturally into corruption and the abuse of
power; the politics of party and debate would seem to herald its
demise.

Michelet, once again, both concurs with Robespierre's critique of government and redirects it at the Jacobin chief himself. "All governments
are brothers," intones the historian, insofar as "government" represents that "form" which, in seeking to establish "calm and order
through the extinction of vital energies," drains a society of its "content [*fond*]." And Robespierre—a "measured, careful, inflexible, man
of politics" in Michelet's description—"*was a government*" (Michelet's emphasis).[95]

The historian in fact apologizes in his revolutionary chronicle for
accentuating the "intrigues" of the emerging state rather than its
"toils," for emphasizing the "all-too-blameworthy leaders and heads
of parties" instead of the numerous "enlightened, modest, impartial
men" who carried out the administrative tasks of the Revolution. Yet
he typically denigrates even the latter, for example, as "lawyers . . .
who spoke frequently and at great length, trusting too much to language," or as men of "paper liberty" who believed that "everything
would be saved once the constitution was established." Still more
damning—and familiar—is Michelet's tale of "the Gironde" and its
brief ascendancy within the revolutionary government. Made up

largely, he contends, of obscure young men from the provinces, the Girondins found themselves thrust "suddenly into the limelight and a world of luxury entirely new to them." Not surprisingly, therefore, they "became almost completely ensnared"—like so many Julien Sorels— "by the society of Paris." But unlike Stendhal's hero, they proved unable in Michelet's narrative to extract themselves from this corrupting net of "bankers and men of money," of "salons" and "fashionable women." Thus, the Gironde, Michelet writes, rapidly degenerated into "factions, groups, [and] coteries," and became ultimately, "in general, the enemy of unity." By the summer of 1792, the historian laments, these "founders of the Republic" were easily marked by their enemies as "the vanguard of the rich and the halfhearted" and even as "hypocritical patriots."[96] Once again, in other words, the revolutionary government—no less than any other—would seem to represent for Michelet a source of social sterility, dissipation, and hypocrisy.

Nor would the historian appear any more enamored of "the politics of transaction" than his Jacobin nemesis. Michelet's *Histoire* is suffused with a scorn for "political machination," for "political schisms" between "republican and republican," for the "interests," "politics," and "reasonings of the man of State," which contrast so sharply with "*absolute Justice*" (Michelet's emphasis). Indeed, if the Girondins come to symbolize in Michelet's narrative the party of debauchery, the Jacobins represent the "machiavellian party" par excellence. The majority of the Jacobins, the historian laments, "embraced without difficulty . . . the grave axiom of revolutionary corruption" that "there exist two moral principles, one public and one private, and that the former, when necessary, may extinguish the latter."[97]

In the final analysis, Michelet concludes, the "Girondins and Jacobins were fellow political logicians" who "differed little in principle"; for both represented that aspect of the Revolution which was "political and superficial." These "parties of reasoners" and "ardent scholastics," he charges, these "political geometricians" and "fanatics of abstraction," lacked the Revolution's authentic "vitality and depth." In *Le Peuple,* as well, Michelet assaults the "administrative" and "political machines" of the modern age whose functionaries—those "dreadful *abstractors* of ultimate essences"—have "armed themselves with five or six formulas" which they employ, "like so many guillotines, *to abstract* men" (Michelet's emphasis). In such men of state the historian again finds a chilling "lack of substance, life, and the feeling for life"; and in such political "machinism" he discerns precisely "[t]he genius of the inquisition and the police, which astonished many in Robespierre and Saint-Just."[98] For Michelet, government would appear innately predisposed to a tyranny that party politics does more to exacerbate than alleviate.

On the surface, Bergson would seem no more an adversary of the state than of the church; nor does the master himself voice that explicit condemnation of parliamentary politics, which, as shall shortly be seen, such disciples as Péguy would derive from his nominally apolitical philosophy. Yet immanent in the philosopher's account of the human psyche and its "latent geometricism" would appear a profound if metaphorical critique of government. "The mechanistic instinct of the mind," the philosopher charges, with its "fixed requirements, its established explanations, its irreducible propositions," is guilty of nothing less than "forcing" the real into "a pre-existing framework"—into "the ready-made garments of our ready-made concepts." Hence, "when it undertakes the study of life," he cautions in L'Évolution créatrice, the intellect "necessarily treats the living like the inert," and when we allow it free reign over our psyches, he warns in his Essai sur les données immédiates de la conscience, its "fixed terms" will eventually become "solidified" and "crystallized," and "automatism" will "little by little . . . overlay freedom." In short, our own "mechanicism" will end up "governing" us entirely.[99]

For Bergson, in other words, the "mechanistic intellect" underlies the reductive church of positivism, and its barren universe of the "ready-made [tout fait]" would seem to comprise for him a pervasive and unyielding bureaucracy of the mind; an internal governmental framework which, like that of Michelet, tends invariably to sap humanity of its "vital energies." Indeed, like Michelet's political "machinism" and Rousseau's degenerating "executive power," this psychic bureaucracy threatens perpetually to institute its own tyrannical regime over the human soul.

Through his much acclaimed concept of "politique," Péguy once more makes manifest what had remained tacit in the master. "Politique," it will be recalled, connotes most broadly for Péguy all that is rigidly determined and barren in the human universe—that which has succumbed, as he put it in 1914, to "metaphysical sclerosis." Accordingly, the essayist characteristically indicts the "placid, sedentary civil servants" of the Sorbonne for their "immobile philosophy"; and he ultimately informs the church's "Roman bureaucracy" that "a dead soul is one which has succumbed to its own accumulation of red-tape, its own bureaucracy."[100] "Politique," then, would seem to comprise for Péguy the institutional embodiment of Bergson's "*tout fait.*"

Not surprisingly, in this light, Péguy reserves his deepest hostility for established government. Having scorned the Third Republic in *Notre jeunesse,* for example, for degenerating from a "living" regime into a sterile "proposition" to be "proven," Péguy suggests—in a passage strongly reminiscent of Michelet—that "the governing republicans and the theoretical monarchists" partake of "the same reasoning." For both, he charges, are "politicians" who "share the language of politics" and "place themselves on the plane of politics." On the other hand, Péguy applauds those heroic Dreyfusards who ranged themselves against all "temporal authorities" and "constituted powers": against "the lycée headmaster, the censor, the academy inspector, the inspector general, the director of secondary education, the minister, the deputies"—against "the entire machine, the entire hierarchy" of "political men." For "instruments as coarse as the government, the Chamber of Deputies, the State, the Senate," Péguy proclaims, are by definition "alien to all that is spiritual."[101]

The ex-Dreyfusard exhibits a similar aversion, moreover, to parliamentary politics, which he typically dismisses as "the game of parties." "The government makes elections," Péguy asserts with Stendhalian scorn, "and elections make the government. Tit for tat." And again he finds the ostensible differences between parties largely inconsequential. Even "more profoundly political," Péguy suggests caustically, than "the professionals, the politicians, the parliamentary men of politics," are "the antipolitical professionals, the antipoliticians . . . the antipolitical antiparliamentarians." He expresses equal disdain, accordingly, for the reigning Radical Party of the political center, and such extraparliamentary movements as the royalist "Action Française" on the right and revolutionary syndicalism on the left. For underlying all political parties and pressure-groups he finds the same political universe: "everywhere," that is, "the same parliamentarianism . . . the same parliamentary shams, the same vacillations." Indeed, proclaims Péguy in *Notre jeunesse,* merely by virtue of practicing "their vocation as politicians," our "men of politics" cannot help but be "guilty in the first degree, criminals in the first degree." For "jaurèsism," as he contemptuously labels party politics in 1913, represents "a system of political prevarication . . . of favors, oppression, [and] iniquity . . . of fraud and turpitude."[102] Once again, in other words, the realm of government and parliamentary procedure remains for Péguy inescapably sterile, two-faced, and corrupt.

Political decay—"the contamination, the degeneration, the dishonor, the deviation, the degradation of mystique into politique"—appears as inevitable in Péguy's narrative as in that of Rousseau, Robespierre, or Michelet. In fact, the historian's previously cited dictum that in government "form exterminates content" would seem a striking anticipation of Péguy's more famous axiom that "everything begins in mystique and ends in politique." The repercussions of such political degeneration are equally familiar. Bureaucratic "tranquility," Péguy proclaims, spells "the death of vitality and liberty"; and "parliamentary politics" not only fails to revive them, but, on the contrary, stands "diametrically opposed to the mystiques which it claims to perpetuate." In truth, Péguy admonishes, "[n]othing" poses a greater threat "to the mystiques of liberty than the politicians of liberty." [103]

For Sartre, the corruption of the state would seem as self-evident as that of established religion and the bourgeoisie; indeed, the existentialist's oeuvre virtually abounds with disdain for government officials and politicians. *La Nausée*'s Roquentin, for example, symbolically assaults the state in the bronzed person of "Gustave Impétraz," a fin-de-siècle school inspector whose statue overlooks Bouville's town square. Holding "his hat in his left hand," details Sartre's protagonist, and "placing his right hand on a stack of papers," the "bronze giant" remains ever "at the service" of the town's "narrow and solid little ideas" by virtue of "the authority and immense erudition drawn from the papers crushed in his hands." Equally unforgiving is Roquentin's portrayal of "Olivier Blévigne," a "great cotton merchant" who "went into politics" and became a parliamentary deputy. Only "five feet tall" in real life, Roquentin reports, the politician "sprang out at you from the canvas" of his official portrait "like a jack-in-the-box" or "a bad-tempered midget." Nor do government officials fare any better in *Les Chemins de la liberté,* where a former socialist minister is described as a "little red-eared mouse," and where Mathieu—who is indicted, it will be recalled, on the same charge by his brother—chronically castigates himself as "merely an official and nothing more." Indeed Sartre's protagonist finally joins the French army in 1938 only out of "the dismal stoicism characteristic of the bureaucrat who endures everything—poverty, illness, and war—from motives of self-respect." What is more, Mathieu reflects wryly, "I don't even respect myself." [104] For Sartre, then, the domain of government would seem at best a breeding-ground for petty ambition, hypocrisy, and sterility.

Nor does the existentialist, as evidenced both by the previous examples and his own public behavior, reserve any sympathy for parliamentary politics. Indeed, nothing has earned Sartre more lasting notoriety than his own self-transformation from "government official not interested in politics"—as he disdainfully describes his fictional alterego, Mathieu—into committed political revolutionary and Marxist. "I was not made for politics," Sartre mused autobiographically in 1972, but "politics has changed me a great deal. . . . and finally I became obligated to engage in it." And after 1945, of course, he increasingly—and controversially—styled himself the champion of extraparliamentary politics: for example, in the Soviet Union and China between 1952 and 1956; in Algeria in 1958; in Cuba in 1960; and in France in May of 1968. Yet, as has also been seen, even Marxism constituted neither a philosophical orthodoxy nor an official political party for Sartre. Repudiating its penchant for historical determinism and "dehumanization," he decreed in 1957 that Marxism must "study real men in depth" and "not dissolve them."[105]

Once again, in fact, all political practice for Sartre would seem subject to spiritual ossification—to "death within the soul," as he labels the phenomenon in *Les Chemins de la liberté*, echoing Bergson's critique of "the ready-made" and Péguy's of "metaphysical sclerosis." In their shared "passion" for "order," for example, the God of *Les Mouches* as well as his anointed head of government, Aegisthus, seek to foster remorse in the citizens of Argos, so that their "sins" will "harden on them—like cold fat." Even the Revolution itself, as delineated in Sartre's *Critique de la raison dialectique* of 1960, would seem destined to degenerate à la Rousseau into an "Institution": a bureaucratic "praxis bogged down in matter," a "petrified practice." In the revolutionary "Institution," Sartre laments, "freedom is perfectly hidden" and "[p]owerlessness and imperative, terror and inertia, become reciprocally established."[106] Established government, in other words, whether parliamentary or revolutionary, would appear to represent for Sartre yet another instance of that human craving for ontological "facticity" or "Being-in-itself" which leads inexorably toward servitude.

Much of Foucault's oeuvre, finally, might be interpreted as a repudiation of the modern state—of those "bureaucrats" and "police" who "see that our papers are in order," and, more broadly, of that "new physics of power" which has superseded the "body of the King" as the true source of political sovereignty in the modern age. The poststructuralist maintains, for example, that the foundation of the police in modern times as a "single, rigorous, administrative machine" has furnished the modern state with an "instrument of permanent, exhaustive, omnipresent surveillance capable of making all visible, as long as it could itself remain invisible." The police of eighteenth-century Paris, Foucault contends, comprising "forty-eight commissioners [*commissaires*], twenty inspectors," as well as paid "'observers,'" "secret agents," "informers," and even "prostitutes," "sanctioned a generalization of the disciplines that became coextensive with the state itself." For the police force was "invented" not only "for maintaining law and order" and "assisting governments in their struggle against their enemies," but also "for assuring urban supplies, hygiene, health, and standards considered necessary for handicrafts and commerce." [107]

No less would the modern professions of teaching and medicine seem to function as a normative police force in service of the state. "The Normal," Foucault asserts in *Surveiller et punir,*

> is established as a principle of coercion in teaching with the introduction of a standardized education and the establishment of *écoles normales;* it is established in the effort to organize a national medical profession and a hospital system capable of operating general norms of health. [108]

Hence, human sexuality, for example, Foucault famously contends in *La Volonté de savoir,* emerged in the modern age as something "one administered. . . . it called for management procedures; it had to be taken charge of by the analytical discourses." It became "a concern of the state," which, in turn, helped foster "*a biopolitics of the population,*" a "political technology of life" (Foucault's emphasis). [109] Thus, the phenomenon of "normalization," for Foucault, encompasses not only the ubiquitous discourse of social science and its "experts," but quite literally a government—and one which constitutes, in the tradition of Michelet, Péguy, and Sartre, a duplicitous, debilitating, bureaucratic machine.

Foucault, moreover, characteristically dismisses "political parties" as well as that "liberal conception of political power" which ostensibly guarantees "everyone, by virtue of the sovereignty of the State, the exercise of his proper sovereign rights." Such a "democratized sovereignty," he insists, is "fundamentally determined and grounded in mechanisms of disciplinary coercion." Indeed, it will be recalled that for Foucault "a parliamentary, representative regime" does not deliver government from panopticism so much as mask it. And beneath that mask lies a "state that is both individualizing and totalitarian"; a "'government of individualization,'" which, both in the "'pathological forms'" of "fascism and Stalinism" and in the allegedly benign shape of Western democracy, "makes individuals subjects." Foucault's dissection of this "modern matrix of individualization" details again how established government, even while claiming to guarantee the liberty of its citizens, quite literally helps to constitute them as "subjects." [110]

Thus, as portrayed by the consecrated heretics, civilized society would seem infested by the greed, hypocrisy, and servility of an ever-expanding "bourgeois aristocracy"; by established churches, both religious and secular, that subvert rather than sustain the spirit; and by a government that inevitably drains the body politic of its vital energy. Hence, Stendhal's "bourgeois aristocracy" imbues *la société* not only with its passion for material gain and social advancement, but with a slavish conformity "to the program" prescribed by "public opinion." Both Michelet's Catholic Church and Foucault's social scientific priesthood, by the same token, preside over concealed "lines of penetration"—the "spiritual direction" of "the Wife," the "medical intervention" into the family, the sacerdotal and psychiatric rites of confession—that actively foster social subservience. And both government and parliamentary politics, whether in the form of Rousseau's "executive power," Péguy's "politique," or Foucault's "matrix of individualization," remain doomed to degenerate into a sterile and self-serving machine that saps society of its vitality. Just as "other people," in short, menace the freedom of the individual in the heretical narrative, so too does the institutional Other embodied by the bourgeoisie, the church, and the state, jeopardize that of society as a whole.

FIVE

THE MOMENT OF FREEDOM

I

The heretical narrative, as has been seen, decries not only the impending collapse of liberty in society, but also what it construes as "bourgeois society" and its liberal ideal of "negative freedom," both economic and political. Thus, Robespierre denounces the "capitalists" and "the rich" as "profiteers" and "pitiless vampires," and Michelet, too, condemns "bourgeois materialism" along with its counterparts: "egoism, well-being, comfort, liberty without sacrifice." Bergson, by the same token, assaults the liberal-utilitarian calculus of "pain and pleasure" as an "automatism," which threatens to eradicate true freedom; Péguy condemns that bourgeois "prudence" which "calculates" and "economizes," and thereby "alienates . . . liberty." The likes of Stendhal's obsequious political liberal, Monsieur Sainclair, Michelet's "political logicians" and men of "paper liberty,"

Péguy's "parliamentary shams" and "criminals," and Sartre's parliamentary "midget," Olivier Blévigne, betoken not the restoration of freedom in the heretical narrative so much as its demise.[1]

For liberty does not comprise the unfettered pursuit of economic, spiritual, and political gain within the radical tradition, but rather that absolute autonomy of will even within civil society itself which may subsist only when one repudiates personal dependency on others. It will be recalled that Rousseau's Émile, by contrast to the civilized man who "lives constantly outside himself," remains impervious to "the weight of popular opinion" and therefore "independent as God himself"; that Bergson champions an autonomous *"moi intérieure"* against the psyche's "parasitic" intellect, which incarnates the demands of conventional society; that Sartre glorifies the "authentic," self-creating individual who overthrows the invading "Look" of the societal "Other"; and that Foucault advocates the liberation of "subjugated knowledges" from the panoptic social gaze of "the disciplines." In short, the consecrated heretics identify liberty with willful independence as opposed to the liberal "pursuit of happiness," and each envisions the prospect of freedom's regeneration—be it through an ideal "social contract," the patriotic re-education of French manhood, the "deep introspection" of the psyche, or the individual's unwavering acceptance of the responsibility for self-creation—notwithstanding bourgeois society and the crippling psychic dependency it engenders. Indeed, the myth of the consecrated heretic, as suggested in chapter 2, recounts liberty's salvation within the very heart of the established order.

Yet how, given an intellectual tradition that so explicitly belittles the economic and parliamentary freedoms of classical liberalism, might the concrete experience of true liberty be revisited in society? Under what circumstances might psychic autonomy, both individual and societal, resurface within the debilitating established order of *les autres*?

Once again, *Le Rouge et le noir* offers a point of departure. Julien Sorel, as previously suggested, emerges in the novel as an independent "man of spirit" entangled in a corrupt and servile social universe—a youth whose "horror of contempt" and penchant for "extraordinary deeds" prevents him from achieving "what constitutes happiness for everyone else in the world: esteem, money, social position." Within the craven Stendhalian cosmos of *la société*, in fact, Julien stands apart as an individual of "violent temper" who possesses "the look of a criminal outlaw . . . at war with his society"—as a man whose "strength of character" might "get him condemned to death."[2]

Stendhal's protagonist, of course, comes to fulfill this prophecy quite literally. Yet Julien's attack on Madame de Rênal, while an avowedly "premeditated act" in violation of "article 1342 of the penal code," constitutes not the random crime of "a vulgar murderer" within the narrative universe of *Le Rouge et le noir* so much as "a noble act of vengeance," which displays "the full loftiness" of his "soul." For Julien himself the crime represents a "supreme moment" and one for which he refuses to feel remorse. Having been "insulted in an atrocious manner," he ruminates: "I deserve death, but that's all. I die after settling my score with humanity." Indeed, Julien's misdeed ultimately serves to unmask the hypocritical social order against which it was committed: "There is no *right*," the lawbreaker reflects on the eve of his execution,

> except where there's a law to prevent one from doing a given thing on pain of punishment. Beyond the law, there is nothing *natural* except the strength of the lion, or the need of the creature who is hungry, *need* in a word. . . . No, those who stand well in the world are simply sneak thieves lucky enough not to have been caught in the act. . . . I attempted a murder, I am rightly condemned, but except for this one action, the Valenod who condemned me is a hundred times more harmful to society (Stendhal's emphasis).[3]

Julien's transgression would seem to embody for Stendhal a symbolic eruption of autonomy—of true freedom—within a debased social universe; a willful, and indeed ethical, refusal to be governed either by the laws of the state or the conventional mores of *les autres*.

Furthermore, the hero's crime would seem righteous insofar as it is carried out on behalf of "society" as a whole and, above all, the dispossessed and oppressed. Such, it will be recalled, is precisely how the accused represents himself at his public trial: "[Y]ou see in me," Julien proclaims, "a peasant in open revolt against his station." And throughout *Le Rouge et le noir* he is intimately identified with the savage but liberating force of revolutionary violence. Infuriated early in the novel, for example, by the insults of Monsieur de Rênal, Julien "violently" frees himself from the grasp of his master's wife (who has just become his mistress) and dreams "of the most atrocious vengeance." Such "moments of humiliation as this," reflects the narrator forebodingly, are "no doubt responsible for figures like Robespierre." Subsequently, in fact, we find Julien declaring, amidst the quintessentially civilized milieu of a Parisian ball: "[I]f I had a little power, I would have three men hanged to save the lives of four." Should not "a man who wants to drive ignorance and crime from the earth," he implores Mathilde de La Mole, "pass through it like a whirlwind and do evil blindly?" The Parisienne Mathilde, moreover, after becoming Julien's mistress, finds that her lover "reigns" over her "by terror." Having previously speculated that her "little Julien" might become "another Danton," she ultimately boasts to her father: "[I]f there is a revolution, I am sure he will have a leading role in it." Stendhal's protagonist also likens himself to the same revolutionary populist who, he reflects admiringly, had once "infused strength into a nation of coxcombs, and prevented the enemy from getting into Paris." Only "I myself," Julien muses while awaiting his execution, "know what I might have done."[4]

Thus, if Julien's violent deed represents for Stendhal a moment of individual liberation from *les autres,* its author would seem to incarnate symbolically the revolutionary emancipation of society as a whole: the unbridled assertion, both terrible and just, of the nation's authentic will against a corrupt and enervated establishment. Yet Julien's freedom—and by metaphorical extension, that of society as well—proves tragically ephemeral. On the scaffold, the hero recollects "the sweetest moments he had ever known in the woods of Vergy"; moments of sublime isolation, during which others would "never be able to get at [him]"; moments "stirred only by his dreams and the delight of freedom." And "[n]ever," concludes Stendhal's narrator, had Julien's "head been so poetic as at the moment when it was about to fall."[5] Never, that is, had the hero's liberty, his independence of will, been more absolute than at the instant of its final demise.

Freedom, then, would seem to emerge in Stendhal's allegory as a transcendent moment of unsullied will within a degenerate social universe; an eruption of righteous violence during which the hero reasserts his primal autonomy against the corrosive gaze of "other people," and, in so doing, symbolically evokes the liberation of society as well. But foreordained by the tale's structure is the protagonist's demise, and, accordingly, the hour of revolutionary insurrection—of absolute freedom and hence absolute value—is itself doomed to collapse. It will be argued below that essentially the same narrative framework underlies some of the most renowned works of the consecrated heretics; in other words, that (1) liberty, arises within the heretical narrative as a fleeting instant of sometimes violent, but always just and meaningful transgression, during which both the individual and "the people"—that mythic collective body of the alienated demos—repudiate psychic dependency and reassert their autonomy of will against the established order; and (2) such revolutionary moments of personal and communal sovereignty, while forever possible to achieve within the heretical narrative, remain ever destined for tragic dissolution.

II

The revolutionary tradition in modern France, indeed the *myth* of revolution and its continued potency within French political culture, has long been recognized and debated by scholars.[6] Keith Baker, for one, has recently traced the evolution of the term "revolution" from the late seventeenth century, when it referred to accidental and undesirable "disruptions" in the "stability" of human affairs, through 1789, by which time it had taken on its modern meaning as the "decisive expression of the will of a nation reclaiming its history." Indeed, once the philosophes had "expanded the concept of revolution to universal significance," Baker writes, it could then come to signify, in the face of the event itself, "a moment of life or death in the social body," a daily "'choice between death and liberty.'"[7]

The role played by Rousseau in this recasting of the "revolutionary moment" has also been the subject of scholarly debate inasmuch as several passages from the Genevan's works would seem to attest to his political conservatism.[8] In dedicating his second discourse to Geneva, for instance, Rousseau compares his city of origin favorably with those regimes of more "recent institution" whose "revolutions" tend to confound liberty with "unbridled license." The ideal community of *Du Contrat social,* moreover, is a relatively small and homogeneous polis that would unite "the consistency of an ancient nation with the docility of a new one." Rousseau emphasizes, furthermore, that revolutionary "changes" of government "are always dangerous"—indeed that "established government should never be touched except when it becomes incompatible with the public good."[9]

Clearly, then, Rousseau is no unequivocal champion of revolution; yet neither, on the other hand, would he seem entirely hostile to it. For equally prominent in Rousseau's oeuvre stand several vivid and laudatory accounts of "revolution," both personal and political. Julie, for example, the heroine of *La Nouvelle Héloïse,* suggests that a "corrupted" soul might on rare occasions recover "its primitive character" through the "violent shock" of an "unexpected revolution." Once its "habits" are "broken," she continues, and "its passions" are "modified in this general upheaval," such a soul might become "like a new creature formed by nature's hand." In *Les Confessions* it is Rousseau's own persona that undergoes a psychic "revolution," as he himself labels it. Having portrayed "Jean-Jacques" as a Genevan Émile, struggling to maintain his natural liberty within the Babylon of Paris, the author recounts his suddenly acquired capacity, in 1756, to proclaim his public "contempt . . . for the customs, the principles, and the prejudices of [his] age." In fact, Rousseau declares: "If ever there was a moment in my life during which I became another man and ceased to be myself, it was at that time." Following this conversion to "virtue," he recollects: "I was truly transformed. . . . Bold, proud, and fearless, I now carried with me wherever I went a self-assurance which owed its firmness to its simplicity." At the level of the individual psyche, then, "revolution" would seem to represent for Rousseau a unique episode, as he puts it, of "intoxication" and "exhilaration," a "celestial fire" within the soul which both emancipates it from society and sets it into virtuous opposition against the established order.[10]

In select cases, moreover, political revolution would seem to promise the same liberation for society as a whole. Having asserted in his second discourse, for example, that the man of nature "prefers the most turbulent state of liberty to the most peaceful slavery," Rousseau voices a straightforward admiration for "the prodigious efforts of every free people to save itself from oppression." Indeed, that "popular insurrection," he later elaborates, "which ends in the death or deposition of a Sultan, is as lawful an act as those by which he disposed, the day before, the lives and fortunes of his subjects." Similarly, in *Émile,* Rousseau notes approvingly—and somewhat presciently—that the "present order" is "subject to inevitable revolutions"; that "we are approaching a state of crisis and a century of revolutions" which will see the "great become small, the rich poor, the king a commoner." In *Du Contrat social,* finally, Rousseau goes so far as to suggest that political revolution might be as essential to the regeneration of society as is personal revolution to that of the individual. In "the history of States," he submits, there arise select "periods of violence" during which "revolutions do for peoples" what "certain crises do for individuals: horror of the past takes the place of forgetfulness, and the State, set on fire by civil wars, is born again, so to speak, from its ashes, and takes on anew, fresh from the jaws of death, the vigor of youth."[11]

Such interludes of political disruption and rejuvenation would seem etched, in point of fact, into the very fabric of Rousseau's political narrative. Even while disavowing revolution as a rule, Rousseau, it will be recalled, makes an exception for those cases when "the established government . . . becomes incompatible with the public good." Indeed, "the instant the government usurps the sovereign," he asserts in a celebrated passage, "the social compact is broken, and all private citizens recover by right their natural liberty, and are forced but not bound to obey." In fact, even regular political assemblies take on the character of institutionalized crisis in Rousseau's dramatic formulation. "The moment the people is legitimately assembled as a sovereign body," he declares, "the jurisdiction of the government wholly collapses, the executive power is suspended, and the person of the meanest citizen is as sacred as that of the first magistrate." Such "intervals of suspension" represent for Rousseau "the aegis of the body politic"—inviolable moments, that is, during which the "general will" reigns supreme and "superior" over all government.[12]

Thus, rightful revolution, within the Rousseauian narrative, whether in the form of a personal or societal upheaval, signifies nothing less than a sacred event; an opportunity for the will, both individual and "general," to purge itself of corruption and reassert its autonomy against the powers that be. Yet such moments of freedom would seem no less singular and transitory for Rousseau than they would subsequently for Stendhal. Hence, "Jean-Jacques's" personal revolution endured, by his own account, only while he remained in "Paris and the sight of that great city's vices." After leaving the capital, the author of *Les Confessions* reports that his "soul" fell into a "state of disturbance" and has since "enjoyed only a passing moment's equilibrium" from its "perpetual oscillations." Rousseau insists in *Du Contrat social,* by the same token, that legitimate political revolution is at best a "rare" occurrence. "Such events," he writes, are "exceptions," which "cannot even happen twice to the same people." Indeed, even the most robust of communities remains doomed for Rousseau to lose "its civic impulse" and degenerate into corruption and slavery. "Free peoples," the Genevan admonishes, "be mindful of this maxim: 'Liberty may be gained, but can never be recovered.'"[13]

In sum, Rousseau does not renounce revolution so much as recast it as a rare and climactic moment of emancipation. His would seem, accordingly, a "turbulent liberty" indeed; for while freedom in Rousseau's narrative may be seized in a righteous—not to say violent—outburst of will, either personal or popular, such episodes remain for him both exceptional and subject to inevitable dissolution.

If Rousseau styles himself the Émile of prerevolutionary France—the natural man, pure of will, amidst the corruption of civilization—Robespierre, as has been seen, styles himself the Rousseau of revolutionary Paris: the virtuous patriot amidst the cabals, factions, and plots of the National Convention. Indeed, through his renowned refusal to compromise his own purity of will—"[t]here are not two ways of being free," Robespierre proclaimed in 1791, "one must be so entirely or one becomes once more a slave"—the Incorruptible both extends his mentor's endorsement of individual autonomy and submits his own public persona as its prototype. No less than Rousseau does the Jacobin identify such personal sovereignty of will with that of the social body as a whole. "The nation possesses in itself all the rights that each man possesses in his person," he declared in 1792; "and just as each isolated individual is governed by his particular will, so too does the general will govern society." [14]

Robespierre also follows his Genevan forbear in championing the theoretical defense of liberty, both personal and societal, by violence. Within his "Proposed Declaration of the Rights of Man and Citizen" of 1793, the Jacobin inscribes the right of "each and every section of the assembled sovereign" to "repel by force" every "act against liberty." The document pointedly emphasizes, in fact, that "when the government violates the rights of the people, insurrection is the most sacred of rights and most indispensable of duties for the people and for each and every portion thereof." [15]

But rightful insurrection, of course, represents for the revolutionary radical not so much a theoretical abstraction as a pressing reality; and the demand for violence, therefore, remains perpetually at hand. Even while opposing war with Austria and Prussia in 1791, for example, Robespierre allows that in the case of "treachery" there would remain "only one recourse left to the nation: a sudden salutary explosion of anger by the people of France." And the same Rousseauian logic leads the Jacobin leader, who had once opposed the death penalty, to call for the beheading of the king in 1792. "Louis must die," he declares, "so that our country may live." The execution of the traitorous monarch, the Jacobin asserts, "will nourish in the hearts of peoples the love of their rights . . . and in the souls of tyrants a wholesome terror of popular justice." [16]

For Robespierre, in fact, the Revolution would seem to epitomize that rare interlude in the Rousseauian narrative when "the people" rise up as one against a decadent and tyrannical state and reclaim their liberty; that exalted time, as the Jacobin puts it in his "Report on the Principles of Political Morality" of 1794, "when, by prodigious efforts of courage and reason, a people breaks the chains of despotism" and "leaves, as it were, the arms of death in order to recapture the vigor of youth." Indeed, "nations," exclaimed Robespierre in 1790, in a striking echo of his Genevan idol, "have only a moment to become free";

and he reiterated two years later that the nation "truly releases its energies only during moments of insurrection." [17]

Yet the Jacobin chieftain also accepts the Rousseauian theory of degeneration,[18] the belief that political communities tend naturally to lose their "character" and "liberty," and to pass, therefore, "from democracy to aristocracy or monarchy." For while "the people," for Robespierre, stand "naturally upright" and "pure," comprising a veritable Rousseauian man of nature writ large, they remain perpetually menaced by the revolutionary enemy, both within and without. Revolutionary violence, accordingly, represents not merely the justifiable defense of freedom against oppression for the Jacobin, but an ongoing "war of liberty against its enemies." And while "revolutionary government," therefore, owes "good citizens . . . the full protection of the state, to the enemies of the people it owes only death." [19]

In his "Report on the Principles of Political Morality," Robespierre notoriously expands this defense of revolutionary violence by associating it explicitly with democratic liberty—that is, by linking "terror" with "virtue." Virtue, it will be recalled, comprises Robespierre's version of Rousseauian "moral liberty": the transformation of "the people's" innate purity of will into a selfless love of the nation.[20] "Democratic government," he contends, echoing not only Rousseau but political theorists from Aristotle to Montesquieu, must embrace "virtue" as its "fundamental principle." For the citizens of any "state in which the sovereign people" is "guided by laws of [its] own making" must constantly prefer the "public interest over all particular interests" in order to survive. But the Jacobin cautions that while virtue is "natural to the people," the present "passions and . . . whirlwinds of intrigue" place it in constant jeopardy. How, he implores the Convention, "can the slave of avarice or ambition be made to sacrifice his idol for the good of the country?" How, in other words, may virtue—the very "soul" of republican liberty—be rescued from the revolutionary enemy, both internal and external? Responding to his own appeal, Robespierre enjoins the Convention to "adopt . . . and establish" everything "that tends to excite love of country, to purify morals . . . to direct the passions of the human heart toward the public interest." Revolutionary "terror," in this light, betokens not a random and meaningless act of violence but rather "prompt, severe, inflexible justice"; not a criminal misdeed but rather "an emanation of virtue," indeed "the despotism of liberty against tyranny." [21]

"Terror," in other words, constitutes nothing less for Robespierre than an act of sacred transgression: a public rite of violent purification through which both the individual and the nation purge themselves of self-interested vice and restore their primal unity of will, their moral liberty. Urging all "French republicans" in June of 1794 to "purify the earth that has been soiled," Robespierre reminds the nation that "[l]iberty and virtue spring together from the breast of the same divinity." Likewise, in his final speech before the Convention, he exhorts his fellow revolutionaries "to purify the national system of surveillance instead of covering up vice," to "purge the Committee on Public Safety itself," and to reconstitute "a unified government." For "rightly understood," the Jacobin proclaims, "revolutionary government" represents "the thunderbolt of retribution launched by the hand of liberty against crime."[22]

Ultimately, then, the Terror reflects Robespierre's aspiration to suspend the revolutionary moment of liberty in time; to sustain indefinitely what Lynn Hunt has called the "'mythic present,' the instant creation of the new community, the sacred moment of the new consensus."[23] It comes as no surprise, in this light, to find the Jacobin imploring the Convention in 1794 to "[m]aintain . . . the sacred spring of republican government instead of letting it decline"—that is, to preserve the hallowed hour of revolutionary purity against its ever-impending dissolution. Nor is it surprising to find Robespierre, as noted previously, anticipating the Revolution's demise and linking it to his own. As early as 1790 Robespierre had warned his fellow revolutionaries that once the "moment" of freedom "is passed," the "cries of good citizens are denounced as acts of sedition" and "freedom disappears." And evoking the same Rousseauian prophecy in his final speech before the Convention, the Jacobin offers up his own life "without regret." For,

> [w]hat friend of the fatherland can wish to survive the moment he is no longer permitted to serve it or his country and defend oppressed innocence! Why seek to dwell in an order of things where intrigues eternally triumph over truth, where justice is a lie, where the vilest passions or the most ridiculous fears occupy in men's hearts the place of humanity's most sacred interests?[24]

In truth "the time is not yet arrived," concludes the embattled revolutionary, "for honest men to serve the country with impunity; the defenders of liberty will be no better than banished so long as the hordes of cheats and traitors are dominant."[25] In the final analysis, then, Robespierre too—like Rousseau before him and Stendhal after—casts liberty as a provisional and unstable moment of heroic violence and unity of will, both individual and collective, within an ever-decadent universe. Indeed, even his attempt to perpetuate freedom's moment through the Terror would seem a tragic portent, within the framework of his own narrative, of its inevitable collapse.[26]

No less than his Jacobin nemesis does Michelet identify individual liberty with that innate "simplicity of heart," that "instinct and action," that "sacred ingenuousness . . . of character" found most often in "the people."[27] The human soul, the historian affirms in his *Histoire de la révolution français,* "follows its nature" when "it remains benevolent" and "void of . . . egoism." And for Michelet, again like Robespierre, freedom demands not only a personal purity of will but a collective one as well. Hence the historian's aforementioned emphasis on a system of education, both public and private, which would bolster the "willpower and moral strength" of all Frenchmen and unite them in a love for the nation. In *Le Peuple* Michelet goes so far as to imagine a "public festival" at which the fathers of France would introduce their sons to "the people," as personified by a ceremonial army, complete with "bayonets flashing and . . . the tricolor flag." During such "fantastic moments of illumination," the historian continues, "when tremendous silence suddenly stills that dark ocean of people," the voice of the fathers would explain that "'[a]ll this is like one man—with one soul and one heart'"; that each "'would die for a single man'"; indeed that "'each one ought also to live and die for all.'"[28]

Michelet's most fundamental model for the regeneration of national liberty, however, remains not public education so much as the Revolution itself: that "living spirit of France," as he calls it in his *Histoire;* that "holy period, when an entire nation, free from all party distinction, as yet a comparative stranger to the opposition of classes, marched together under a flag of brotherly love." The "only government," the historian proclaims in *Le Peuple,* "that devoted itself heart and soul to the education of the people was that of the Revolution." Indeed, "the Revolution," he notes with gratified irony, did not "suppress the nobility" so much as "make nobles of thirty-four million Frenchmen."[29]

Michelet's celebrated account of the event unfolds, in Lionel Gossman's apt phrase, as "a long weary road punctuated by moments of brilliant illumination";[30] as a chronicle, that is, of adversity and corruption interrupted periodically by sacred episodes—the Festival of Federation in 1790, the popular insurrection of 10 August 1792, climactic military victories over European armies—during which Michelet's collective hero, "the people," rises up as one and reasserts its primal sovereignty of will. The historian evokes the General Confederation of 1790, for example, as a time when "everything was possible. All divisions had ceased: there was no longer either nobility, bourgeoisie, or people. The future was present. That is to say, time itself was no more. It was a flash of eternity." Even more telling is Michelet's account of the 10 August uprising and its preparatory confrontation, on 20 June, between the crown and the Parisian mob. "June 20," he insists, "must not be viewed as a riot, a simple fit of anger. The people of Paris became the violent but legitimate organ of the true sentiment of France." By the same token, 10 August may be attributed "neither to the Assembly, the Jacobins, nor the Commune," according to Michelet. For it represents "a great act of the people," an "act of energy, of devotion, of desperate courage." At "this supreme moment," the historian proclaims, France was "saved" by a "magnificent burst of national fury." Indeed, even "the egoism of private interest," he maintains, while not "disappearing entirely," became "completely secondary" during "this rare moment of patriotic enthusiasm." The "conquerors" of 10 August, accordingly, must be regarded not as "a band of brigands or barbarians" but rather as "the people, one and complete." For even while "the most furious passions" were openly displayed among them, no "base or ignoble appetites" arose at "this moment of heroic exaltation." [31]

For Michelet, revolutionary liberty unfolds as a hallowed occasion of spiritual unity, both individual and collective, and as a just, at times brutally violent, act of popular deliverance—a "noble act of vengeance," as Julien Sorel might put it, which must not be mistaken for "vulgar murder." [32] The historian in fact distinguishes sharply between the "humane and benevolent epoch of our Revolution," which "had for its actors the people itself, the whole people, everyone," and those periods of criminal violence, of "sanguinary deeds," which included "only a minimal, an infinitely small, number of men." The "September Massacres" of 1792, for example, represent an instance of "hypocritical violence" for Michelet, which diverged entirely from "the naively exalted sensibility" of the people. "'We were all there at the 10th of August,'" asserts a living witness cited by Michelet, "'and not one at the 2nd of September.'" And above all, as has been seen, the historian repudiates the "Jacobin inquisition," which was, again, "by no means in the hands of the people." [33]

Indeed, revolutionary violence, as Gossman again points out, becomes "sanctified" for Michelet only by a "selfless dedication" to national unity, only when it constitutes a universal uprising against "the outsider or alien within, the absolute and absolutely evil Other, who seeks to obstruct the reintegration of what in its essence is One." Thus again, for example, with the king still alive following the August uprising, and France not only overrun by foreign armies but internally "disorganized" and "betrayed," the historian hails the "terrible and violent convulsion" of popular fury that saved the nation. "Never," he exclaims, "had the world witnessed" such a "flame," which, erupting "like a volcano of life," illuminated "the entire dominion of France." Such violence—a "burning jet of heroism," in Michelet's orgasmic imagery, a "divine burst . . . of will"—manifests for the historian a "singular moment" of "profound solidarity" and emancipation. Likewise, such military victories as Valmy and Jemmappes emerge in Michelet's epic as "sacred" or "supreme" moments of "accord, unanimity, [and] mutual sacrifice"—of "warlike fraternity" in the face of "implacable foes."[34]

Once again, in short, episodes of legitimate violence and communal concord unfold in Michelet's narrative as rare and sacred moments— and they remain destined for tragic dissolution. "Can such a state last?" the historian asks rhetorically, referring to the aforementioned solidarity of classes during the Festival of Confederation. "Was it possible that the social barriers, on that day leveled, should be left on the ground?" Earlier in his account Michelet had responded to his own entreaty: "The union was sincere at that sublime moment which I have the happiness to describe; it was true but transient; and soon the disunity of classes and opinions reappeared." The historian depicts the original convocation of the Estates General of 1789 in nearly identical terms:

> Who would not be moved by the memory of that unique moment when we first came to life? It was short-lived, but it remains for us the ideal. . . . Oh sublime Concord, in which the emerging liberties of the classes, subsequently in opposition, embraced so tenderly, like brothers in the cradle—shall we never more see you return unto this earth?[35]

Most broadly, Michelet's narrative recounts the tragic dissipation of the Revolution's "living unity" in favor of that "artificial association" and "mechanical unity" offered by the Jacobins. Acknowledging, for example, that "for a moment" at the end of 1793 "the dictatorship of the Committees" was necessary to the nation's "defense" and "safety," he argues that its notorious extension thereafter signified not only the

Republic's loss of "vitality" but its veritable "fall." Indeed, one final occasion, the "civic feast" commemorating Bastille Day in 1794, reconfirms for Michelet this bleak revelation. "Rich and poor sat down together," he recounts, "and there was truly a moment of sincere fraternity." But while "the spectacle" was indeed "admirable" and "very touching," he concludes, "it lasted but a single day"; for "the true situation" rendered "such reconciliations" increasingly impossible.[36]

Michelet's revolutionary chronicle, in sum, would seem once again to gravitate toward singular moments of absolute unity, both individual and collective; moments which entail—in an unwitting echo of Robespierre—a righteous and liberating violence against the revolutionary Other, both within and without. Such interludes of authentic freedom, however, remain inescapably ephemeral in the historian's narrative, ever destined to dissolve into the divisive social universe of self-interest.[37]

The manifestly political tale of liberation discernable in Michelet or Robespierre re-emerges as a metaphysical melodrama in the fin-de-siècle philosophy of Bergson. To recapitulate, the philosopher partitions the human psyche into a "fundamental self," which remains intuitively linked with *la durée,* the ceaseless and dynamic flow of reality, and its "parasitic" twin the "intellect," which "continually encroaches upon the other" with its "insatiable desire to separate," to impose a fixed spatial grid upon the temporal flux of pure duration. Bergson identifies the intellect, it will be recalled, with social scientific determinism and with the daily, utilitarian demands of "social life"; and he suggests that this eternal intellectual Other—this perpetual bourgeois bureaucrat of the soul—will render us "more and more lifeless, more and more impersonal," the more we submit to its demands. "Many live this kind of life," the philosopher laments in *Essai sur les données immédiates de la conscience,* "and die without having known true freedom."[38]

It will also be recalled that for Bergson genuine freedom amounts to an expression of "the whole of the self," of the "deep-seated" will, absolute and autonomous, on those occasions when it "allows itself to live" in *la durée.* "We are free," the philosopher asserts, "when our acts spring from our whole personality," when they correspond to "the whole of our most intimate feelings, thoughts, and aspirations."[39]

Concerning the concrete emergence of such liberty, moreover, Bergson's account becomes uncharacteristically personal and dramatic—and increasingly familiar. At "those moments of our lives," he writes in *Essai,* "when we make a serious decision," our fundamental self "heats up and becomes impassioned." Having expected, perhaps, to follow social convention or the dictates of reason, we find that something "revolts within us." This, the philosopher professes, "is the deep-seated self rushing to the surface." We experience "in the depths of the self" a "sudden boiling over of feelings and ideas." And finally, reaching a "great and solemn crisis," which is "decisive of our relationship to others, and even more with ourselves," we "choose in defiance of what is conventionally called a motive." Indeed, during such interludes, Bergson reiterates in *L'Évolution créatrice,* "our whole personality" becomes concentrated into "a point, or rather a sharp edge, pressed against the future and cutting into it ceaselessly"; and it is only then, he concludes, "that life and action are free."[40]

For Bergson, then, the advent of liberty would seem once again to comprise an uprising of undivided will against the eternal enemy, both within and without; a moment, again, of sacred transgression during which one renounces one's own internal establishment as well as that of society. By framing such moments of liberation in the rhetoric of "defiance," "crisis," and "revolt," Bergson demarcates—at least metaphorically—an arena of sanctified violence, not to say revolution. The "abrupt intervention of will" in our decision making, he asserts in *Essai,* amounts to a psychological "coup d'état which our intellect foresees and tries to legitimate beforehand through a formal deliberation." And in *L'Évolution créatrice,* the philosopher goes so far as to characterize life itself as a magnificent combat between a free, vibrant, and "indivisible" energy—the celebrated "*élan vital*"—and that inert matter which constitutes its eternal nemesis. "The movement" instigated by the "vital impetus," Bergson claims, "is sometimes turned aside, sometimes divided, always opposed" by the material world; "the evolution of the organized world," accordingly, represents "nothing more" that the perpetual "unfolding" of the "contest" between the two.[41]

Freedom itself, therefore, emerges within Bergson's philosophical universe not only as a vital and figuratively violent upsurge of primal will, both in the human psyche and the collective "life force" as whole, but as a phenomenon that is innately transitory. "The life force [*élan*]," cautions the author of *L'Évolution créatrice,* "is finite. . . . It cannot overcome all obstacles." Worse yet, our own "fleeting intuitions" of life's vitality resemble "a lamp almost extinguished, which only glimmers now and then, for a few instants at most." In truth, laments Bergson in *Essai,* "the moments at which we . . . grasp ourselves are rare, and that is why we are rarely free." Genuinely "free acts," in fact, remain highly "exceptional" for the philosopher. They constitute "moments unique of their kind" that will "never be repeated, any more than the past phases in the history of a nation will ever come back again"; for truly "free activity" would seem inevitably to gravitate back toward "conscious automatism." [42]

Beneath Bergson's philosophical tale of emancipation, in other words, may be discerned the unmistakable echo both of Rousseau —whose "exceptional" interludes of revolutionary regeneration may never "happen twice to the same people"—and of Michelet, whose revolutionary "volcanoes of life" and communal "flashes of eternity" embody "moments" both "sublime" and "transient." For Bergsonian liberty, like that of Rousseau and Michelet—not to mention Stendhal and Robespierre—must relapse, in the final analysis, into the realm of mundane self-interest from which it came.

The crypto-political allegory underlying Bergson's metaphysics resurfaces quite explicitly in the inflammatory rhetoric of Péguy. Indeed, the latter extols that "Bergsonian revolution" which, in his view, has sought to overthrow the "barrenness, servitude, and intellectual death" of the modern world on behalf of a "universal liberation." [43]

Individual freedom consists for Péguy, it will be remembered, of a primal purity of soul, "a completely organic and living" spirituality; in a word, of "mystique," which refers to the lived experience of Bergsonian "duration." [44] Péguy's prototypical instance of such a "mystique" is, again, "Dreyfusism," which constitutes "a system of *absolute liberty, absolute truth,* [and] *absolute justice* . . . of a profoundly spiritual order" (Péguy's emphasis). Indeed, "our Dreyfusism," proclaims the essayist in *Notre jeunesse,* amounted to nothing less than "a religious movement": the sacred quest for "a *single* and *living* Justice and Truth" (Péguy's emphasis). [45]

The Dreyfus affair, moreover, manifests for Péguy the latest and most supreme leap of that "heroism" and "mystique," that "heroic upsurge among us all," which occasionally takes hold of "the people." We Dreyfusards, he boasts, were "infinitely proud . . . infinitely full, infinitely swelled with *military* virtues" (Péguy's emphasis). He continues: "[placing our] whole life, our whole career, our whole health, our whole body and soul," at the service of the cause, "we declared that a single injustice, a single crime, a single illegality, above all if it is officially registered and sanctioned; a single wrong to humanity, a single wrong to justice and to law, especially if it is universally, legally, nationally, commodiously accepted; that a single crime shatters and is sufficient to shatter the whole social pact, the whole social contract." For "a single dishonor," Péguy concludes, "is enough to dishonor an entire people. It is a touch of gangrene which corrupts the entire body."[46]

Echoing both Rousseau and his Jacobin disciple, Péguy portrays the Affair as a singular occasion of self-purification, both for the individual and the nation as a whole. Nor, furthermore, does he shrink from the discourse of violence and revolution. The Dreyfus affair, Péguy contends, represents one of those "great trials of a whole people," comparable to the "great trials of war." Such ordeals, he affirms, are noteworthy more for their "internal energy"—the "violence" of their "eruption"—than for any specific historical cause. For when such an event occurs, he explains, "when a great war breaks out, a great revolution," it is because "a great people . . . has the impulse to break free." Having had "enough of peace," such a people becomes "seized" at "a given moment" by the "profound need for glory, for war," and it therefore generates "an explosion, an eruption." The Dreyfus affair, Péguy argues, epitomizes one such moment. Arising out of a "need for heroism, for *military* war, for military glory . . . for sanctity," which "seized an entire generation," it signified nothing less than "*the temporal salvation of the people and the race*" (Péguy's emphasis). Through participating in it, therefore, he continues, "we remained very precisely in the purest French tradition"—that tradition, as Péguy labels it in a subsequent work, "of *revolutionary energy*," "spirit," and "instinct," which constitutes "the honor and the grandeur of this people" (Péguy's emphasis).[47]

In this way, the Dreyfus affair appears to represent for Péguy the political counterpart of a Bergsonian "free act"—the abrupt and decisive revolt of a popular will against the eternal foe of "politique"—and his rendition of the affair seems clearly to recapitulate the archetypal moment of liberty so fundamental to the heretical narrative. Like Julien Sorel's "supreme moment" of "noble vengeance" or Robespierre's "war of liberty against its enemies," Péguy's Dreyfusism constitutes an upsurge of violent and purifying transgression against the established order during which both the individual and "the people" symbolically reclaim their primal integrity of will.

The structure of the heretical narrative, however, dictates that such freedom must ultimately perish; and Péguy's rendering of the saga, as has been seen, portends nothing if not tragic decline. "Everything begins in mystique," intones the essayist's most celebrated aphorism, "and ends in politique." Indeed, *Notre jeunesse* chronicles, at bottom, as previously detailed, the "*decomposition of Dreyfusism in France*," the "degradation of the Dreyfusard mystique into the Dreyfusard politique" (Péguy's emphasis). Once victorious, Péguy charged in 1913, Dreyfusism became "a system of political prevarication, a system of favors, oppression, [and] iniquity." Following the Affair, he elaborates, the Republic itself degenerated into "a base politique and a system of government founded on the satisfaction of the basest appetites and the fulfillment of the basest interests." For "that is the law," Péguy laments in *Notre jeunesse,* "that is the rule: . . . all parties live by their mystique and die of their politique."[48] And so again, in the foreboding cadences of an Old Testament prophet, Péguy invokes that parable so peculiar to modern France: the rise and fall of freedom's moment.

Sartre's oeuvre as well, as its author seems well aware, would appear to gravitate toward the same narrative framework. "It was called to my attention several years ago," Sartre confesses in *Les Mots,* "that the characters in my plays and novels arrive at their decisions suddenly and through crisis"; that "a single instant, for example, was sufficient for Orestes of *Les Mouches* to achieve his conversion."[49]

The very structure of the existentialist's ontology would seem, in fact, to lend itself to such moments of individual liberation. For Sartre, again, human consciousness consists of an ontological "nothingness," a yearning for self-complete essence, or "Being." Yet owing to that inner "lack" which constitutes both our consciousness and our freedom, we remain inherently unable to complete ourselves—to achieve, that is, the "facticity" of a chair or a tree. We stand "condemned," therefore, ceaselessly to create and recreate ourselves through our daily choices of action. But characteristically, in Sartre's view, we either flee our self-made "essence"—as does *Huis clos*'s Garçin, for instance, by denying his cowardice—or our perpetual possibility of "transcendence," as does the waiter from *L'Etre et le néant,* who plays "*at being* a waiter in a café*" in the same way that "an inkwell is an inkwell" (Sartre's emphasis). Authentic liberty, accordingly, requires that we repudiate such "bad faith" and forthrightly embrace both our "facticity" and our "transcendence"; that we act with the conscious recognition of our complete and perpetual responsibility for self-creation.[50]

Recalling, then, Bergson's eruption of "deep-seated" will within the mechanistic realm of the intellect, freedom characteristically unfolds for Sartre as an upsurge of lucid "transcendence," of conscious and unsullied will, within the constricting realm of "Being." Thus, in *L'Etre et le néant,* for example, the existentialist exalts in "those extraordinary and marvelous instants when the prior project collapses into the past in the light of a new project which arises on its ruins." And in *Saint Genet,* by the same token, Sartre focuses upon "the *fatal instant*" when his subject is "caught in the act" of stealing; for "an instant," reiterates the existentialist, "is sufficient to destroy, to enjoy, to kill, to get oneself killed" (Sartre's emphasis). Returning to the case of *Les Mouches,* it is not surprising to find liberty "crash[ing] down" on Sartre's protagonist "suddenly," like "a thunderbolt."[51]

Indeed, like Robespierre's "thunderbolt of retribution"—for once again, such occasions of self-defining liberty tend to emerge in Sartre's oeuvre as moments of sanctified violence,[52] of just transgression against the prefabricated moral code of bourgeois society, which amounts itself, as noted previously, to a species of communal "bad faith." Hence, Orestes's "thunderbolt" of freedom precipitates the brutal murder of his mother and stepfather, which he carries out in defiance of that conventional "Goodness" personified by Jupiter. "Why should I feel remorse?" Orestes asks the dying Aegisthus. "I am only doing what is right." And having pronounced his bloody deed "good," Sartre's protagonist proclaims himself "free. Beyond anguish, beyond remorse. Free. And at one with myself." Likewise, Mathieu of *Les Chemins de la liberté* redeems his own liberty through an abrupt and lethal burst of gunfire at German soldiers, which Sartre's narrator renders as an all but explicitly Jacobin outburst of righteous transgression and cleansing violence: "He fired, and the tables of law crashed about him—Thou shalt love thy neighbor as thyself—bang! in that bastard's face—Thou shalt not kill—bang! . . . He was firing on his fellow men, on Virtue, on the whole world: Liberty is Terror. . . . he was pure, he was all-powerful, he was free. Fifteen minutes."[53]

Such interludes of transgressive violence tend to evoke not only individual freedom in the Sartrean narrative but, once again, the emancipation of "the people"—of the oppressed social body as a whole. Hence, Orestes seeks through his bloody deed to vanquish his own "bad faith" and "to overthrow" Jupiter's oppressive "empire" over "the people of Argos." In his final address to the town's citizens, Sartre's protagonist proclaims, in a remote echo of Julien Sorel: "it was for your sake I killed." In fact, existentialism itself, insisted Sartre in 1945, is fundamentally a philosophy of "action and commitment" which maintains that each individual is responsible not only for "his own individuality" but "for all men." In "seeking my own liberty," therefore, "I am obliged to seek that of others."[54]

Ultimately, indeed, the liberation of society would become, for Sartre, more a political than a literary or philosophical issue; hence his notoriously wide-ranging support for revolutionary violence during the postwar years. The "violence" of the industrial proletariat, he declared in 1952, for instance, amounts to "a positive humanism"; and that of Castro, Che Guevara, and the Cuban revolutionaries, Sartre reiterated in 1961, constitutes not "madness" so much as "[n]egation, refusal, rebellion against the inhuman order." Likewise, Frantz Fanon's "irrepressible violence" against African colonialism, he proclaimed two years later, represents neither "sound and fury, nor the resurrection of savage instincts," but rather the heroic spectacle of "man recreating himself." [55]

In his proto-Marxian *Critique de la raison dialectique* of 1960, Sartre went so far as to offer a programmatic phenomenology of revolutionary insurrection, for which he drew in large part upon the archetypal events of 1789–94.[56] Driven no longer by an ontological "lack" in a universe of "Being," but rather by material "need" in a human world of "scarcity," the individual in Sartre's revolutionary saga is characteristically alienated from his fellow beings. Indeed, discovering "each of them as the material possibility of his own annihilation," he lives in a state of wary and isolated "seriality." At the outset of the narrative, accordingly, the lower class remains unified only by its common "impotence." As the revolutionary situation unfolds, however, the dispossessed classes become consolidated first "from the outside" by the revolutionary enemy—"the government constitutes Paris as a totality," writes Sartre, referring to the summer of 1789—and thereafter each individual begins "to see himself in the Other." Once each man has come to recognize the entirety of "his own future in the Other," the crowd spontaneously arms itself and forms "a fused group." Owing, furthermore, to the "scarcity of time"—for while "the enemy is not there yet," he "could arrive at any minute"—the first act of the newly unified group is one of violent expropriation. That deed, the taking of the Bastille in Sartre's illustration, unfolds for "everyone as the urgent discovery of a common freedom." In fact, "the explosion of the revolt" reveals "the essential characteristic of the fused group" to be precisely "the sudden restoration of freedom." For "in the spontaneous praxis of the fused group," Sartre explains, "free activity is realized by everyone as unique (*his own*), multiple . . . and total." Therefore, "*the battle in progress*" embodies "for everyone, an absolute reciprocity" (Sartre's emphasis).[57]

Sartre's "fused group" amounts, at least metaphorically, to an existential hero writ large. For like Orestes or Mathieu, it achieves both inner unity and absolute freedom in an apocalyptic explosion of willful violence against the societal Other. Plainly recalling the "warlike fraternity" of Michelet's "people" or the "heroic upsurge" of Péguy's Dreyfusards, Sartre's revolutionary drama renders liberty yet again as a sacred moment of unsullied will—both individual and collective— during which a community of comrades arises through the conscious and willful participation of autonomous individuals in a collective political deed.

The climactic hour of freedom, however, can be sustained no more for Sartre than for Péguy or Michelet. Existential freedom, as has been seen, remains doomed by definition to collapse into the realm of "Being." For while we may occasionally "apprehend" ourselves, Sartre remarks in *L'Etre et le néant*, as "a freedom which perfectly reveals itself and whose being resides in this very revelation," such occasions must dissipate all but immediately owing to the harsh ontology of being human. Trapped within the unending dialectic between "facticity" and "transcendence," we remain "condemned" either to suffer the perpetual "anguish" of ontological incompletion or "to flee" that "anguish in bad faith." Thus, at the instant when Mathieu first beholds his freedom, "his joy" changes "on the spot to a crushing anguish." And Orestes, following his "thunderbolt" of liberating violence, finds himself "without excuse, beyond remedy, except what remedy I can find within myself." [58]

Nor, by the same token, may Sartre's "fused group" perpetuate itself following its violent birth in the revolutionary womb. Having no more achieved "actual totality" than the existential hero achieves ontological self-completion, the revolutionary group remains at best "a ceaselessly developing totality" which seeks an "organic unity" it may never acquire. First through an "oath"—Sartre cites the French Revolution's "Tennis Court Oath" as his example—and later through the internal reassertion of "group praxis" against the revolutionary enemy—that is, through "Terror"—it attempts to render itself permanent. But ultimately the "fused group" must degenerate, like Rousseau's "general will," into a "petrified practice," a corrupt and bureaucratically inert "*institution*" (Sartre's emphasis). By contrast, that is, to the revolutionary epic of Marx, Sartre's yields no happy ending, no tranquil social utopia. While history, for Sartre, offers the perpetual possibility of revolutionary liberation, "group action is always doomed to diachronic alienation." [59] While genuine freedom, in other words, remains ever possible to achieve in the Sartrean narrative, it proves once again tragically ephemeral.

If one accepts, finally, the previously cited interpretation of James Miller, the saga of freedom's moment would seem to frame the very life history of Foucault. Every culture, maintained Foucault in a 1962 essay cited by Miller, establishes absolute behavioral limits: "the de-limitation of madness," for example, or "the prohibition of incest." But "the moment" such cultural boundaries "mark a limit," the post-structuralist asserts, "they create a space of possible transgression." And portraying Foucault's biography as a quest for "the pure violence" of such "limit-experiences," Miller goes so far as to suggest that his subject gravitated toward the supremely transgressive—and consum-mately fleeting—violence of suicide, through which, as the young Fou-cault once put it, "a totally free existence could arise, . . . one that would no longer know the weight of living but only that transparency where love is totalized in the eternity of an instant."[60]

Whether one concurs with Miller's biographical musings or not, however, the centrality to Foucault's oeuvre of liberating flights of transgression would seem evident enough. Liberty, it will be recalled, arises for Foucault from *"a certain decisive will not to be governed"* (Foucault's emphasis).* In fact, insofar, as "the recalcitrance of the will and the intransigence of freedom" remain "at the very heart of the power relationship," he declared in 1983, institutional "power" itself "cannot be separated" from "the refusal to submit." It would therefore be impossible "for power relations to exist," Foucault contends, "with-out points of insubordination."[61]

For Foucault, moreover, such "points" characteristically entail crim-inal and even violent transgression against "disciplinary" discourses and their "normalizing" institutions. One striking, if ambiguous, case in point is that of Lacenaire, a celebrated nineteenth-century felon whom Foucault cites in *Surveiller et punir* as "the typical 'delin-quent'": a criminal by-product, that is, of the era's recently instituted panoptic penal system. Born, Foucault remarks, at "more or less the same time as Julien Sorel," Lacenaire was "a ruined petty bourgeois of good education" who personified a species of minor transgression—

---

*This account of Foucaultian liberty refers above all to the writer's "middle period" and does not encompass the final two volumes of his *History of Sexuality* (both pub-lished in 1984), in which Foucault advances the possibility of a freedom that might be consciously reconstituted by an historically constituted self in light of—and in opposi-tion to—its given structure. For, as noted in chapter 1, my purpose here is not to explore the multifaceted "individuality" either of Foucault or of any of my subjects, but rather to treat the most visible and celebrated aspects of their lives and works as part of a broad cultural narrative—an impersonal historical discourse, as Foucault himself might put it—rooted in the cultural institutions of modern France. For a lucid account of freedom as envisioned by the late Foucault, see Mark Poster, *Critical Theory and Post-structuralism* (Ithaca: Cornell University Press, 1989), especially 54–60, 91–95.

"swindling, desertion, petty theft, imprisonment," and a "failed attempt at murder"—which came to be as "reassuring" as it was threatening to "the Parisian bourgeoisie." Yet had he "been a contemporary of Robespierre," Foucault contends, the delinquent's "rejection of the law would have taken a directly political form"; indeed, he would have been "a revolutionary, a Jacobin, a regicide." According, moreover, to the "Fourierist" social critics of the 1830s, whom Foucault cites approvingly, delinquency itself manifests "'an outburst of protest in the name of human individuality,'" which might ultimately prove "precious to the liberation of our society."[62]

Through this would-be subversive, then—this explicitly Stendhalian antihero—Foucault links society's emancipation to criminal transgression and to the political violence of revolutionary Jacobinism. Nor, of course, does he shrink from extending the same logic to contemporary society and politics. In 1971, Foucault endorsed a policy of "Revolutionary action" against "the university, the prisons, the domain of psychiatry." We must "engage" the system, he declares with the militancy of a latter-day Péguy, "on all fronts."

> We strike and knock against the most solid obstacles; we persist. It seems that we're winning but then the institution is rebuilt; we must start again. It is a long struggle; it is repetitive and seemingly incoherent. But the system it opposes, as well as the power exercised through the system, supplies its unity.[63]

The following year, by the same token, Foucault announced that "[w]omen, prisoners, conscripted soldiers, hospital patients, and homosexuals, have now begun a specific struggle against the particularized power . . . exerted over them." And such struggles, he adds, remain "part of the revolutionary movement to the degree that they are radical, uncompromising, and nonreformist." In 1976, Foucault famously championed an "*an insurrection of subjugated knowledges*" against "the institutions" and "effects" of "scientific discourse" (Foucault's emphasis). For present "everywhere in the power network," he reiterates in *La Volonté de savoir,* are "points of resistance": some "that are possible, necessary, improbable," and "others that are spontaneous, savage, solitary, concerted, rampant, violent, irreconcilable." Such "points, knots, or focuses of resistance," Foucault elaborates, calling to mind Bergson's "points" of "vital impetus" within the universe of matter, "are spread over time and space at varying densities." They might "inflame . . . certain points of the body, certain moments of life, certain types of behavior." In fact, his own historical "genealogies," professes Foucault, represent precisely such "Molotov cocktails or minefields" within the established discourse. "I would like them to self-destruct after use," he joked in 1977, "like fireworks."[64]

Characteristically, then, Foucault advocates what he calls "specific struggles" against the "normalizing" institutions and discourse of modernity: that is, localized, and at least nominally violent disruptions of the established order. Yet broad communal insurrection and violence would seem also to exercise a genuine fascination for the poststructuralist. Thus, at a public forum with French Maoists in 1972, as has been seen, Foucault defended the French Revolution's infamous "September Massacres" as "an act of war against internal enemies, a political act against the manipulations of those in power, and an act of vengeance against the oppressive classes"—as "an approximation," in a word, of "popular justice." Foucault obviously differs here with Michelet, who repudiated the same event as a criminal and "sanguinary deed." Yet their dispute would seem not over the abstract moral legitimacy of political violence so much as which particular acts of violence constitute a genuine expression of popular will. Later during the same exchange, Foucault applauds "[t]he Resistance, the Algerian War, [and] May '68" as "crucial episodes" in "the revival . . . of clandestinity, of arms, and of action in the streets." Most telling of all, however, is the poststructuralist's notorious panegyric to the Iranian Revolution in 1979. Exclaiming, in an unmistakable echo of Rousseau and Robespierre, that "few peoples in history" have experienced such an event, he contends that the "collective will," which has remained nothing more than "a political myth" in "our theories," achieved "an absolutely clear, particular aim" in the Iranian uprising; that the Revolution, in a word, manifested the tangible "erupt[ion]" of "an absolutely collective will" onto the historical stage. For in its "rejection of submission to foreigners," Foucault declares, in its "disgust at the looting of national resources," in its "rejection of a dependent foreign policy," the Iranian people literally and *"tirelessly demonstrated its will"* (Foucault's emphasis). Indeed, what lends the Iranian Revolution "its beauty," he explains, is the remarkably clear "confrontation" between an "entire people" and a corrupt and powerful "state" which had threatened the former "with its weapons and police." Through their insurrection, the Iranians "sa[id]" not only "'we have to change this corrupt administration'" and overhaul the nation's "'political organization,'" its "'economic system,'" and its "'foreign policy,'" but also "'above all we have to change ourselves.'" Thus, during the revolutionary event itself, attests Foucault, "[t]here was literally a light that lit up" within the Iranian people, "and which bathed all of them at the same time."[65]

In the Iranian Revolution, then, Foucault would seem to find—or perhaps construct—his own version of Sartre's "fused group," Michelet's "magnificent burst of national energy," and Robespierre's rare interlude "when, by prodigious efforts, a people breaks the chains of despotism"—of that violent but sacrosanct upheaval, that is, whereby both the individual and "the people" purge themselves of psychic dependency and reclaim their autonomy of will. "[B]ehind all the submissions and coercions," Foucault rhapsodized in 1979, "and beyond the menace, the violence, the persuasion," there remains the "moment when life will no longer barter itself, when the powers can no longer do anything, and when, before the gallows and machine guns, men revolt." For, again, he summarizes, "there is no power without potential refusal or revolt."[66]

But of course "revolt," whether a personal "limit-experience," a "specific struggle" against the "norm," or a political insurrection, remains no less evanescent for Foucault, no less tragically fleeting, than it does for Sartre, Michelet, or Robespierre. While the modern network of power, Foucault argues in *Surveiller et punir*, defines "innumerable points of confrontation" which might allow "an at least temporary inversion of the power relations," the "overthrow of these 'micropowers' does not . . . obey the law of all or nothing." Indeed, repudiating such "global, *totalitarian theories*" of revolutionary liberation as Marxism, Foucault cautions in *La Volonté de savoir* that there is "no *single* locus of Great Refusal, no soul of revolt, source of all rebellions or pure law of the revolutionary" (Foucault's emphasis). Even that singular "phenomenon" of the Iranian Revolution, he laments, which "has traversed [an] entire people," remains destined "one day" to "stop." In fact, the "revolutionary experience itself" will "die out," and so too will that light that once bathed all Iranians "at the same time." And "[a]t that moment," Foucault concludes, in a striking echo of Péguy, "all that will remain are the different political calculations that each individual had had in his head the whole time."[67] "Mystique," in other words, will disintegrate, leaving only "politique" in its wake, and freedom's moment will once again collapse back into the realm of institutionalized power from which it came.

SIX

CONCLUSION

I. PAROXYSMS, "TOTALITARIANISM," AND FREEDOM

"French intellectuals," the philosopher Richard Rorty once noted in a forum on Foucault, "often strike Americans as hoping for paroxysms where nobody should want them—in politics."[1] In light of the foregoing, Rorty's remark rings true on more levels than one. As a meditation, first of all, on political discourse in modern France it would seem not at all without foundation: since the eighteenth century, as has been seen, several culturally acclaimed—indeed "consecrated"—members of the French intelligentsia have gravitated conspicuously toward "political paroxysms" of a sort.

Rorty's comment would also appear faithfully to reflect the often fervent disapproval expressed by American as well as other Western scholars for such "paroxysms" and their presumably ominous political implications. Indeed, as noted in chapter 1, more than a few members of the Western liberal intelligentsia since World War II have posited a link between the revolutionary intellectual tradition in modern France, as framed initially by Rousseau and the Jacobin Terror, and the phenomenon of twentieth-century "totalitarianism." Thus, the Israeli political scientist J. L. Talmon, writing in 1952, found Nazi Germany and the Stalinist Empire to be modern visitations of a "totalitarian democracy," which he traced to the revolutionary Jacobins and their intellectual master, Rousseau. In 1957, the previously cited English historian and philosopher Isaiah Berlin also charged Rousseau and his revolutionary disciples with championing that "'positive' freedom of collective self-assertion" which betrays a utopian yearning for "final solution(s)." During the 1970s, moreover, France's liberal intelligentsia itself, in revising the received Marxian account of the Revolution, breathed new life into the linkage between Jacobinism and modern totalitarianism. "Today," wrote François Furet in 1978, "the Gulag is leading to a rethinking of the Terror precisely because the two undertakings are seen as identical." Since that time "revolutionary discourse," particularly in its Jacobin guise, has been routinely taxed in Western scholarship for its "latent illiberalism" and "totalitarian" implications.[2]

Nor, as Rorty's remark reminds us, have France's more recent cultural militants fared better. Already condemned in 1956 by his former comrade Raymond Aron for succumbing to the French intellectual's addiction to "the myth of revolution and salvation by violence," Sartre stands still indicted in the Western academy on charges that range from providing a philosophical cloak for the Cambodian mass murders of the 1970s to, of course, Stalinist collaborationism. In seconding Tony Judt's recent assault, for example, both on Sartre and the postwar French intellectual community as a whole, John Weightman recalls "the almost hysterical pro-Communist atmosphere" on the Left Bank during the postwar years and judges it "an incipiently totalitarian situation." Foucault, too, particularly in response to his early support for the Iranian Revolution, has attracted more than his share of moral derision from liberal critics in the West.[3]

It is hard to escape the impression, in light of such indictments, that the term "totalitarian" has undergone an enormous historical inflation since World War II; indeed, that the scholarly appraisal of the revolutionary intellectual tradition in modern France has become distorted by what Keith Baker has called the historical "force field" of the contemporary age: that "master event" which "constitutes, in effect, the outer limits of historical intelligibility," and into which "all other events are drawn." Baker refers here most specifically to the Nazi Holocaust, but he might just as well have extended his "master event" to include such atrocities as Stalin's mass executions and internments of the 1930s, 1940s, and 1950s, and the state-sponsored terrorism of Mao's "Cultural Revolution" in the 1960s; to encompass, in other words, the most unfathomable evils of twentieth-century "totalitarianism" as a whole.[4]

Western scholarship, moreover, has not been drawn alone into the historical force field of "totalitarianism": the likes of Sartre and Foucault themselves, extending the time-honored heretical assault on "bourgeois liberalism," have not shrunk from denouncing the "bourgeois West" for its own alleged "totalitarianism." Responding, for example, to the execution of the Rosenbergs in 1953, Sartre declared: "Fascism is not defined by the number of its victims, but by the way it kills them." And Foucault, by the same token, in painting such ostensibly humane Western institutions as mental hospitals and prisons in notoriously Orwellian hues, has repeatedly underscored the potential for "totalitarian" intervention inherent in the relationship between "rationalization and the excesses of political power"—a potential, which, he claims, one should not need "bureaucracy or concentration camps to recognize."[5] Paradoxically, then, both "the French intellectuals" and "the bourgeois West"—as they have been designated by mutual caricature—have periodically implicated the other, be it as actual perpetrators or unwitting accomplices, in the most heinous political crimes of the twentieth century or their moral equivalent. Each side, in formulating its respective allegations, has readily invoked the specters of governmental terrorism, state-sponsored murder, and the concentration camp; and each has either directly or implicitly labeled the other "totalitarian," an adjective which has come universally to signify the ultimate horror chamber of modern politics.

Such accusations cannot help but lead one to ask if every political phenomenon of the modern era may, without serious historical distortion, be understood and judged within the bipolar moral and intellectual universe of the "master event"—assessed, that is, as either contributing to "totalitarian subjugation" or "democratic liberation." Shouldn't Foucault have acknowledged, for example, as political philosopher Alan Ryan suggests in what seems to epitomize the Western academy's grievance against "French intellectuals" as a whole, that "liberal Western societies" have been "freer and more humane than their totalitarian competitors"?[6] One might equally ask, on the other hand, if it is just or accurate to couple the political discourse of the Rousseaus, Robespierres, Sartres, and Foucaults of modern France

with that of Hitler, Stalin, and Mao. Does the Jacobin Terror constitute a true historical analogue to the Soviet Gulag? Are all "political
paroxysms" created historically equal?

This is not the place for an in-depth historical comparison of the
Jacobin Reign of Terror with its alleged twentieth-century counterparts in Nazi Germany, Soviet Russia, or Maoist China. But one may
perhaps fruitfully compare the archetypal totalitarian model of state,
society, and freedom in the modern age with that advanced by France's
consecrated heretics. The term "totalitarianism" refers, of course, to a
diverse and immensely complex series of historical events. Yet even in
the mutual accusations of the heretics and their Western detractors one
may discern a common outline of what it must encompass, at bare
minimum, to merit the name: (1) a permanent and monolithic central
government that lays claim to absolute domination over its subjects
and their lives; (2) the absence or elimination, accordingly, of autonomous political parties and parliamentary institutions; (3) the promotion by the state of a utopian collectivism or group organicism—Hitler's "*volksgemeinschaft*," for example, or the Marxist-Leninist vision
of proletarian class solidarity in the communist "final stage"—in
which the individual's freedom is forever bound to that of the social
body as a whole; and 4) a state-sponsored cult of violence and terror
that entails the forced expulsion, imprisonment, or extermination of
society's putatively "undesirable" members.[7]

There would seem, at first glance, several parallels between aspects
of this model and that suggested by the heretical narrative. The characteristic contempt of the consecrated heretics, for example, for parliamentary politics—for the divisive "debates," political "intrigues," and
"factions" of Rousseau and Robespierre, the "paper liberty" of Michelet's revolutionary parliamentarians, the "game of parties" practiced by Péguy's men of "politique," the "parliamentary, representative
regime," which, for Foucault, merely veils "panopticism"—has been
detailed above. The heretical narrative might equally be charged with
promoting a species of "utopian collectivism." For, again, whether
through the "general will," the revolutionary will of "the people," "the
Dreyfusard mystique," the "*groupe en fusion*," or the "collective will"
of the Iranian masses, the likes of Rousseau, Robespierre, Michelet,
Péguy, Sartre, and Foucault have characteristically exalted the solidarity of the social body as a unified whole. It would be difficult to deny,
finally, that a "cult of violence" stands virtually at the core of the heretical narrative. For underlying its distinctive philosophical vitalism
—perhaps best exemplified by Bergson but equally discernable, for

instance, in Rousseau, Péguy, and Sartre—would appear an all but Nietzschean proclivity for deeds of transgressive, self-affirming will and even violence in the face of "civilized society." Thus, Julien Sorel's "premeditated" act of "open revolt" against *la société* finds clear counterparts, for example, in Michelet's "divine bursts" of popular "will" against the Revolution's enemies, Bergson's "deep-seated" eruptions of "*élan vital*" within the mind's "geometrical realm," Sartre's cleansing "thunderbolts" of violence against the bourgeois order, and Foucault's "Molotov cocktails" of "insubordination" and "resistance" against the modern "society of normalization." In the case of Robespierre, furthermore, the heretical cult of violence would seem linked even to a monolithic and all-powerful state, which aspires, through legally sanctioned terror, to purge society of those political parties and individuals it deems undesirable.[8]

Under closer examination, however, the analogy between the two models does not hold up for long. The customary heretical scorn for parliamentary institutions, first of all, as plausibly alarming as it might appear to its critics, betokens not a latent partiality for monolithic government so much as a deeply ingrained suspicion of political power and its natural inclination toward corruption. And so Stendhal's satire of the Restoration's liberal parliamentary "opposition" for colluding with and groveling before the established state lives on, for example, in Péguy's critique of the Third Republic's "parliamentary shams" and "political prevarication," and in Sartre's inevitably caustic snapshots of vain and self-serving politicians. Indeed, government itself, it will be recalled, remains forever subject within the heretical narrative to degeneration and ossification. Hence, Rousseau's previously cited axiom that government inclines invariably to engender its own self-serving "corporate will" mirrors Bergson's contention that the psyche tends innately to capitulate before its own bureaucratic "automatism" and Sartre's that even revolutionary government will ultimately degenerate into an entrenched "Institution." For Michelet, likewise, government constitutes by definition that "form" which drains society of its "*content*" (Michelet's emphasis), just as "politique," for Péguy, constitutes the inescapable decay of "mystique." Even Robespierre repeatedly cites the "mistrust" of government as a cardinal political principle. "[I]n every free state," he proclaimed in his "Proposed Declaration of the Rights of Man and Citizen" of 1793, "the law must, above all, defend public and individual liberty against the abuse of authority by those who govern." In fact, "revolutionary government" itself, insists the Jacobin, even as he defends the Terror, must remain "trusting of the people and severe to itself." For all government tends, "according to the natural course of things," to "lapse into the hands of corrupt individuals."[9]

Nor may the consecrated heretics be accused of espousing a group organicism or permanent community of "comrades"—a closed human "circle," in the arresting image of Czech novelist Milan Kundera, which forms "a single body and a single soul, a single ring and a single dance."[10] The "hell" constituted by "other people" in the heretical narrative has been amply characterized above. And indeed, the heretical account of society seems if anything to disclose a profound dread—rooted, no doubt, in the Enlightenment critique of the Old Regime's corporate particularism—of immutable social ties and groups.[11] Hence, Rousseau, once again, conceives both the "general will" and the government it appoints as the artificial creations of an assembly of entirely discrete individuals. He seeks even to dissolve in advance any "partial associations" that might breed within that assembly were it formed either by elected representatives or even private citizens who had prior "communication with one another." Robespierre, as well, while embracing representative government, not only concurs that "[e]ach and every section of the assembled sovereign must enjoy the right to express its will with entire liberty," but manifests an equal fear of those "coteries" and "cabals" which might "factionalize" the "National Representation." Likewise, Sartre, notwithstanding his early regard for Hegel and Heidegger and his later appreciation for Marx, unfailingly denies the reality of corporate groups. Having repudiated Heidegger's notion of an ontologically stable "being-with-others [*Mitsein*]," insofar as "[t]he essence of the relations between consciousnesses ... is conflict," he insists again in *Critique de la raison dialectique* that neither the "fused" revolutionary group nor, by consequence, the revolutionary state itself, might ever acquire "organic unity." Foucault, too, recoils in his own way at the prospect of the organic group: that "corpus of knowledge, techniques, [and] 'scientific' discourses" which comprises, for him, the perpetual menace of "disciplinary power;" that "tightly knit grid of material coercions," which would seem to represent nothing if not the concealed—and institutionally congealed—corporatism of the modern age.[12]

The "utopian collectivism," then, which would appear so pronounced in the heretical narrative advances neither communal organicism nor the primacy of the state; it exalts rather the revolutionary insurrection of "the people," of that quasi-mythical body of the nation-as-one which materializes only on rare occasions of unified national will. In this light, accordingly, the heretical "cult of violence" would seem to entail not so much the deification of government or national community as of freedom itself; and freedom in the heretical narrative comprises a flight of autonomous will, both individual and collective, which remains forever tragically abbreviated. Thus, the head of the dauntlessly independent lawbreaker Julien Sorel, it will be recalled, is never quite "so poetic as at the moment" it is "about to fall." And Bergson's "fundamental self," while able occasionally to seize its freedom in an "abrupt intervention of will," a "coup d'état" against its own internal ordinances, must recognize that such "free acts" are highly exceptional—that they constitute "moments unique of their kind." Michelet, too, while identifying liberty with episodes of communal concord and revolutionary brutality—of "terrible and violent convulsion" and "warlike fraternity"—ultimately finds such "divine flashes" to be perhaps "true" but inevitably "transient." And Péguy, while depicting the "Dreyfusard mystique" as a "heroic upsurge" among a people who must periodically "break free" and express their "need for heroism, for *military* war," underscores nonetheless the inescapable "*decomposition of Dreyfusism*"—the tragic evanescence, that is, of all "mystiques" and therefore of freedom itself (Péguy's emphasis). Fated equally to collapse into the "anguish" of impermanence are Sartre's existential "thunderbolts" of liberty; and so too is his revolutionary "*groupe en fusion*," ultimately "doomed to diachronic alienation." No less does Foucault repudiate those "global, *totalitarian theories*" of liberation which promote an eternal "locus of Great Refusal" or "pure law of the revolutionary," in favor of those "limit-experiences" and "specific struggles" against the "norm" which remain by definition "temporary" (Foucault's emphasis).[13]

Even Robespierre, finally, by virtue of his longing to "maintain . . . the sacred spring of republican government instead of letting it decline"—his calamitous attempt, that is, to suspend by force the "sacred moment" of revolutionary "consensus"—tacitly concedes the inevitability of revolutionary decline. For within his own theory of revolutionary government lies not only the requirement that government officials "sacrifice" their "pride in power to equality" and submit "ceaselessly" to public inspection, but the Rousseauian tenet that the "body politic" tends naturally to lose its "character" and "liberty" and fall into "decrepitude."[14] Indeed, one is tempted to concur with political scientist Anne Sa'adah that the Jacobin philosophy of government, notwithstanding its immediately deplorable repercussions, yielded not so much a permanent dictatorship as an "inherently destabilizing" politics whose final casualty was Jacobin rule itself.[15]

At worst, in sum, the heretical narrative would seem to lend a mythological aura to such bloody political episodes as the Terror or the various communist and Third World revolutions of the twentieth century. Indeed, the glorification of violent transgression and revolutionary emancipation within the narrative of consecrated heresy might help illuminate the gravitation of several twentieth-century French thinkers—Georges Sorel, Georges Bataille, Maurice Blanchot, Georges Canguilhem, Gilles Deleuze, and Jacques Derrida, for instance, not to mention Foucault—toward Nietzsche,[16] as well as the conspicuous appeal of Marxism within modern French political culture.[17] Yet it has been seen that Foucault, for one, remains in his own way as faithful as Rousseau to the sovereign will of "the people"—that he betrays none of Nietzsche's antidemocratic elitism, his forthright repudiation of "'the slaves,' 'the mob,' 'the herd,'" and their "supreme rights."[18] Nor does the Marxist "convert" Sartre embrace the master's utopian teleology—his conviction that the proletarian revolution will generate an eternal community of comrades. In short, if the heretical narrative might reasonably be accused of nurturing a disconcerting ideological blind spot for the mythos of popular revolution, it cannot be charged either with shaping or justifying the ideological framework of modern totalitarianism.

II. FREEDOM AND THE "BUREAUCRATIC PHENOMENON"

What, then, if not the specter of totalitarianism, do the conspicuous "paroxysms" of the heretical narrative signify within the political culture of modern France? How, indeed, does the heretical account of freedom and its emergence in self and society relate to the notorious pendulum swings—cited in chapter 1—of the modern French polity?

Again, no groundwork has been laid here for a detailed comparative analysis of such political eruptions in modern France as the Napoleonic coups of 1799 and 1851, the revolutions of 1830 and 1848, the Paris Commune of 1870–71, the Dreyfus affair at the turn of the century, Vichy's "National Revolution" of 1940, the Algerian Crisis of 1958, or "the events" of May 1968. The French sociologist Michel Crozier, however, in such widely influential works as *The Bureaucratic Phenomenon* (1963) and *The Stalled Society* (1970) among others, has formulated a model of modern French political culture and its putative irregularities, which accords rather strikingly with the archetype of consecrated heresy.[19]

A disciple of Tocqueville, Crozier maintains that French society has been wedded since before the Revolution to a stifling centralized bureaucracy. Yet the French state has functioned, according to him, not as a totalitarian monolith imposing its will on the individual, but rather as an impersonal set of rules and regulations meant to secure each individual against "face-to-face dependence relationships"—a view which recalls, on the one hand, Rousseau's ideal of an objective, impersonal "general will," and on the other, Foucault's often cited craving "to have no face." When the rules, explains Crozier, remain abstract universals applied equally to all, then no individual will be forced to submit directly to the will of another, and each will possess a private "zone of autonomy, of caprice, of creativity"—in short, of "*bon plaisir*": that absolute and "arbitrary will" once granted only to the Old Regime monarch. Thus, the "bureaucratic system of organization," he summarizes, has afforded modern French citizens, at least in principle, the widest possible "freedom from interference" by others and therefore "some participation in *bon plaisir* to the greatest number of persons."[20]

Bureaucratic regulations, however, invariably ossify and weaken in their application, and any system based on them remains inherently too rigid to reform itself. The inevitable "stalemates" therefore generated by such a system may "be broken," Crozier contends, only through periodic "regime crises" and "revolutions." Hence the "alternation of routine and crisis" so emblematic of modern French organizations in particular and of modern French history in general. In fact, France's famed oscillations, suggests the sociologist in *The Stalled Society,* between "long periods of routine" and "short bursts of crisis," may help explain "the permanence" of its "revolutionary tradition."[21]

It is not surprising, in this light, to find in Crozier's 1970 account of the still fresh uprising of May 1968 an all too familiar image. The "*enragés,*" he writes, "managed, *for at least a moment in the paroxysm of their revolt,* to square the circle of direct democracy: they created a crowd in which individuals could express themselves, an action without organization, permanent spontaneity" (emphasis added). Yet the May crisis, he concludes, amounted only to a passing "carnival," which wrought no permanent change; indeed, it didn't represent an attack on the institutions of "the stalled society" so much as "their clearest expression."[22]

In sum, it would be difficult not to detect in Crozier's portrait of the "bureaucratic phenomenon," with its radically circumscribed safeguards against "face-to-face dependency relationships" and its sporadic paroxysms of popular rage—its finite interludes, that is, of individual *"bon plaisir"* and collective violence—a mirror-image of the heretical saga of liberty. Freedom, for the consecrated heretics, remains structured by an irresolvable tension between autonomous human will, both individual and "general," and that enervating societal Other that continually invades it.[23] Indeed, heretical liberty comprises nothing if not a radical disruption of the norm, an outburst of violent will, an exalted moment of crisis during which "the people" purge both society and their own psyches of bureaucratic petrification and decay. Once again, however, for the consecrated heretics no less than for Crozier, such flights of liberation must remain fleeting; for while ever possible to launch, they are destined to return to the realm of the mundane and corrupt from which they arose.

Crozier's model, then, would seem to offer a compelling interpretation not only of modern French politics and its legendary volatility, but of the apparent ideological role played therein by the heretical chronicle of liberty. Evoked thus far as a "master narrative" within French political culture, which has resurfaced under various guises since the eighteenth century, it would appear by Crozier's account to pervade the very institutional structure of modern France and even to underlie, at least in part, the nation's periodic gravitation toward "political paroxysms." Like his colleague Pierre Bourdieu, in fact, Crozier contends that the cultural habits of mind that structure French society and politics in the modern age have been instilled and perpetuated by its famously centralized educational system and the ongoing reproduction of intellectual elites. Above all, the *grandes écoles,* he charges, which "exist in symbiosis with the French social and bureaucratic system . . . whose stability they help to preserve," have propagated a "mandarin class," which, while "ostensibly independent of the system," remains "in fact, its necessary counterpart." Hence, the archetypal French intellectual, reiterates Crozier in another work, "so progressive in his intentions," so devoted to "sovereign, unbridled, creative liberty," has "remained aristocratic in his style"; and such figures as Sartre, by consequence, have in truth represented a "cultural conservatism disguised as social progressivism."[24]

As penetrating and even persuasive as Crozier's diagnosis of modern French society and its ills might be, it remains precisely that: an ingenious exercise in social criticism, which seeks not to reconstruct

France's revolutionary tradition—or, for that matter, the French idea of freedom—on its own historical ground so much as to reform it. Contributing to an ongoing liberal critique of modern French society and values, which emanates explicitly from "Tocqueville's tirade"—as Crozier himself labels it—and extends through recent calls for an "end to the French exception," Crozier laments the "bureaucratic, paternalistic straightjacket" of France's "stalled society," its chronic "dysfunction" and "vicious cycles," the "irresponsibility" of its intelligentsia, and even the "radical totalitarian character" of those "demands for change" that "do occur." He goes on to prescribe a therapeutic social regimen which features radical decentralization (especially of the university system) as well as the exchange of France's bureaucratic model of society, which promises only "isolation and independence from others," for a consensual model of change and a liberal-utilitarian vision of freedom.[25]

Crozier's analysis, in other words, however insightful and in some ways "correct" it appears, does not altogether elucidate the historical import of the heretical narrative in modern France. One is left wondering if the saga of liberty disseminated by the consecrated heretics may be fully or exclusively understood as the traumatic symptom of a "stalled society"—as a "dysfunction" to be cured, that is, or an "exception" to the rule of liberal Western politics to be "ended." What, apart from institutionalized habit, accounts for its indisputable cultural potency? And what, from the standpoint of those who have fostered it, constitutes its abiding value and significance?

III. FREEDOM, "NOBILITY," AND MASCULINITY

Such questions, of course, which profess to encompass the normative framework of modern French political culture as a whole, may hardly expect to find a definitive answer here. Yet Crozier himself, ever attuned, like his mentor Tocqueville, to the deeply ingrained continuity of cultural mores in modern France, suggests one possible avenue of inquiry by grounding his model in such prerevolutionary norms as the monarch's "*bon plaisir*" and the growing "insistence," at all levels of the Old Regime's social hierarchy, on "personal autonomy."[26] For the conception of liberty as the absolute sovereignty of the individual psyche within its own sphere calls to mind at least one more premodern ideal: that of "nobility."[27]

Inasmuch as the heretical saga of liberty, not to mention the French Revolution itself, stands in direct historical opposition to that legal hierarchy of privilege, status, and estate of which the Old Regime nobility was the very emblem, any presumed affinity between the two would appear absurd at first glance. Yet before the seventeenth century, as Ellery Schalk has documented, the term "nobility" in French cultural discourse signified less a social caste demarcated by privilege and blood than a code of behavior grounded still in the feudal military ethos of "action." At least in principle, that is, nobility constituted a "profession of virtue," which entailed "loyalty to one's monarch or military leader" as well as "courage and prowess in battle, selflessness when defending the weak and the poor," "uprightness," and "honesty." Thus, "in theory," Schalk elaborates, "ennoblement" was earned neither through estate nor "riches" but rather "'virtuous' deeds, which were, of course, supposed to take place on the battlefield." Lineage and hierarchy notwithstanding, in other words, the noble ethos accented a bold sovereignty of spirit that resisted both political and economic dependency. But owing in part, Schalk concludes, to the "new absolutist state of the seventeenth century," which had "no room" for "an independent nobility," the Old Regime noble came ultimately to be defined according to legal estate and ancestral "pedigree," while "virtue," on the other hand, evolved into a cultural value unto itself.[28]

Regardless, then, of how fully it was ever embodied in practice, "noble virtue" and its attendant qualities of courage, military prowess, moral integrity, selflessness on behalf of the weak, contempt for monetary gain, and fierce personal autonomy would seem to have represented a powerful cultural ideal in premodern France[29]—and evidently well beyond. Tocqueville, for one, voices a famous nostalgia in *The Old Regime and the French Revolution* for that noble liberty which, he laments, was betrayed and squandered by the Old Regime aristocracy and had all but evaporated by his own time. While undoubtedly "subservient" to "the king's authority," he proclaims, "the Frenchman of the old regime" knew nothing of "that craving for material well-being which leads the way to servitude," that obsequiousness "before an illegitimate or dubious authority," or "that type of obedience which comes of a servile mind." Surely, he chides his mid-nineteenth-century French readers, we would all do well to regain the "heroism," the "nobility of mind," and the "ill-adjusted, intermittent freedom" of "our ancestors."[30]

The saga of the consecrated heretic outlined in chapter 2, moreover, with its stress on the hero's humble origins and willful repudiation of personal dependency and economic gain, his figurative conquest of civilized society and subsequent isolation therein, his resolute public probity, and his final deed of symbolic transgression on behalf of "the people," would seem a transparent recasting of the noble ethos in the mold of modern democratic liberty. In fact, both the consecrated heretics and their fictional alter-egos frequently find themselves endowed with unmistakable marks of medieval nobility. Julien Sorel, for example, depicted more than once in *Le Rouge et le noir* as a man with "nobility" in his "heart" if not his blood—a man concerned more with "heroism" and "extraordinary deeds" than "commerce"—is identified explicitly by Mathilde de La Mole with her noble ancestor, Boniface, who had been beheaded in 1574 by Catherine de Medici for his daring attempt to liberate two captured princes—one of whom would later become King Henri IV. Indeed, ultimately, in the wake of Julien's crime, Mathilde beholds "Boniface de la Mole . . . reborn in him, but in an even more heroic mold."[31]

Rousseau, likewise, who figuratively "ennobles" Saint Preux by virtue both of a crypto-aristocratic name and a noble virtuosity of spirit, does the same for his celebrated "noble savage": that "robust and strong" man of action who, it will be recalled, remains not only incapable of deceit, but entirely "solitary" and "self-sufficient." It will be recalled as well that Rousseau's Émile, not to mention the self-portrayed "Jean-Jacques" himself, finds himself ultimately obliged "to sacrifice" his own interests for "the common interest"—to undertake "the painful task" of "telling men useful but unwelcome truths with some vigor and courage." Similarly, the youthful persona of Jean-Paul Sartre, as fashioned two centuries later in the existentialist's own self-lacerating account, makes "heroism the sole object" of his "passion" and bestows upon "the writer," consequently, "the sacred powers of the hero." Thus, the juvenile "knight-errant," summarizes Sartre, transformed himself into the "writer-knight" who will "run the wicked through" with his "sharp pen." It comes as no surprise, in this light, to find the existentialist's fictional hero Orestes—that scion of the Greek nobility and allegorical hero of the Resistance—liberating both himself and "the people of Argos" through his murderous, but nonetheless "virtuous," deed. In fact, existential freedom, elaborated Sartre in 1944, amounts precisely to "acting alone for the good of all."[32]

No less, furthermore, do the virtues of nobility tend to emerge in the heretical portrait of "the people." Hence, for Robespierre, the revolutionary "people" of France would seem to embody a Rousseauian "noble savage" writ large and defined by its natural "uprightness," its "freedom from burdensome passions," and above all, its heroic self-sacrifice on behalf of the nation. Indeed, the infamous "virtue" of Robespierre's moral discourse, insofar as it embraces such qualities as "integrity," "a sense of duty," "self-respect," "grandeur of soul," and "love of glory," and stands opposed to "the tyranny of fashion," "formal codes of honor," "insolence," "vanity," and "love of money," appears to allude not only to that classical virtue cited by Montesquieu and Rousseau as the wellspring of all republics, but also, once again, to a noble "profession of virtue"—indeed military virtue—in republican guise. It will be recalled, by the same token, that Julien Sorel exalts Danton as the man who "infused strength into a nation of coxcombs [*freluquets*]," and that Péguy discerns in the "need for heroism," "great trials," "military glory," and "even martyrdom," which "periodically seizes this people," the very "honor" of the French nation as a whole, not to say "the historical honor of our whole race, the honor of our ancestors, the honor of our children." Likewise, Michelet, who again submits—paraphrasing Rousseau—that "[m]an is born noble" and "dies noble" but becomes "coarse and ignoble" by virtue of civilization, proclaims that the French Revolution did not "suppress the nobility" so much as "the opposite: it made nobles of thirty-four million Frenchmen."[33]

It is tempting, in light of such passages, to view the heretical saga of liberty as the reverse side, in Norman Hampson's formulation, of the "nationalization of honor" during the revolutionary age, or as mirrored again—in Robert Nye's more recent formulation—in the modern democratic demand to "inculcate" the "courage and sangfroid of the nobleman into the mass of men" through military service.[34] Such speculation, however, clearly falls beyond the confines of the present inquiry. Yet Nye's study of "male codes of honor in modern France" from which the preceding passage is taken does bring to mind one final historical motif that seems to pervade both the early modern ethos of nobility and the heretical model of liberty: that of "masculinity."

The present study, to be sure, cannot hope to treat the complex question of what constitutes "masculine" and "feminine," male and female, within French cultural discourse in anything but a cursory fashion. Nevertheless, the heretical narrative would seem manifestly to echo and refashion those "primordial qualities of manliness" which had been fostered, according to Nye, in "male-dominated warrior societies" and embodied in the code of "the noble gentleman."[35] Julien Sorel, for one, would appear to epitomize militant as well as military masculinity in postrevolutionary France: as the fervent apostle of Napoleon, he devours his idol's memoirs as well as the published "bulletins of the Grande Armée"; as an aspirant after "military glory," he considers "the novel of [his] career" completed once he has earned a commission in the cavalry; and as the sexual conqueror of Mathilde de La Mole, he likens himself to "a general" who has "just half won a great battle."[36]

Indeed, the heretical narrative itself, as has been seen, literally climaxes in "paroxysms" of liberation—in spasms of individual and collective release, which all but explicitly evoke male orgasm. Thus, Michelet's "supreme moments" of revolutionary liberty arise as "magnificent bursts" and "convulsions" of national energy, "volcanoes of life," and "burning jets of heroism," while Péguy's episodes of "mystique" manifest themselves as "heroic upsurges" and "eruptions" of national will. Bergson, likewise, represents freedom itself as a universal life-bearing essence, an "*élan vital*" or "vital impetus," which might at any moment "rush to the surface" but may only sustain itself "for a few instants at most." And Sartre—who once described existential "anguish" as that "virile uneasiness [*inquiétude virile*]" which constitutes the precondition for "action"—portrays freedom as a "marvelous instant" or "thunderbolt" of "nothingness," which must collapse immediately back into "Being." Even Foucault, finally, whose avowed homosexuality would seem to make him an unlikely icon of conventional masculinity in modern France, appears to conform nonetheless to the masculine archetype—if not to champion, indeed, a model of gay masculinity. Apart from his pronounced predilection, noted in a 1977 interview by Bernard Henry-Lévy, for "military metaphors," such as "power and resistance, tactics and strategy," he identifies liberation with the "overwhelming" intensity, the "complete and total pleasure," of metaphorically orgasmic "limit-experiences"—be they political "eruptions" of "collective will" or the "eroticization of power" and "strategic relations" achieved through sadomasochistic sexual practice.[37]

None of which is to suggest, it must be emphasized, that the heretical saga of liberty is reducible to male sexuality in any classically "Freudian" sense. For the recurrence of male sexual imagery in the heretical narrative would seem to betoken not so much its submerged or subconscious "meaning" as the hallmark itself of historically masculine norms and anxieties. One final look, accordingly, at that fear of personal dependency that pervades the heretical narrative—that "*horreur du face à face*" as Crozier would have it—might help to illuminate those norms.

It will be recalled that personal dependency as such generally translates in the heretical narrative into a humiliating servility before male figures of power and authority. Thus, Julien Sorel escapes from the domination of a brutal father into a social universe that requires him to submit to Monsieur de Rênal and the Marquis de La Mole. No less, both literally and figuratively, do Robespierre's "tyrants" and "revolutionary enemies," Michelet's calculating Jacobins and subversive priests, Péguy's Jaurèsian traitors and "men of politics," and Sartre's "right-thinking" bourgeois "*salauds*"—not to mention his imperious Zeus—evoke the oppression of masculine authority; as do equally, for that matter, with their overtones of "scientific" dominion over both the psyche and society, Bergson's "geometrical intellect" and Foucault's modern panoptic "disciplines." The penetrating, subjugating "Look" of the "Other," in a word, remains at least symbolically male in the heretical narrative.

Dependency on women, on the other hand, as characterized both in the public biographies of the consecrated heretics and in their works, seems to constitute no particular obstacle to liberty. On the contrary, the likes of Rousseau's Madame de Warens, Robespierre's Duplay women, Julien Sorel's Madame de Rênal, Péguy's Madame Favre, and Sartre's lifelong mistress, Simone de Beauvoir, seem to offer their respective charges a steadfast maternal support, as it were, which actually nurtures their sense of personal autonomy within a menacingly masculine universe. "I am adored, therefore I am adorable" is the message the young Sartre receives from his biological mother—and ultimately, by all accounts, from Simone de Beauvoir as well. He represents his father's death, on the other hand, as the "great event of my life," which "gave me my freedom." Foucault's mother, similarly, insofar as she promotes his choice of an academic career, is portrayed as having bolstered her son's independence from an oppressive father. And Michelet not only professes a profound debt to his own mother, but glorifies maternal love more generally in *Du Prêtre, de la femme, et de la famille* as the fount of "primal individuality" in great men. For, again, while the father's instinct is to suppress the son's "natural impulse," the mother's is to sustain his "will," his "works," and his "freedom."[38]

Yet if liberty would seem symbolically enhanced by female support within the heretical narrative and stifled by male authority, its actual surrender constitutes nothing less than a "feminization." Here, Rousseau's celebrated critique of the Republic of Letters and of civilization itself invites particular reassessment. Apart, that is, from literally assaulting the domain of the Parisian salon, where he complained: "Nothing is achieved . . . except by help of the ladies," Rousseau tends—as has been noted by more than one scholar—to divide the moral universe into masculine and feminine spheres. On the one side stands that "natural" *amour de soi,* or love of self, which betokens the simplicity, transparency, vigor, and unyielding autonomy—in short, the "manly" Spartan virtue—of the free individual; on the other, that "civilized" *amour-propre,* that lust after approval, wealth, rank, and appearances, which signifies "effeminate" corruption and subjugation to society. And given that "every woman in Paris" now "gathers in her apartment a harem of men more womanish than she," protests Rousseau in the *Lettre à d'Alembert* for example, it can come as no surprise that "man" has "fallen" and "degenerated" since the time of Greece and Rome. In repudiating "enlightened" society, in other words, for rendering men "womanish"—and thereby implicitly representing himself, in Dena Goodman's words, as "the only man left in an effeminate and therefore false society"—Rousseau identifies liberty expressly with masculinity, and liberty's surrender with emasculation.[39]

It would be difficult to deny either the enduring resonance of this Rousseauian dichotomy within the heretical narrative or its identification of the "female" with psychic subservience. Both would seem unmistakable, for instance, in Robespierre's repudiation of "vanity," "love of money," and "the tyranny of fashion" in favor of "integrity," "grandeur of soul," and "self-respect"—that is, of "virile" virtue, as Robert Darnton has put it; in the civilized impotence of such Stendhalian men as Rênal, the Comte Thaler, and Monsieur Sainclair, as well as in Julien's final renunciation of Mathilde de La Mole and, with her, "the ideal of Paris"; in Michelet's charge that the church undermines the masculinity, and thereby the liberty, of French husbands through the priest's spiritual "penetration" of their psychologically malleable wives; in Foucault's corresponding critique of the "medicalization" of sexuality through the so-called "idle," "nervous," or "hysterical" woman; and in Sartre's well known "binary aesthetic," as Tony Judt phrases it, which characteristically places "masculine heroes" in opposition to "feminized victims (of both sexes) collaborating in their own servitude."[40]

All of which is not to suggest that the heretical narrative is inherently "misogynistic," or that it excludes women as such from the empire of freedom in any literal social or political sense; for again, the actual role of women in society, constructive or otherwise, would seem a subject of conspicuous ambivalence for the consecrated heretics. The point is rather that the heretics appear to cast freedom itself in a fundamentally masculine mold. Their espousal, on the one hand, of individual prowess and valor, of willful autonomy and social transparency, of heroic

outbursts of violence and will on behalf of the weak and disenfran-
chised, and their renunciation, on the other, of personal dependency
and the hypocrisy of appearances, of economic well-being and the pursuit of material gain, of conventional society and established hierarchy,
would seem rooted, as suggested above, in the warrior virtues of
premodern "manliness." Indeed, the zeal with which the consecrated
heretics have historically condemned "negative liberty"—that false
and ignoble freedom, as they would have it, to increase one's personal
status and fortune in the corrupt social and political universe of the
"bourgeoisie"—would seem to represent, in this light, more a "noble"
assault on bourgeois liberal masculinity than any yearning for "totalitarian" alternatives.

Should such reflections ultimately prove persuasive, moreover, they
suggest that the heretical model of liberty—framed as it is by eruptions
of uncompromised will that remain forever possible to achieve yet forever fated to dissolve—remains profoundly imbedded in the institutions and political culture of modern France. Indeed, so laden would
it seem with historical and even mythic potency, that one must wonder
if the French Revolution is in fact over, as the contemporary historical orthodoxy suggests,[41] or rather awaiting its prescribed moment to
resurface.

NOTES

CHAPTER I

1. Isaiah Berlin, *Four Essays on Liberty* (Oxford: Oxford University Press, 1969), 123–30. See also J. G. Merquior, *Liberalism Old and New* (Boston: Twayne, 1991), 8, 10, 15, 29–32, 3.

2. Berlin, *Four Essays*, 131–34; Leonard Krieger, *The German Idea of Freedom* (Chicago: University of Chicago Press, 1957), ix, 138. See also Merquior, *Liberalism,* 12–13.

3. On the opposition between liberal and radical intellectual traditions in revolutionary and postrevolutionary France, see Jean Rivero, "The Jacobin and Liberal Traditions," and George Armstrong Kelly, "The Jacobin and Liberal Contributions to the Founding of the Second and Third Republics," respectively, in *Liberty/Liberté: The American and French Experiences,* ed. Joseph Klaits and Michael H. Halzel (Baltimore: Johns Hopkins University Press, 1991), 116–30 and 131–49; see also Anne Sa'adah, *The Shaping of Liberal Politics in Revolutionary France* (Princeton: Princeton University Press, 1990) and Merquior, *Liberalism,* 10–11, 33, 51, 53–58, 14. On the roots of both traditions in the French Revolutionary "Declaration of the Rights of Man and Citizen," see Dale Van Kley, ed., *The French Idea of Freedom: The Old Regime and the Declaration of Rights of 1789* (Stanford: Stanford University Press, 1994). On the radical intellectual tradition in particular and its historical repercussions, see, for example, Jacques Julliard, *La Faute à Rousseau: essai sur les conséquences historiques de l'idée de souveraineté populaire* (Paris: Seuil, 1985); Sunil Khilnani, *Arguing Revolution: The Intellectual Left in Postwar France* (New Haven: Yale University Press, 1993); Sudhir Hazareesingh, *Political Traditions in Modern France* (New York: Oxford University Press, 1994); Claude Nicolet, *L'Idée républicaine en France (1789–1924)* (Paris: Gallimard, 1982); Stanley Hoffmann, *Decline or Renewal? France since the 1930s* (New York: Viking Press, 1974). On the peculiarities of the French liberal tradition—specifically, its stress on "mores" over abstract rights and its ambivalence about Rousseau—see Larry Siedentop, "Two Liberal Traditions" in *The Idea of Freedom: Essays in Honor of Isaiah Berlin,* ed. Alan Ryan (Oxford: Oxford University Press, 1979), 153–74; and André Jardin, *Histoire du libéralisme politique: de la crise de l'absolutisme à la constitution de 1875* (Paris: Hachette, 1985), 35, 50–58.

4. Van Kley, *French Idea of Freedom,* 18.

5. The classic works that first linked the French revolutionary tradition to

totalitarianism are J. L. Talmon, *The Rise of Totalitarian Democracy* (Boston: Beacon Press, 1952), and Raymond Aron, *The Opium of the Intellectuals,* trans. Terence Kilmartin (New York: Doubleday, 1957). Since the 1970s, this cold war thesis has experienced a powerful resurrection (for a summary, see Khilnani, *Arguing Revolution,* 146–73). See, for example, François Furet, *Interpreting the French Revolution,* trans. Elborg Forster (Cambridge: Cambridge University Press, 1981); Tony Judt, *Past Imperfect: French Intellectuals 1944–1956* (Berkeley: University of California Press, 1992); Ferenc Fehér, *The Frozen Revolution: An Essay on Jacobinism* (Cambridge, UK: Cambridge University Press, 1987); Mona Ozouf, "La Révolution française et l'idée de l'homme nouveau," in *The Political Culture of the French Revolution,* vol. 2 of *The French Revolution and the Creation of Modern Political Culture,* ed. Colin Lucas (Oxford: Pergamon Press, 1988), 214; and Isser Woloch, "On the Latent Illiberalism of the French Revolution," *American Historical Review* 95 (December 1990): 1452–70. Anne Sa'adah (*Shaping of Liberal Politics*), as well as J. G. Merquior (*Liberalism,* 11) mount a convincing challenge to the totalitarian thesis.

For a survey of the ongoing debate over whether Rousseau specifically may be linked to modern totalitarianism, see Carol Blum, *Rousseau and the Republic of Virtue* (Ithaca, NY: Cornell University Press, 1986), 17. A cogent defense of Rousseau against the charge can be found in Raymond Polin, *La Politique du solitude* (Paris: Sirey, 1970), 135–38. Two more defenses of Rousseau are to be found in J. G. Merquior, *Rousseau and Weber: Two Studies in the Theory of Legitimacy* (London: Routledge, 1980), 35–57, and James Miller, *Rousseau, Dreamer of Democracy* (New Haven: Yale University Press, 1984).

6. Berlin, *Four Essays,* 162.

7. Quoted in Didier Eribon, *Michel Foucault,* trans. Betsy Wing (Cambridge, MA: Harvard University Press, 1991), 131.

8. On Péguy's influence, see Stanley Hoffmann, ed., *In Search of France* (New York: Harper and Row, 1963), 32, 35.

9. See Pierre Bourdieu, *Homo Academicus,* trans. Peter Collier (Stanford: Stanford University Press, 1988), xviii.

10. See Michel Crozier, "The Cultural Revolution: Notes on the Changes in the Intellectual Climate in France," in *A New Europe?* ed. Stephen R. Graubard (Boston: Houghton Mifflin, 1964), 606–7, 611; Victor Brombert, *The Intellectual Hero: Studies in the French Novel, 1880–1995* (New York: J. P. Lippincott, 1960), 33; Hoffmann, *Decline or Renewal?* 127; Jean-François Sirinelli and Pascal Ory, *Les Intellectuels en France de l'affaire Dreyfus à nos jours* (Paris: Armand Colin, 1986), 9; Keith Reader, *Intellectuals and the Left in France since 1968* (London: Macmillan, 1987), 138.

Similar assessments may be found, for example, in Jeremy Jennings, ed., *Intellectuals in Twentieth-Century France* (New York: St. Martin's Press, 1993), 8, 75–76, 192; Theodore Zeldin, *Intellect and Pride,* vol. 2 of *France 1848–1945* (Oxford: Oxford University Press, 1977), 205–9; Herbert R. Lottman, *The Left Bank* (Boston: Houghton Mifflin, 1982), 47; Judt, *Past Imperfect,* 230, 248–53; and Hazareesingh, *Political Traditions,* 36.

11. Bourdieu, *Homo Academicus,* xix, 105, 223. On the French education system in the modern age, see Antoine Prost, *Histoire de l'enseignement en*

France, 1800–1967 (Paris: Armand Colin, 1968); and Fritz K. Ringer, *Education and Society in Modern Europe* (Bloomington, IN: University of Indiana Press, 1979). On the university system and the *grandes écoles,* see Terry N. Clark, *Prophets and Patrons: the French University and the Emergence of the Social Sciences* (Cambridge, MA: Harvard University Press, 1973); George Weisz, *The Emergence of Modern Universities in France, 1863–1914* (Princeton: Princeton University Press, 1983); and Zeldin, *Intellect and Pride,* 316–45.

12. Bourdieu, *Homo Academicus,* xix; Zeldin, *Intellect and Pride,* 209, 107. On the École Normale, see Robert Smith, *The École Normale Supérieure and the Third Republic* (Albany: State University Press of New York, 1982); and Sirinelli and Ory, *Les Intellectuels,* 28–30.

13. Zeldin, *Intellect and Pride,* 341–42; Eribon, *Foucault,* 213; Bourdieu, *Homo Academicus,* ix.

14. Bourdieu, *Homo Academicus,* xviii, xix, 105–6, 109.

15. Bourdieu, *Homo Academicus,* xix. On Michelet, see Roland Barthes, *Michelet,* trans. Richard Howard (New York: Hill and Wang, 1987), 223–26; on Bergson, see R. C. Grogin, *The Bergsonian Controversy in France 1900–1914* (Calgary, Canada: University of Calgary Press, 1988), ix.

16. On Péguy, see H. Stuart Hughes, *Consciousness and Society* (New York: Vintage Books, 1958), 345–54; on Sartre, see John Gerassi, *Protestant or Protestor?* vol. 1 of *Jean-Paul Sartre: Hated Conscience of his Century* (Chicago: University of Chicago Press, 1989), 31.

17. While several contemporary scholars, noting the coinage of the term during the Dreyfus affair, have situated the birth of "the intellectual" in modern France at the turn of the twentieth century (see, for example, Sirinelli and Ory, *Les Intellectuels,* 5–6; and Christophe Charle, *Naissance des "intellectuels" 1880–1900* [Paris: Éditions de Minuit, 1990], 7–8), most have followed Tocqueville in tracing it to the Enlightenment. See Alexis de Tocqueville, *The Old Regime and the French Revolution,* trans. Stuart Gilbert (Garden City, NJ: Doubleday Anchor, 1955), 146–47; and, for example, Jürgen Habermas, *The Structural Transformation of the Public Sphere: An Inquiry into a Category of Bourgeois Society,* trans. Thomas Burger and Frederick Lawrence (Cambridge, MA: Harvard University Press, 1989); Reinhart Koselleck, *Critique and Crisis,* trans. Berg Publishers (Cambridge, MA: Harvard University Press, 1988); Paul Benichou, *Le Sacre de l'écrivain 1750–1830* (Paris: Libraire José Corti, 1973); Priscilla Clark, *Literary France* (Berkeley: University of California Press, 1987); John Lough, *Writer and Public in France* (Oxford: Oxford University Press, 1978); and Robert Darnton, "The Facts of Life in Eighteenth-Century France," in *The Political Culture of the Old Regime,* vol. 1 of *The French Revolution and the Creation of Modern Political Culture,* ed. Keith Michael Baker (Oxford: Pergamon Press, 1987), 261–88.

Already during the preceding century the man of letters had acquired a certain prestige in Parisian high society, but only under the latter's careful tutelage and surveillance. The Académie Française, for example, established by Richelieu in 1635 in order to sponsor literary activity under the auspices of the crown, mirrored both the rising esteem in which the intelligentsia was held during the age of royal absolutism in France and its continued state of dependency. For while now granted his own distinct social rank, the writer in seven-teenth-century France amounted to little more than a pawn in the struggle between a centralizing crown and the traditional aristocracy; he remained liter-ally a *"créature"* of patronage, be it royal or noble. See Claudette Delhez-Sarlet, "L'Académie Française et le Mécénat," in *L'Age d'or du Mécénat (1598–1661)*, ed. Roland Mousnier and Jean Mesnard (Paris: Editions du Centre national de la recherche scientifique, 1985), 241–46. On the "writer" or man of letters in seventeenth-century France and his place in the system of patronage, see Alain Viala, *Naissance de l'écrivain* (Paris: Éditions de Minuit, 1985); Orest Ranum, *Artisans of Glory: Writers and Historical Thought in Seventeenth-Century France* (Chapel Hill: University of North Carolina Press, 1980); and Sharon Kettering, *Patrons, Brokers, and Clients in Seventeenth-Century France* (New York: Oxford University Press, 1986). For a comprehen-sive account of the Republic of Letters in the eighteenth century, see Dena Goodman, *The Republic of Letters: A Cultural History of the French Enlight-enment* (Ithaca, NY: Cornell University Press, 1994).

18. See Keith Michael Baker, *Inventing the French Revolution* (Cambridge, UK: Cambridge University Press, 1990), 114–16, 170. On the idea of "the public" in eighteenth-century France, see also Baker's introduction to *French Revolution*, 1: esp. xvi—xix; and Mona Ozouf's article, "L'Opinion pub-lique," in the same volume (419–34); as well as Habermas, *Structural Transfor-mation*.

19. See Baker, *Inventing the Revolution*, 5; Furet, *Interpreting the Revolu-tion*, 29; and Lynn Hunt, *Politics, Culture, and Class in the French Revolution* (Berkeley: University of California Press, 1984), 12–16.

20. Habermas, *Structural Transformation*, 33; Dénis Diderot, "The Defi-nition of an Encyclopedia," in *The Old Regime and the French Revolution*, vol. 7 of *Readings in Western Civilization*, ed. Keith Michael Baker (Chicago: University of Chicago Press, 1987), 73, 71–72, 83, 81, 82, 77, 75–76. On the consolidation of the eighteenth century's Republic of Letters around the *En-cyclopédie*, see Goodman, *Republic of Letters*, 23–33. On the *Encyclopédie's* social and intellectual agenda, see Herbert Dieckmann, "The Concept of Knowledge in the *Encyclopédie*," in *Essays in Comparative Literature*, ed. Herbert Dieckmann, Harry Levin, and Helmut Motekat (St. Louis: Washing-ton University Studies, 1961), 73–107.

21. Jean d'Alembert, "Essai sur la société des gens de lettres et des grands," in *Oeuvres complètes de d'Alembert*, vol. 4 (Paris: A. Belin, 1822), 342, 359, 354, 360, 362, 372. On d'Alembert's essay and the self-fashioned image of the "heroic philosophe" in eighteenth-century France, see Robert Darnton, *The Great Cat Massacre* (New York: Vintage Books, 1984), 208; as well as Ranum, *Artisans*, 334–36.

22. Koselleck, *Critique*, 113, 116, 114, 119.

23. For Bourdieu's concept of "cultural capital" see his *Distinction*, trans. Richard Nice (Cambridge, MA: Harvard University Press, 1984). This inter-pretation of the Republic of Letters is almost universally held by scholars. It is noteworthy, for example, that in identifying it as a "sphere of criticism of pub-lic authority" (*Structural Transformation*, 51), the Marxist philosopher Jürgen Habermas concurs with the above cited assessment of Reinhart Koselleck, who

scarcely belongs to the same political camp. Literary scholar Priscilla Clark designates the Republic of Letters similarly as an "adversary subculture" (*Literary France*, 59), and historian Tony Judt refers to a "counterestablishment of the mind" (*Past Imperfect*, 250) in prerevolutionary France. Paul Benichou, by the same token, writes that "[t]his intelligentsia born of the bourgeoisie" first dethroned society's traditional "spiritual powers" and then became its "new clergy"; hence, the Enlightenment men of letters, he asserts, offered themselves as "both the judges of society and its support" (*L'Écrivain*, 20).

24. Dena Goodman notes that d'Alembert's previously cited "Essai sur la société des gens de lettres et des grands" represented not only a manifesto on behalf of the Republic of Letters but a defense of civilized "sociability" against Rousseau's assault on it in his first discourse. She also argues compellingly that by virtue of attacking the Republic's discourse of sociability, Rousseau was championing the ostensibly masculine virtue of independence against the corrupt, "'civilizing force'" of women (*Republic of Letters*, 35–36, 54–55)— a thesis which will be addressed here more fully in the concluding chapter.

25. Darnton, "Facts of Life," 278; Jean-Jacques Rousseau, *Discours sur les sciences et les arts/Lettre à d'Alembert sur les spectacles* (Paris: Garnier-Flammarion, 1987), 143, 296, 213.

26. As quoted in Darnton, *Cat Massacre*, 229–30; Koselleck, *Critique*, 159.

27. Rousseau's peculiar double stature as "the great critic of the Enlightenment"—or "antiphilosophe" as Sara Maza has put it—and "a central figure (perhaps *the* central figure)" of same is discussed in a recent forum on the public sphere within eighteenth-century France. See Daniel Gordon, David Bell, and Sarah Maza, "The Public Sphere in the Eighteenth Century: A Forum," *French Historical Studies* 17 (1992): 882–956 (especially 900, 945). See also Goodman, *Republic of Letters*, 35–39; and Mark Helliung, *The Autocritique of the Enlightenment: Rousseau and the Philosophes* (Cambridge, MA: Harvard University Press, 1994).

28. Goodman, *Republic of Letters*, 4, 226.

29. On the "Voltaire versus Rousseau" issue, which he identifies as "one of the deepest ones in our culture," see P. N. Furbank, "On Not Knowing Thyself: The Unresolved Conflict between Voltaire and Rousseau," *Times Literary Supplement* (London), 7 October 1994.

30. See Voltaire, *Letters on England*, trans. Leonard Tancock (New York: Penguin Books, 1981).

31. See Goodman, *Republic of Letters*, 97–99, 226. See also Peter Gay, *Voltaire's Politics: The Poet as Realist* (Princeton: Princeton University Press, 1959).

32. Goodman, *Republic of Letters*, 39.

33. Echoing Bourdieu's categories, Shlomo Sand makes a distinction between Rousseau the "marginalized writer," and Voltaire the philosophe-as-"courtier" and representative of "the worldly intellectualism of the capital." See Shlomo Sand, "Mirror Mirror on the Wall, Who is the True Intellectual of them all? Self-Images of the Intellectual in France," in Jennings, *Intellectuals in France*, 35, 37. Dennis Porter, by the same token, distinguishes sharply between the legacy of Rousseau in modern France, which he identifies with the archetype of the politically "engaged" public "writer," and that of Voltaire,

whom he classifies as a man more of literature than politics (see Dennis Porter, *Rousseau's Legacy* (New York: Oxford University Press, 1995), 8, 64–65.

34. On the symbolic opposition of Bergson and Durkheim, see, for example, Grogin, *Bergsonian Controversy*, 113–15; and Stuart Hughes, *Consciousness*, 57–58. On Péguy and Jaurès see, for example, Basil Guy, "Notes on Péguy the Socialist," *French Studies* 15 (1961): 12–29. On Sartre's breaks with the likes of Aron and Camus, see, for example, Gerassi, *Protestant or Protestor?*, 167.

35. David Jordan, *The Revolutionary Career of Maximilien Robespierre* (Chicago: University of Chicago Press, 1985), 4–5, 33–35; Furet, *Interpreting the Revolution*, 59, 61. On the evolution of the Enlightenment's salons into revolutionary clubs—and above all the Jacobin Club—see Goodman, *Republic of Letters*, 233–34, 288–300.

36. Stendhal, *Vie de Henri Brulard* (Paris: Garnier frères, 1961), 89, 162, 291, 391. On Stendhal's relative obscurity during his own lifetime as well as his ultimate repudiation of political commitment, see Porter, *Rousseau's Legacy*, 71–105. See also Gita May, *Stendhal and the Age of Napoleon* (New York: Columbia University Press, 1977), 2, 234.

37. Michel Crouzet, *Nature et société chez Stendhal* (Lille: Presses Universitaires de Lille, 1985), 31, 27–28; Marjorie Taylor, *The Arriviste* (Wales, UK: Dragon Books, 1972), 60. Taylor goes so far as to list the parallels between the Rousseau of *Les Confessions* and Stendhal's protagonist (49–64). For similar assessments of Rousseau's influence on Stendhal, and especially *Le Rouge et le noir*, see also Victor Brombert, *Stendhal: Fiction and the Themes of Freedom* (New York: Random House, 1968), 11–12, 63; Porter, *Rousseau's Legacy*, 80–81; and May, *Stendhal*, 11, 219–20.

38. Nancy Rosenblum, *Another Liberalism* (Cambridge, MA: Harvard University Press, 1987), 19. Among the scholars who note the remarkable cultural salience of Stendhal's protagonist within modern France and beyond are, again, Taylor, *Arriviste*, 16, 14; Fritz K. Ringer, *Fields of Knowledge* (Cambridge, UK: Cambridge University Press, 1992), 83; Victor Brombert, *Intellectual Hero*, 14; Raymond Giraud, *The Unheroic Hero in the Novels of Stendhal, Balzac and Flaubert* (New Brunswick, NJ: Rutgers University Press, 1957), 80–83; and Priscilla Clark, *The Battle of the Bourgeois* (Paris: Didier, 1973), 155–56.

39. These eight figures are meant, of course, to represent the category of consecrated heretic in modern France, not exhaust it. Alongside Foucault, Bourdieu himself lists such "postmodern" intellectuals as Louis Althusser, Jacques Derrida, and Gilles Deleuze (*Homo Academicus*, xvii); and a more historically encompassing inventory might include the likes of Louis Antoine de Saint Just, Victor Hugo, Pierre-Joseph Proudhon, Émile Zola, Alain [Émile Chartier], Georges Sorel, and André Gide, to name several of the most obvious candidates.

40. See Michel Foucault, *Power/Knowledge: Selected Interviews and Other Writings, 1972–1977*, ed. Colin Gordon, trans. Colin Gordon et al. (New York: Pantheon Books, 1980), 93, 97–102. Underlying these questions is the methodological assumption that "discourse," or the given historical categories of language, powerfully shapes social and political reality by virtue of its monopoly on what Hayden White has called "meaning-production." Such an ap-

proach, White argues, permits historians "to regard ideology as a process . . . in which certain sign systems are privileged as necessary, even natural ways of recognizing a 'meaning' in things and others are suppressed, ignored, or hidden in the very process of presenting a world to consciousness." Recent historical accounts of the French Revolution's "political culture" clearly manifest this recent "linguistic turn" in intellectual history, as it has been dubbed. Hence, Keith Baker, for example, has sought to reconstruct that "set of discourses or symbolic practices" whereby individuals or groups in prerevolutionary France made political claims. Indeed denying that "there are social realities independent of symbolic meanings" and defining intellectual history as the history of such meanings, he concludes that "political authority is, in this view, linguistic authority." Lynn Hunt, by the same token, has endeavored to chart the political culture of the Revolution itself by focusing upon its repeated "key words and principles," that is, upon "the general principles of revolutionary language" as well as the "operation of revolutionary symbols" and rituals. See Hayden White, "Method and Ideology in Intellectual History: The Case of Henry Adams," in *Modern European Intellectual History: Reappraisals and New Perspectives,* ed. Dominick LaCapra and Stephen L. Kaplan (Ithaca: Cornell University Press, 1982), 307; John E. Toews, "Intellectual History after the Linguistic Turn: The Autonomy of Meaning and the Irreducibility of Experience," *American Historical Review* 92 (1987): 879–907; Baker, *Inventing the Revolution,* 4, 13, 5; and Hunt, *Politics,* 10–11, 14–15.

41. Several proponents of "the linguistic turn" have borrowed not only from poststructuralism but from anthropological, linguistic, and literary theories of narrative. Hence, White, for example, has in recent years powerfully underscored the "fictive character" of all cultural discourse. Indeed, for White, ostensibly non-fictional narratives, such as scientific treatises, autobiographies, and works of history as well, contain "a deep structural content which is generally poetic," a "pre-critically accepted paradigm" that might be grasped by a reader "as part of his cultural endowment." Thus, in order to reveal the cultural "mythos" underlying *The Origin of Species,* for example, or *The Education of Henry Adams,* White counsels the methodologically self-conscious historian to analyze the "emplotment" of these texts as if they were fictional allegories, and to map out those preconscious linguistic paradigms—the repeated motifs, narrative strategies, and tropes—that structure the narrative and lend it meaning. Employing the well known schema of literary theorist Northrop Frye, White himself has classified the nineteenth-century histories of Tocqueville and Michelet according to the "generic plots" of romance, tragedy, comedy, and satire, which would seem to frame them. Lynn Hunt as well, in seeking to reconstruct the means through which the French revolutionaries appropriated political authority, has regularly invoked narrative theory. Like White, she employs Frye's "generic plots" in order to reveal "the narrative structures" that "informed revolutionary rhetoric" and thereby helped shape the Revolution itself; and citing the anthropological model of Clifford Geertz, she seeks to identify the "cultural frame" or "master fiction" within which the revolutionary radicals defined themselves and made their claims. See Hayden White, *Metahistory* (Baltimore: Johns Hopkins University Press, 1973), ix, 1–2, 7–8, and *Tropics of Discourse* (Baltimore: Johns Hopkins University

Press, 1978), 84–86, 133; Hunt, *Politics,* 34–37, 87. For a similar method-ological perspective, see Lionel Gossman, *Between History and Literature* (Cambridge, MA: Harvard University Press, 1990). For a critical account of the interaction in recent years between intellectual history and literary theory see David Harlan, "Intellectual History and the Return of Literature," *American Historical Review* 94 (1989): 581–609.

42. Michelet's unpublished autobiographical works have been collected and edited: see Jules Michelet, *Écrits de jeunesse,* ed. Paul Viallaneix (Paris: Galli-mard, 1959).

43. My "marginalization" of Foucault's late works, especially the last two volumes of his *History of Sexuality* (both published in 1984), might appear somewhat arbitrary or problematic to some readers. Yet Foucault's reading public, as Mark Poster suggests, proved more often than not "disappointed" by these latter works, which lacked "the powerful problematic" and the "mag-nificent writing" of *Surveiller et punir* and *La Volonté de savoir.* See Mark Poster, *Critical Theory and Poststructuralism* (Ithaca: Cornell University Press, 1989), 88–89.

44. Again, the previously cited linguistic and narrative "turns" obviously challenge the methods and assumptions of intellectual history as it has tradi-tionally been practiced. Rather than tracing, for example, the evolution of "unit ideas" in history, such as "reason" or "progress," over the course of time, practitioners of the "linguistic turn" tend to seek within a clearly delineated historical community a common discursive "archive" that comprises its "intel-lectual stock." By the same token, they eschew the conventional focus of in-tellectual history upon "unitary authors"—upon the intentions, influences, in-tellectual evolution, and "psychobiographical" lives of individual thinkers— as well as that "social history of ideas" which seeks to place given individuals and texts into their "historical contexts." For such approaches, they argue, require the historian to embrace assumptions and models that are foreign to the works actually under analysis: the presumed identity between lives and texts, for instance, or the unproblematic existence of so-called "contexts," con-ceived as "nondiscursive" realms of concrete historical "fact." Proponents of the "linguistic turn," on the other hand, claim to ground historical interpreta-tion solely upon the categories and meanings imbedded within its designated texts, and they openly acknowledge the constitutive character of such interpre-tation. See, for example, Baker, *Inventing the Revolution,* 15, 5. For a sum-mary of the linguistic critique of traditional intellectual history, see Dominick LaCapra, "Rethinking Intellectual History and Reading Texts," in *Modern Eu-ropean Intellectual History,* ed. LaCapra and Kaplan, 47–85 (Ithaca, New York: Cornell University Press, 1982). For an intelligent recent example of the traditional approach, see Jack Hayward's *After the French Revolution* (New York: New York University Press, 1991), which places intellectual biographies of six "representative" thinkers within their respective historical contexts in nineteenth-century France.

My own position in this methodological debate is firmly agnostic—or rather, I propose to take the best from both worlds. By extending Bourdieu's sociology of the contemporary "academic field" to demarcate a heretical "ar-chive," or "community of discourse," within the centralized political and intellectual institutions of modern France, I seek to ground my argument if not in a specific historical "context" or series of "contexts," certainly in an historically identifiable—and culturally stable—*"longue durée."* Whether or not the linguistic approach, and most particularly its narrative variant, is intrinsically superior to more traditional historical methods, it would seem especially well suited to the study of cultural paradigms, mythologies, or "communities of discourse"; to the reconstruction, that is, of the shared suppositions, motifs, and stories through which social meanings are constituted within a particular historical community over time. For in attempting to retrieve the common narrative structure underlying a given historical community, such an approach must deliberately privilege the repeated linguistic patterns and archetypal plot structures shared within its designated texts over the intentions, peculiarities, inner contradictions, or personal lives of their authors; indeed, it must do so regardless of whether or not the latter information is directly knowable. Finally, insofar as it focuses explicitly on what remains relatively constant within a historical community over time, the narrative approach must treat its texts as an aggregate rather than attempting to reconstruct the specific "historical context" of each or the historical evolution of all.

CHAPTER II

1. Joseph Campbell, *The Hero with a Thousand Faces* (Princeton: Princeton University Press, 1968), 30.

2. Annie Cohen-Solal, *Sartre: A Life,* ed. Norman Macafee, trans. Anna Cancogni (New York: Pantheon Books, 1987), 506; Ronald Hayman, *Writing Against: A Biography of Sartre* (London: Weidenfeld and Nicolson, 1986), 446; James Miller, *The Passion of Michel Foucault* (New York: Simon and Schuster, 1993), 13, 16.

3. Hayman, *Writing Against,* 439.

4. Clark, *Literary France,* 158, 196, 208; Daniel Mornet, *Les Origines intellectuelles de la révolution française* (Paris: Armand Colin, 1933), 227; Miller, *Passion,* 13; see also Eribon, *Foucault,* 3-4.

5. Philippe Lejeune, *L'Autobiographie en France* (Paris: Armand Colin, 1971), 10, 32, 84, 85, 19, 21.

6. David Jordan, *Revolutionary Career,* 7, 12, 33. The influence of *Les Confessions* over the revolutionary generation is well documented. The Prince de Ligne, for example, a cosmopolitan noble of the late eighteenth century, wrote his *Fragments de l'histoire de ma vie* in conscious imitation of *Les Confessions,* and Saint-Just, construing Rousseau's work as a political fable, viewed its author as "the archetypal 'revolutionary man.'" See Basil Guy, "Rousseau Improv'd: The Prince de Ligne's *Fragments de l'histoire de ma vie,*" *Romanic Review* 71 (1980): 281-94; and Miller, *Dreamer,* 136-37.

7. Stendhal, *Henri Brulard,* 218, 275-76; Crouzet, *Stendhal,* 27, 52, 71, 94-95.

8. See Michelet, *Écrits,* 182; Charles Péguy, *Souvenirs,* ed. Pierre Péguy (Paris: Gallimard, 1938), 26, 29, 43-45, 73. On Sartre's *Les Mots* and the poststructuralist critique of autobiography see Lejeune, *L'Autobiographie,* 75, 100. Foucault's confessional remarks are quoted in Miller (*Passion,* 31), who notes that the first comment was "slipped" into an interview with Didier Eri-

bon in 1981. Eribon cites it as well in his own biography of Foucault, which he justifies on the grounds that the philosopher routinely employed "prefaces, articles, and interviews" as a means of playing "the commentary game" on his own life and work. See Eribon, *Foucault,* 29, ix.

9. See Grogin, *Bergsonian Controversy,* 125–26; Eribon, *Foucault,* x, 110. Gerassi, *Protestant or Protestor?* 27, 7. Gerassi, in fact, seeks explicitly to salvage Sartre's "genuine audacity" from the overly conventional portrait of Annie Cohen-Solal, which he denigrates as an attempt to domesticate the radical for "mainstream" bourgeois consumption (27, 29).

10. Stendhal, *Le Rouge et le noir* (Paris: Garnier-Flammarion, 1964), 46, 49. 183, 476, 42, 437. On the topics of Julien's struggle to maintain his independence and innate nobility, see Brombert, *Themes of Freedom,* 69, 71–76, 87, 98–99.

11. Stendhal, *Le Rouge et le noir,* 49, 162.

12. Ibid., 285, 291, 298, 319, 326.

13. Ibid., 195, 309, 302, 305, 246, 331.

14. Ibid., 446, 465, 466.

15. Ibid., 476.

16. The conclusion of *Le Rouge et le noir* has long been a subject of academic controversy. More than a few literary scholars have maintained that Julien's sudden decision to sacrifice himself and defy the established order is entirely out of character, that it represents a "radical psychological shift"—see, for example, Sandy Petrey, *Realism and Revolution* (Ithaca: Cornell University Press, 1988), 123—entirely unwarranted by Julien's previous character, which betrays above all an unwavering zeal for personal success. Regardless of whether this is so—and I have argued in this chapter that it is not—the fundamental structure of Stendhal's tale remains unchanged. Indeed, Julien's mythic stature within French culture would hardly be imaginable without his ultimate revolt against the powers that be on behalf of "the people."

17. Dennis Porter's definition of the Rousseauian "writer" surely overlaps that of the legend of the consecrated heretic as I have outlined it: "The idea of the 'writer' transmitted by Rousseau to subsequent generations . . . is of someone who puts his or her private self on display for the purpose of personal witness, self-affirmation, and sociopolitical emancipation, and whose writings address themselves to humanity at large." Thus the "writer," Porter goes on to summarize, is distinguished through "his radical political theory, his suspicious attitude toward art and literature, the disclosures from his private life, and the stance he adopts toward his public and toward the sociopolitical world in need of moral renewal" (*Rousseau's Legacy,* 12, 68).

Nor is Porter the first scholar to note the archetypal character of the "writer" or "consecrated heretic" within modern French culture, or to associate it with Rousseau. Stanley Hoffmann, for one, commenting on the intellectual tradition in modern France as a whole, cites the striking "similarities between Rousseau and Sartre." Both, he writes, "were in revolt against the social order of their time," indeed against their respective "established disorders"; both "grounded their political philosophy in psychology"; and both believed man "free only when he was either by himself or in . . . communities whose members are fused by voluntary striving toward a single common goal" (*De-*

cline or Renewal? 127). Victor Brombert, likewise, in tracing the modern "figure of the intellectual" in French fiction from "Rousseau's Saint Preux, Stendhal's Julien Sorel, [and] the ambitious young men of Balzac" to the protagonists of such twentieth-century *normaliens* as Péguy, Jules Romains, and Sartre, ultimately lists the following among his traits: "the utilization of culture as an instrument for criticizing tradition; the unselfish gratuitous pursuit of truth, but simultaneously the pursuit of a humanitarian ideal; the transmission or preaching of moral values; the sensation, now proud, now humiliating, of existing outside the social framework, and yet, on the whole, an obvious sympathy for the laboring groups of the country and a consequent attraction to Leftist political parties; a feeling of 'not belonging' and impotence; jealousy of men of action; the cult of revolt, sometimes even of anarchy" (*Intellectual Hero,* 13, 14, 34).

18. A reading of his autobiographical *Henri Brulard* would suggest that many of the heroic portents that Stendhal projected onto Julien Sorel mirror both the Rousseauian narrative and his view of himself. By his own account, Stendhal detested his father, felt isolated as a child, came by his anticlericalism at the age of four, demonstrated an early misanthropic streak, and possessed an inconvenient "nobility of soul." Moreover, while the son of an *haute-bourgeois* family with pretensions to nobility, he frequently vents his contempt for the bourgeoisie. See *Henri Brulard,* 15–16, 38, 42, 114–15.

19. Jean-Jacques Rousseau, *Les Confessions* (Paris: Garnier, 1964), 164, 606, 186, 481.

20. Ibid., 10, 42, 67.

21. Ibid., 4, 7, 304, 760, 44, 94, 9.

22. See Pierre Trahard, *Les Maîtres de la sensibilité française au XVIIIe siècle (1715–1789),* vol. 1 (Paris: Boivin, 1931), 107–8.

23. Both David Jordan and Norman Hampson note that Robespierre's biographers have typically either demonized him as a tyrant or lionized him as a revolutionary hero; indeed, both biographers, in expressing their frustration at finding the man beneath the myth, describe the myth quite clearly (Jordan, *Revolutionary Career,* 16–22; and Norman Hampson, *The Life and Opinions of Maximilien Robespierre* (London: Duckworth, 1974), 1–9. For an excellent account of how Robespierre's historical portrait has evolved since the Revolution, see George Rudé, *Robespierre, Portrait of a Revolutionary Democrat* (New York: Viking Press, 1975), 57–95. Another useful evocation of Robespierre's public mythology may be found in Ann Rigney, "Icon and Symbol: The Historical Figure Called Maximilien Robespierre," in *Representing the French Revolution,* ed. James Heffernan (Hanover: Dartmouth University Press, 1992): 106–22.

24. Hampson, *Robespierre,* 5; Jordan, *Revolutionary Career,* 24–27. See also Rudé, *Revolutionary Democrat,* 15–18.

25. See Guy, "Péguy the Socialist," 25–26.

26. Péguy, *Souvenirs,* 27, 95, 96–97, 13, 17–18; Jérome and Jean Tharaud, *Notre Péguy,* 20, 145–54; Halévy, *Péguy,* 4, 45–47; Stuart Hughes, *Consciousness,* 348.

27. See Jacques Chevalier, *Henri Bergson,* trans. Lilian A. Clare (New York: Macmillan, 1928), 42–47; Stuart Hughes, *Consciousness,* 58.

28. Jules Michelet, *Le Peuple* (Paris: Flammarion, 1974), 13, 24, 21.

29. Sartre, *Les Mots*, 196, 94, 19, 32–33, 168, 150, 122; Gerassi, *Protestant or Protestor?* 59, 76–77; Hayman, *Writing Against*, 35–36, 58; Cohen-Solal, *Sartre*, 44, 61–62.

30. Michel Foucault, *Politics, Philosophy, Culture: Interviews and other Writings, 1977–1984*, ed. Lawrence D. Kritsman, trans. Alan Sheridan (New York: Routledge, Chapman, and Hall, 1988), 4; Miller, *Passion*, 39–40, 45; Eribon, *Foucault*, 5, 25–26.

31. Hayman, *Writing Against*, 17.

32. Michelet, *Écrits*, 183; Sartre, *Les Mots*, 11, 91; Eribon, *Foucault*, 11; Miller, *Passion*, 63, 365–66.

33. Rousseau, *Discours sur l'origine et les fondements de l'inégalité parmi les hommes/Discours sur les sciences et les arts* (Paris: Garnier-Flammarion, 1971), 181, and *Les Confessions*, 178, 332, 197, 111, 387.

34. Ibid., 38.

35. Ibid., 40, 94, 428, 422.

36. Ibid., 425, 41, 434, 429.

37. Maximilien Robespierre, *Oeuvres de Maximilien Robespierre*, 10 vols. (Paris: Société des Études Robespierre, 1950–1967), 7: 163. Jordan, *Revolutionary Career*, 40.

38. Ibid., 59. Norman Hampson also dates Robespierre's public celebrity from the spring of 1791 (*Robespierre*, 72) as does Alfred Cobban in *Aspects of the French Revolution* (New York: George Braziller, 1968), 145. George Rudé notes that even Michelet—for whom Robespierre, as shall be seen, constitutes anything but a revolutionary hero—portrays the Jacobin leader as "a solemn, solitary, brooding figure, devoted to the cause of justice" (*Revolutionary Democrat*, 67).

39. Charles Péguy, *Oeuvres en prose complètes* (Paris: Gallimard, 1992), 3: 524–25. On Péguy's rise to celebrity, see, for example, Halévy, *Péguy*, 45–86, 138–51; and Stuart Hughes, *Consciousness*, 347–52.

40. Sartre, *Les Mots*, 166–67, 156; Cohen-Solal, *Sartre*, 222, 248; see also Hayman, *Writing Against*, 113, 182–83.

41. See above, p. 9.

42. Eribon, *Foucault*, 212–13.

43. Kippur, *Michelet*, 116–17, 92, 121; Barthes, *Michelet*, 5.

44. Stuart Hughes, *Consciousness*, 114–15, 122; Grogin, *Bergsonian Controversy*, 113, 120, 123–24; Raissa Maritain, *Les Grands Amitiés* (Paris: Desclée de Brouwer, 1958), 171. Grogin's book addresses Bergson's wide-ranging influence in politics, the arts, and religion at length.

45. Eribon, *Foucault*, 238, 212–13, 210, 222; Miller, *Passion*, 148–49, 178–79, 285.

46. Eribon, *Foucault*, 135–36, 201.

47. Rousseau, *Les Confessions*, 335; Jordan, *Revolutionary Career*, 57 (see also, Hampson, *Robespierre*, 86–87); Michelet, *Écrits*, 183, and quoted in Kippur, *Michelet*, 10; Barthes, *Michelet*, 7; Halévy, *Péguy*, 2; Péguy, *Souvenirs*, 13, 17–18; Sartre, *Les Mots*, 19, 32–32, 168; Eribon, *Foucault*, 14, 11 (see also Miller, *Passion*, 39). Péguy's lifelong dependency on women—and retreat from the influence of men—is noted by Basil Guy in "Péguy the Socialist," 26.

Sartre's dependency on Simone de Beauvoir as well as numerous other women is outlined in varying degrees of detail by all three of his biographers. See, for example, Hayman, *Writing Against*, 70–80.

48. Rousseau, *Les Confessions*, 461.

49. Ibid., 494–95.

50. Ibid., 652.

51. Ibid., 428–29, 516, 613, 477, 257.

52. Ibid., 324, 580.

53. Jordan, *Revolutionary Career*, 146, 150, 169.

54. Robespierre, *Oeuvres*, 10: 274, 277, 354, 356.

55. Péguy, *Oeuvres complètes*, 3: 1306, and *Souvenirs*, 74–75; Halévy, *Péguy*, 223; Tharaud and Tharaud, *Notre Péguy*, 210–11. Rolland is quoted by Basil Guy, who offers the following summary of Péguy the "[h]eretic and apostate and renegade": "by refusing to temporize, by refusing to tarnish a 'mystique' in the name of political expediency, [Péguy] is at last alone, surrounded from a distance by a curious mixture of exasperation and respect" ("Péguy the Socialist," 27, 25).

56. Gerassi, *Protestant or Protestor?* 31; Cohen-Solal, *Sartre*, 276, 414, 449. It should be noted that Sartre's aversion to political parties was not as complete as his public legend suggests. In the late 1940s, the philosopher sought himself to found a party, the Rassemblement Démocratique Révolutionnaire; he rather quickly abandoned the effort, however. See Hayman, *Writing Against*, 248, 258.

57. See above, p. 16.

58. For recent indictments of Sartre's "Stalinism," see Judt, *Past Imperfect;* and John Weightman, "Fatal Attraction," *The New York Review of Books*, 11 February 1993.

59. Cohen-Solal, *Sartre*, 314; Gerassi, *Protestant or Protestor?* 186.

60. Hayman, *Writing Against*, 372; Jean-Paul Sartre, *Situations* (Paris: Gallimard, 1948), 2: 7, and *Plaidoyer pour les intellectuels* (Paris: Gallimard, 1972), 12, 77, 66, 73, 82; Cohen-Solal, *Sartre*, 415, 426.

61. Foucault, *Politics*, 124; Eribon, *Foucault*, 161, 281; Michel Foucault, *The Foucault Reader*, ed. Paul Rabinow (New York: Pantheon, 1984), 383–84; Miller, *Passion*, 227. Miller even more so than Eribon, argues that the young Foucault found "Sartre's challenge . . . irresistible" and sought above all to equal and surpass him as a public intellectual (Ibid., 45, 179).

62. Ibid., 89, 200, 204, 206, 313; Eribon, *Foucault*, 242–49.

63. Foucault, *Politics*, 265, 107, 155, and Michel Foucault, *Language, Counter-Memory, Practice*, ed. Donald F. Bouchard, trans. Donald F. Bouchard and Sherry Simon (Ithaca: Cornell University Press, 1977), 208, 214; Miller, *Passion*, 189.

64. Kippur, *Michelet*, 124, 133–34, 139; Orr, *Michelet*, xiii; Grogin, *Bergsonian Controversy*, 190–91. In confining the "Bergsonian controversy" to the era of the philosopher's lectures at the Collège de France (1900–14) Grogin also—perhaps unintentionally—reconfirms those as the years of his subject's public legend, noting that thereafter "his career was no longer as controversial as it once was" (ix).

65. Jean Starobinski has convincingly argued this point in his *Jean-Jacques*

Rousseau: Transparency and Obstruction, trans. Arthur Goldhammer (Chicago: University of Chicago Press, 1988).

66. Rousseau, *Les Confessions,* 64, 198, 322. Dennis Porter notes as well that Rousseau employed confession, "public self-abasement," and even "martyrdom" as "a sign of 'the writer's' self-testing and integrity" (*Rousseau's Legacy,* 56).

67. Jordan, *Revolutionary Career,* 41; Robespierre, *Oeuvres,* 10: 545–46, 556, 566.

68. Jordan, *Revolutionary Career,* 33, 9, 212; Robespierre, *Oeuvres,* 10: 543, 546, 565–66.

69. Barthes, *Michelet,* 19; Michelet, *Le Peuple,* 3, 26, and *Écrits,* 182.

70. Grogin, *Bergsonian Controversy,* 143. Stuart Hughes asserts as well, again citing Jacques Chevalier as his source, that "it was only a sense of solidarity with the sufferings of his Jewish co-religionists under Nazi rule that held him back from formally adhering to Catholicism" (*Consciousness,* 119–20).

71. Halévy, *Péguy,* 282, 292; Tharaud and Tharaud, *Notre Péguy,* 249; Stuart Hughes, *Consciousness,* 354.

72. Péguy, *Souvenirs,* 74–75, 6, 11, 29, 43, 96, 102.

73. Sartre, *Les Mots,* 158, 135, 139, 144–45, 147, 210, 136.

74. Dennis Porter notes similarly that such "enduring concepts" in Sartre as "'transparency' and 'authenticity'" betoken the latter's "continuity with the Rousseauist tradition." Indeed, Porter finds in Sartre's last interview with Michel Contat, entitled "Self-Portrait at Seventy," "a more utopian conception of the lost transparency of human communication" than one may discover "even in Rousseau" (*Rousseau's Legacy,* 148, 151).

75. Sartre, *Les Mots,* 67, 127, 212, 207–8, 210–11.

76. Michel Foucault, *La Volonté de savoir,* vol. 1 of *Histoire de la sexualité* (Paris: Gallimard, 1975). Eribon quotes this famous passage from the preface of Foucault's *Archeology of Knowledge* in *Foucault,* 186, and Miller cites it several times in *Passion,* 123, 163.

77. Eribon, *Foucault,* 327, 329; Miller, *Passion,* 362–63.

78. Ibid., 372; Foucault, *Politics,* 156, 16.

79. Ibid., 321, 330, 263; Miller, *Passion,* 163, 295 (see also Eribon, *Foucault,* 277). Miller, who discusses the "masked philosopher" interview in his text, muses at one point that "[t]he man who 'wrote in order to have no face' succeeded most spectacularly" at the task of "becoming a world-famous intellectual in the process" (*Passion,* 320, 163).

80. In this light, it is worth citing—with Dennis Porter—Rousseau's defense of Molière's famous "misanthrope," Alceste, against the play's author: "What is Molière's misanthrope then? A good man who hates the morals of his time and the wickedness of his contemporaries; who precisely because he loves his fellow men hates in them the evils they do to each other and the vices these evils cause." See Porter, *Rousseau's Legacy,* 39.

CHAPTER III

1. Rousseau, *Les Confessions,* 422.

2. In fact, the centrality of this theme in modern French discourse has long

been noted. See, for example, Michel Crozier, *The Bureaucratic Phenomenon,* trans. Michel Crozier (Chicago: University of Chicago Press, 1964), 220–24; Merquior, *Liberalism,* 9–14; Hoffmann, *Decline or Renewal?* 122–24, 146; and Nicolet, *L'Idée républicaine,* 468–69, 500–506. A more complete discussion especially of Crozier's model of "face-to-face" dependency relationships and their avoidance in modern France will be taken up in chapter 6.

3. Stendhal, *Le Rouge et le noir,* 36, 500, 142, 465, 476.

4. See above, p. 26.

5. Stendhal, *Le Rouge et le noir,* 294–95.

6. Ibid., 91–92, 97.

7. Ibid., 197, 107, 100, 95.

8. Ibid., 273, 319, 440.

9. Ibid., 469, 481.

10. The pivotal role of personal dependency and its avoidance in Rousseau's oeuvre has often been noted by scholars. See, for example, Polin, *La Politique,* 7–10; Blum, *Rousseau and the Republic,* 93, 117, 123; and Miller, *Dreamer,* 180–86. My own interpretation of the role of personal dependency in Rousseau is indelibly marked by Professor Keith Baker of Stanford University and, above all, Professor Paul Lucas of Clark University. Indeed, my Rousseau is more Lucas's than my own.

11. See above, p. 13.

12. Rousseau, *Discours,* 35, 38, 49, 51, 58, 59.

13. On Rousseau and the myth of origins see Starobinski, *Transparency and Obstruction;* and Jacques Derrida, *Of Grammatology,* trans. Gayatri Chakravorty Spivak (Baltimore: Johns Hopkins University Press, 1974).

14. Rousseau, *Discours,* 158, 225, 171.

15. My use of the masculine pronoun here and throughout conforms to the usage of the subject in question; ibid., 195, 201–2, 196.

16. Ibid., 203, 196 n, 202.

17. Ibid., 213, 196 n, 234.

18. Dennis Porter notes as well that Rousseau, in remarking that the "savage" lives "in himself" while the "social man . . . can live only in the opinion of others," anticipates "Sartre's famous affirmation that 'Hell is other people!'" (see *Rousseau's Legacy,* 58).

19. Jean-Jacques Rousseau, *Émile, ou de l'éducation* (Paris: Garnier-Flammarion, 1966), 39, 148, 99.

20. Ibid., 40, 110, 275, 276.

21. Ibid., 277, 111, 126, 106.

22. Ibid., 100, 110, 101, 207, 75–76.

23. Ibid., 418, 439, 440, 442, 444, 206.

24. Ibid., 583, 618–19.

25. Ibid., 620.

26. Jean-Jacques Rousseau, *Du Contrat social* (Paris: Garnier-Flammarion, 1966), 39, 41, 42, 88, 46.

27. Ibid., 51.

28. Ibid., 52, 51, 54–55.

29. See above, note 22.

30. For the standard critique of Rousseau-as-totalitarian, see chapter 1, note 5. My own view of Rousseau's "general will" is, again, indebted to both Keith Baker and Paul Lucas.

31. Rousseau, *Contrat social*, 69, 64, 74–75, 68, 178, 180.

32. Ibid., 66, 149, 135, 54, 69.

33. Ibid., 55–56.

34. Ibid., 67, 66, 76, 139–40, 127.

35. Ibid., 79.

36. The avoidance of personal dependence for Rousseau—and indeed, for the consecrated heretics more generally—by no means implies a retreat from political engagement. On the contrary, as pointed out by such scholars as Judith Shklar and Lucio Colletti, Rousseau maintains that a perpetually active citizenship is the only means of establishing and maintaining true individual autonomy in society. See Judith Shklar, *Men and Citizens* (Cambridge, UK: Cambridge University Press, 1969), 18, 34–35, 58–60, 75–76, 160–62; and Lucio Colletti, *From Rousseau to Lenin*, trans. John Merrington and Judith White (New York: Monthly Review Press, 1972), 148, 174, 184–85.

37. Jordan, *Revolutionary Career*, 151; Lucien Jaume, *Le Discours jacobin et la démocratie* (Paris: Fayard, 1989), 193, 198. While Joan McDonald argues (*Rousseau and the French Revolution* [London: Athlone Press, 1965]) that the direct influence of *Du Contrat social* over the revolutionaries was negligible, Miller (*Dreamer*, 142–64) and Blum (*Rousseau and the Republic*, 33–35, 139–50) have made a strong case for the powerful symbolic hold of the Rousseauian narrative as a whole over the revolutionary generation.

38. Robespierre, *Oeuvres*, 7: 162, 164; 8: 465, 467.

39. Ibid., 7: 620–21, 622; 9: 113, 116.

40. Ibid., 6: 625; 10: 352, 355, 356.

41. Ibid., 10: 353, 482.

42. Ibid., 8: 59; 9: 116; 10: 355.

43. Ibid., 9: 488; 10: 572, 278, 274, 357.

44. See René Rémond, *L'Anticléricalisme en France* (Paris: Fayard, 1976), 68–70.

45. Michelet, *Du Prêtre, de la femme, et de la famille* (Paris: Hachette, 1845), 255, 285, 294, 234; *Le Peuple*, 85, 147, 166, 169.

46. Ibid., 142, 102, 104–5, 121, 123, 129, 141, 138.

47. Ibid., 129; *Du Prêtre*, 236, 196, 197, 203, 234, 237, 240, 247.

48. Ibid., 266, 200, 262, 210, 205.

49. Ibid., vi, 260, 295.

50. Michelet, *Le Peuple*, 193, 187, 244, 241, 245, 203, 87–88.

51. Michelet, *Du Prêtre*, 287.

52. See above, p. 43.

53. See chapter 2, note 47.

54. Michelet, *Du Prêtre*, 285, 287, 294, 290–91, 289.

55. See above, p. 9.

56. Henri Bergson, *Essai sur les données immédiates de la conscience* (Paris: Presses Universitaires de France, 1927), 93, 126; *L'Évolution Créatrice* (Paris: Presses Universitaires de France, 1941), 5, 159–60.

57. See above, p. 63.

58. Bergson, *L'Évolution*, 264, and *Essai*, 125, 129, 6.

59. Ibid., 125, 95, 98, 123; *L'Évolution*, 17, 166.

60. Bergson, *Essai*, 97, 95, 96, 178, 101, 174, 178, 55.

61. Ibid., 172, 74–75, 174; *L'Évolution*, 267.

62. Péguy, *Oeuvres complètes*, 3: 20, 540, 805.

63. Ibid., 3: 788–89, 821, 1327, 1347.

64. Ibid., 3: 29–30, 89, 796–97, 932; Charles Péguy, *Le Choix de Péguy* (Paris: Gallimard, 1952), 24–25, 28–29.

65. Péguy, *Oeuvres complètes*, 3: 124, 10, 11, 790, 1323.

66. Ibid., 3: 29, 120, 150, 93, 943.

67. Jean-Paul Sartre, *Huis clos/Les Mouches* (Paris: Gallimard, 1947), 19, 89, 48, 51, 91, 42, 93.

68. Jean-Paul Sartre, *L'Etre et le néant* (Paris: Gallimard, 1943), 305, 306, 307.

69. Ibid., 309, 461, 581, 310, 478, 481, 413, 318.

70. Ibid., 674, 499.

71. Ibid., 624, 92, 95, 494, 492.

72. Ibid., 306, 309; *Huis clos/Les Mouches*, 33.

73. Sartre, *L'Etre*, 499, 82, 338, 96.

74. Ibid., 678, 67, 70, 615, 614, and *Huis clos/Les Mouches*, 181, 122, 237.

75. Jean-Paul Sartre, *Saint Genet, comédien et martyr* (Paris: Gallimard, 1952), 23, 24, 27, 55, 75, 453, 457, 521.

76. See above, p. 41.

77. Foucault, *Les Mots*, 335, 397, and *Power/Knowledge*, 98.

78. Michel Foucault, *Surveiller et punir* (Paris: Gallimard, 1975), 207, 202, 209, and *Power/Knowledge*, 148.

79. Foucault, *Surveiller et punir*, 211, 215, 186–87, 173, 224, 189, and *Power/Knowledge*, 94, 107.

80. See above, p. 75.

81. Foucault, *Surveiller et punir*, 172, 34, and *Power/Knowledge*, 98, 93, 94.

82. Michel Foucault, *La Volonté*, 29, 42, 61–62, 158, 145–46, and *Politics*, 68–69.

83. Foucault, *La Volonté*, 110, 122, 189–90, 79, and *Politics*, 70.

84. Mark Poster, *Foucault, Marxism, and History* (Cambridge, UK: Polity Press, 1984), 26; Foucault, *Politics*, 126, and *La Volonté*, 59, 163.

85. Foucault, *Surveiller et punir*, 209, 211, 220, *Power/Knowledge*, 155, and *La Volonté*, 34–35, 183, 185.

86. Foucault, *Surveiller et punir*, 9–13; Michel Foucault, *Madness and Civilization: A History of Insanity in the Age of Reason*, trans. Richard Howard (New York: Vintage Books, 1965), ix, 279, 281, and *Politics*, 119–20. On Foucault's lifelong desire to recover "prediscursive experiences," see Miller, *Passion*, 21.

87. Here I am paraphrasing the views expressed by Poster (*Foucault*, 96–97).

88. Foucault, *Politics*, 36; Foucault quoted in Miller, *Passion*, 304; Foucault, *La Volonté*, 211. Toward the end of his life, Foucault became fascinated by the pagan philosophies of Cynicism and Stoicism, in which he hoped to find "an ideal unity of the will and truth" which would not be tainted by

"normalization." While this late turn toward an "aesthetic individualism," in which a given historical self might consciously reconstitute itself as a work of art, remained incomplete and was never as popularly celebrated as were his works of the 1970s, it would seem remarkably consistent with the Rousseauian project to achieve psychic autonomy from *les autres*. The Cynics, for example, as Foucault noted in 1984, sought "to eliminate all of the dependencies introduced by culture." See Miller, *Passion*, 323, 346, 361; and Poster, *Critical Theory*, 54, 60, 93–95.

89. Foucault, *Power/Knowledge*, 152, 154.

90. Miller, *Passion*, 311.

CHAPTER IV

1. Christophe Prochasson has recently underscored the "aristocratic" contempt of the modern French intellectual for the bourgeoisie and its monetary values. See "Intellectuals as Actors: Image and Reality," in Jennings, *Intellectuals in France*, 68–69.

2. Stendhal, *Le Rouge et le noir*, 62, 476, 388, 309, 443, 378, 361, 104.

3. Ibid., 488, 343–45, 75, 65, 159.

4. Ibid., 38, 159, 396, 142, 465. See also Brombert, *Themes of Freedom*, 86–91.

5. Rousseau, *Discours*, 38, 48, 168.

6. Rousseau, *Lettre à d'Alembert*, 212; Jean-Jacques Rousseau, *Julie ou La Nouvelle Héloïse* (Paris: Garnier-Flammarion, 1967), 3, 164. Rousseau also, as has been seen, reiterates these points in his *Émile* as well as *Les Confessions* (see above, pp. 66, 44).

7. Rousseau, *Discours*, 233, 229, and *La Nouvelle Héloïse*, 165.

8. See above, pp. 62–63.

9. Rousseau, *Discours*, 210, 211, 216.

10. Rousseau, *Lettre à d'Alembert*, 213, and *Héloïse*, 164, 171, 165, 177. Rousseau, of course, famously reiterates this critique of the Republic of Letters in *Les Confessions* (see above, p. 44).

11. Rousseau, *Discours*, 229, 40, 234, and *Héloïse*, 165, 172, 180.

12. Robespierre, *Oeuvres*, 9: 495; 7: 167, 166; 8: 461, 115, 114; Courtois, quoted in Jordan, *Revolutionary Career*, 142.

13. Ibid., 233; Robespierre, *Oeuvres*, 10: 352.

14. Ibid., 4: 170–71; 10: 361, 476–77, 548, 574, 570, 571–72.

15. Ibid., 8: 49; 7: 511; 10: 455, 552, 551, 572.

16. Jules Michelet, *Histoire de la révolution française* (Paris: Robert Laffont, 1979), 1: 717, 687.

17. Ibid., 2: 897; 1: 367, and *Le Peuple*, 132.

18. Michelet, *Histoire*, 2: 775, 460, 375; 1: 389, 449, 346, and *Le Peuple*, 113, 135.

19. Michelet, *Histoire*, 1: 142–43, 367, and *Le Peuple*, 202, 134, 193.

20. Ibid., 145, 163; *Histoire*, 1: 356.

21. See above, p. 74.

22. See above, p. 78.

23. Bergson, *Essai*, 97, 96, 93, 120, 99.

24. Ibid., 126, 125, 174, 178, and *L'Évolution*, 264.

25. Péguy, *Oeuvres complètes,* 3: 104–5, 96, 794, 1447, 135, 1456, 1458, 814.

26. Ibid., 3: 1432, 1423, 149, 105, 1416.

27. Ibid., 3: 813, 790, 1432, 1419, 1420.

28. Ibid., 3: 1417, 105, 794, 787, 944.

29. Sartre, *Plaidoyer,* 30, 44, and *Saint Genet,* 32; Jean-Paul Sartre, *Critique de la raison dialectique* (Paris: Gallimard, 1960), 753, *La Mort dans l'âme* (Paris: Gallimard, 1949), 208, and *La Nausée* (Paris: Gallimard, 1938), 68, 72, 73, 137.

30. Ibid., 137–38.

31. Sartre revisits social avarice in his aforementioned *Critique de la raison dialectique* of 1960. Deducing it, however, from an organic rather than an ontological "lack" in human "Being," he portrays it in even more dire and universal terms. In light of material "scarcity," which, Sartre maintains, "is the foundation of the possibility of human history," each man must recognize in his fellow beings "the simple possibility of consuming an object he needs"; that is, "the material possibility of his own annihilation" (*Critique,* 166, 192).

32. Sartre, *L'Etre,* 650, 651, 654.

33. Sartre, *La Nausée,* 162, 169, 167–68.

34. Jean-Paul Sartre, *L'Age de raison* (Paris: Gallimard, 1945), 266, 55, 131, 132–33.

35. Sartre, *Saint Genet,* 30, and *La Nausée,* 228; Jean-Paul Sartre, *Le Sursis* (Paris: Gallimard, 1972), 341, and *Huis clos/Les Mouches,* 118, 233, 119.

36. Again, in *Critique de la raison dialectique,* Sartre rediscovers social automatism in the isolation and anonymity—the "massification"—that typically characterizes capitalist society. "For each member of the group waiting for the bus," he explains, "the big city is present . . . as the practico-inert group in which there is a movement toward the interchangeability of men and their instruments" (*Critique,* 309).

37. Quoted in Miller, *Passion,* 112, 98.

38. Foucault, *Power/Knowledge,* 98, 156, 203, *La Volonté,* 92, and *Surveiller et punir,* 223.

39. See above, pp. 91–92.

40. Foucault, *Surveiller et punir,* 223, and *La Volonté,* 51, 66.

41. Foucault, *Power/Knowledge,* 105, *Surveiller et punir,* 223, 226, *Politics,* 144, and *La Volonté de savoir,* 145–46.

42. Foucault, *Power/Knowledge,* 160, 104, 105.

43. See René Rémond, *L'Anticléricalisme en France* (cited above).

44. Stendhal, *Le Rouge et le noir,* 128, 330, 199, 462.

45. Ibid., 330, 203.

46. Ibid., 384, 386, 195, 190, 484.

47. Ibid., 275, 71, 452, 492–93.

48. Rousseau, *Émile,* 385, 361.

49. Rousseau, *Héloïse,* 445–46, *Contrat social,* 175, 179, and *Les Confessions,* 465, 669, 670.

50. Rousseau, *Émile,* 391, *Les Confessions,* 70, and *Contrat social,* 177.

51. Rousseau, *Émile,* 347, 348, 408, and *Les Confessions,* 465, 672.

52. Rousseau, *Émile,* 349, 387, 384, 385, and *Contrat social,* 178–79, 174.

53. See, for example, Jordan, *Revolutionary Career,* 197, 287–88.

54. Quoted in ibid., 50; Robespierre, *Oeuvres,* 10: 457, 481.

55. Ibid., 10: 195, 452, 560.

56. Such is the interpretation of David Jordan, for example (*Revolutionary Career,* 287–88).

57. Robespierre, *Oeuvres,* 10: 446, 457, 482, 196.

58. Michelet, *Histoire,* 2: 715, 352, 460, 405, 355, 644, 351.

59. See above, p. 75.

60. Michelet, *Du Prêtre,* vi, 260, and *Histoire,* 1: 252, 298, 290, 349.

61. Ibid., 1: 309; 2: 19, 16.

62. Michelet, *Le Peuple,* 67, and *Du Prêtre,* 303, 306.

63. Michelet, *Le Peuple,* 231, 239, 240, 243.

64. See above, p. 53.

65. Bergson, *L'Évolution,* 196–97, 166, 329, 94, 363, 364; *Essai,* 173, 123.

66. Bergson, *L'Évolution,* 15, and *Essai,* 121, 124.

67. Ibid., 173, 177, 85, and *L'Évolution,* 88, 368–69, 268.

68. Nicolet, *L'Idée républicaine,* 505; Péguy, *Oeuvres complètes,* 3: 31–32, 812–13. On Péguy's secular anticlericalism, see also Paul Cohen, *Piety and Politics* (New York: Garland Press, 1987), 250–53.

69. Péguy, *Oeuvres complètes,* 3: 100, 103, 101.

70. Ibid., 3: 103, 446, 957, 1444, 1448.

71. Charles Péguy, *Oeuvres en prose 1898–1914* (Paris: Gallimard, 1957–59), 1: 482–83; *Oeuvres complètes,* 3: 85, 100, 1330, 1403, 1327.

72. Sartre, *La Nausée,* 68, 79, 80, 69, and *Le Sursis,* 341.

73. Jean-Paul Sartre, *L'Existentialisme est un humanisme* (Paris: Éditions Nagel, 1970), 92, *La Nausée,* 165, 169–70, and *L'Age,* 153.

74. Sartre, *La Mort,* 338.

75. Ibid., 340.

76. Sartre, *L'Existentialisme,* 49, 35, 34, and *L'Etre,* 678.

77. Sartre, *Huis Clos/Les Mouches,* 156, 233, 178, 236, 235, 237.

78. Foucault, *Power/Knowledge,* 80–81, *Politics,* 70, 68, 69, and *La Volonté,* 27, 30.

79. Foucault, *Politics,* 144, 196, 134, *Power/Knowledge,* 107, 85, and *Surveiller et punir,* 27, 17.

80. Foucault, *La Volonté,* 160, 62, 58, and *Surveiller et punir,* 227.

81. Foucault, *La Volonté,* 91, 81, 86–87, 89, 92, and *Surveiller et punir,* 228–29.

82. Foucault, *Power/Knowledge,* 84, 98, 93, 85, 83, 80.

83. The critique of centralized government in modern France finds its most eminent spokesman, of course, in Alexis de Tocqueville (see *Old Regime*). Among the modern scholars who have expanded on Tocqueville's celebrated analysis are Michel Crozier (*Bureaucratic Phenomenon*), Stanley Hoffmann (*In Search of France*), and Anne Sa'adah, (*Shaping of Liberal Politics*).

84. Stendhal, *Le Rouge et le noir,* 35–37, 11, 8, 379–80.

85. Ibid., 244, 246.

86. Ibid., 246, 305.

87. Ibid., 123, 268, 289.

88. Rousseau, *Discours,* 219, 228.

89. Rousseau, *Contrat social,* 51, 140, 101, 113, 103.

90. Ibid., 134, 67, 146, 125.

91. Robespierre, *Oeuvres*, 8: 47, 59; 9: 466, 467; 10: 274, 356.

92. Sa'adah, *Shaping of Liberal Politics*, 99. Sa'adah compellingly details the mistrust of parliamentary politics shared by Robespierre and the Jacobins (see, for example, 149–56).

93. Jordan, *Revolutionary Career*, 61, 142; Robespierre, *Oeuvres*, 10: 360, 545, 556, 570, 551.

94. Ibid., 10: 355, 351, 557, 572.

95. Michelet, *Histoire*, 2: 742–43; 1: 826.

96. Ibid., 1: 582, 132; 2: 102, 144–45, 274.

97. Ibid., 1: 716; 2: 34, 35, 114, 121.

98. Ibid., 1: 616, 615, 794, and *Le Peuple*, 144, 235.

99. Bergson, *L'Évolution*, 197, 17, 49, 48, and *Essai*, 178.

100. Péguy, *Oeuvres complètes*, 3: 1323, 1416.

101. Ibid., 3: 1326, 14, 17–18, 33, 76.

102. Ibid., 3: 29, 22, 15, 96, 1332, 797, 90, 943.

103. Ibid., 3: 90, 20, 1417, 1331.

104. Sartre, *La Nausée*, 49, 133, 136, 135, *L'Age*, 52, 65, and *Le Sursis*, 253.

105. Sartre, *L'Age*, 63, *Situations*, 10: 134, and *Critique*, 37, 58.

106. Sartre, *Huis clos/Les Mouches*, 202, 119, and *Critique*, 631, 636, 585.

107. Michel Foucault, *L'Archéologie de savoir* (Paris: Gallimard, 1969), 28, *Surveiller et punir*, 210, 215, 216; Michel Foucault, "The Subject and Power," in *Michel Foucault: Beyond Structuralism and Hermeneutics*, ed. Hubert L. Dreyfus and Paul Rabinow (Chicago: University of Chicago Press, 1982), 215.

108. Foucault, *Surveiller et punir*, 186.

109. *La Volonté*, 35, 154, 183, 191.

110. Foucault, *Power/Knowledge*, 130, 88, 105, *Surveiller et punir*, 223, *Politics*, 84, and "Subject and Power," 212, 209, 215.

CHAPTER V

1. See above, pp. 100–105, 126, 131, 133, 134.

2. Stendhal, *Le Rouge et le noir*, 437, 476, 100, 459, 83, 298, 331.

3. Ibid., 450, 458, 451, 491.

4. Ibid., 476, 83, 303, 307, 350, 320, 431, 480.

5. Ibid., 498–99, 97.

6. Tony Judt's caustic *Past Imperfect* represents only one recent assessment of the revolutionary tradition in modern France. Claude Nicolet maintains, on the other hand, that underlying the Republic itself remains that "permanent revolution" which consists "first and foremost in the abolition of its eternal enemies: the recourse to religious transcendence; the acceptance of ready-made 'truths'; the egoism of private interests" (*L'Idée républicaine*, 498). Other evaluations of the revolutionary tradition, both critical and laudatory, may be found, for example, in Khilnani, *Arguing Revolution*; Bernard Henri-Lévy, *Les Aventures de la liberté: une histoire subjective des intellectuels en France* (Paris: Gallimard, 1991); Brombert, *Intellectual Hero*; Hoffmann, *Decline or Renewal?*; Aron, *Opium*; and Michel Crozier, *The Stalled Society*, trans. Michel Crozier (New York: Viking Press, 1973), to which I will return in the conclusion.

7. Baker, *Inventing the Revolution*, 206, 211, 214, 223.

8. For a summary of the scholarly debate over Rousseau's view of revolution, and especially the "revisionist" assessment of Rousseau as a political conservative, see Miller, *Dreamer*, 2. Miller himself underscores Rousseau's ambivalence about revolutionary upheaval (89, 130, 138), as does William H. Blanchard (*Rousseau and the Spirit of Revolt* [Ann Arbor: University of Michigan Press, 1967], 142–46). Koselleck, on the other hand, portrays a Rousseau who, in his "quest for the true state, . . . unwittingly unleashed the permanent revolution" (*Critique*, 163).

9. Rousseau, *Discours*, 141, and *Contrat social*, 89, 140.

10. Rousseau, *Discours*, 223, *Héloïse*, 268, and *Les Confessions*, 494–96.

11. Ibid., 494, *Discours*, 223, 233, *Émile*, 252, and *Contrat social*, 81.

12. Ibid., 140, 127, 132.

13. Rousseau, *Les Confessions*, 494–96, and *Contrat social*, 81–82.

14. Robespierre, *Oeuvres*, 7: 164, and *Lettres à ses commettans* (5 January 1793), quoted in Cobban, *Aspects*, 185.

15. Robespierre, *Oeuvres*, 9: 468.

16. Ibid., 8: 60; 9: 130.

17. Ibid., 10: 355; 6: 243; 8: 148.

18. See above, p. 128.

19. Robespierre, *Oeuvres*, 10: 355, 274; 9: 116.

20. See above, p. 73.

21. Robespierre, *Oeuvres*, 10: 353, 355, 354, 357.

22. Ibid., 10: 482, 576, 557.

23. Hunt, *Politics*, 27. Colin Lucas, similarly, interprets the Terror as an attempt to institutionalize and sacralize revolutionary violence, to tame the Revolution's "brief moment of galvanic, cathartic action" and lend it both meaning and order (see "Revolutionary Violence," in *The Terror*, vol. 4 of *The French Revolution and the Creation of Modern Political Culture*, ed. Keith Michael Baker (Oxford: Pergamon, 1994), 73.

24. Robespierre, *Oeuvres*, 10: 354, 566, 576.

25. Ibid., 6: 243.

26. By characterizing Robespierre as the "mouthpiece" and "embodiment" of the French Revolution's "purest and most tragic discourse," François Furet suggests that the Jacobin's personal saga, his ascendancy to that brief and precarious pinnacle of power from which he ultimately fell, has become identified with the revolutionary narrative itself. Hence, Robespierre's demise and the "Thermidorean reaction" that ensued have come to mark the end of "the Revolution in power" and the re-emergence of "society" and its "special interests" (*Interpreting the Revolution*, 61, 58, 74).

27. See above, p. 74.

28. Michelet, *Histoire*, 1: 347, and *Le Peuple*, 193, 203, 240.

29. Michelet, *Histoire*, 1: 31, 38, and *Le Peuple*, 231, 88.

30. See Gossman, *History*, 213. Gossman is not the only scholar to notice Michelet's gravitation, both in the *Histoire* and in other works, toward exalted moments of national unity and liberation. See also White, *Metahistory*, 161–62; Barthes *Michelet*, 61; Kippur, *Michelet*, 158–65; and Orr, *Michelet*, 100.

31. Michelet, *Histoire*, 1: 344, 732, 747, 748, 782.

32. Lionel Gossman portrays Michelet's "ideal" similarly as "the transgressive act of overcoming separation" (*History*, 210, 185).

33. Michelet, *Histoire*, 1: 36, 795, 434.

34. Gossman, *History*, 185; Michelet, *Histoire*, 1: 808, 810. 882; 2: 87.

35. Michelet, *Histoire*, 1: 345, 342, 98.

36. Ibid., 2: 149, 744, 840.

37. Hayden White has classified Michelet as an "anarchist" precisely because the historian's "romantic emplotment of the history of France up to the Revolution was . . . set within a larger Tragic awareness of its subsequent dissipation." Hence, "the ideal itself," White concludes, "could never be realized in time, in history, for it was as evanescent as the condition of anarchy which it presupposed for its realization" (*Metahistory*, 153, 162).

38. Bergson, *Essai*, 125, 95, 97, 101.

39. Ibid., 129, 75, 128.

40. Ibid., 179, 93, 127, 128, and *L'Évolution*, 202.

41. Bergson, *Essai*, 119, and *L'Évolution*, 271, 254–55.

42. Ibid., 254, 268, and *Essai*, 174, 126, 179, 180.

43. Péguy, *Oeuvres complètes*, 3: 1422.

44. See above, p. 82.

45. Péguy, *Oeuvres complètes*, 3: 821, 943, 84.

46. Ibid., 3: 41, 120, 151, 9.

47. Ibid., 3: 146–47, 152, 945.

48. Ibid., 3: 20, 155, 943, 944, 41.

49. Sartre, *Les Mots*, 192. Michel Crozier noted as well, in 1964, that the "moral system" implicit in Sartre's works "is a heroic and individual morality which consists in making the individual assume the whole weight of the world at every moment" (see "Cultural Revolution," 616).

50. See above, pp. 85–87.

51. Sartre, *L'Etre*, 532, *Saint Genet*, 9, and *Huis Clos/Les Mouches*, 210, 236.

52. Sartre's fascination with violence has often been noted by his biographers and critics. See, for example, Hayman, *Writing Against*, 442–47; Judt, *Past Imperfect*, 126; and Aron, *Opium*, 65, 80–81.

53. Sartre, *Huis Clos/Les Mouches*, 205, 210, 224, and *La Mort*, 244–45.

54. Sartre, *Huis Clos/Les Mouches*, 205, 246, and *L'Existentialisme*, 68, 24, 84.

55. Jean-Paul Sartre, *The Communists and the Peace*, trans. Martha H. Fletcher and Phillip R. Beck (New York: George Braziller, 1968), 54–55, *Sartre on Cuba* (New York: Ballantine Books, 1961), 45, 116, and preface to *The Wretched of the Earth*, by Frantz Fanon, trans. Constance Farrington (New York: Grove Press, 1963), 18.

56. For a lucid account of Sartre's synthesis of existentialism and Marxism, see Mark Poster, *Existential Marxism in Postwar France: From Sartre to Althusser* (Princeton: Princeton University Press, 1976).

57. Sartre, *Critique*, 166, 192, 205, 308, 325, 387, 388, 391, 393–94, 425, 420.

58. Sartre, *L'Etre*, 615, *Le Sursis*, 343, and *Huis Clos/Les Mouches*, 237.

59. Sartre, *Critique*, 411, 553, 581, 636, 635. In a 1970 interview, Sartre reiterated that "the idea of a total and instantaneous liberation is a utopia. We could already predict certain limits and constraints which would be imposed upon any future revolution" (*Situations*, 9: 130).

60. Miller, *Passion*, 115, 88–89, 75.

61. Foucault, "Subject and Power," 221–22, 225.

62. Foucault, *Surveiller et punir*, 289, 296.

63. Foucault, *Language*, 228, 230.

64. Ibid., 216, *Power/Knowledge*, 81, 87, and *La Volonté*, 126–27; Michel Foucault, "Interview with Jean-Louis Ezine," *Nouvelles littéraires* 2477 (17–23 March 1975).

65. Foucault, *Power/Knowledge*, 130, 1–2, 18, and *Politics*, 215, 216, 217.

66. Michel Foucault, "Inutile de se soulever?" *Le Monde*, 11 May 1979, quoted in Miller, *Passion*, 313, and *Politics*, 84.

67. Foucault, *Surveiller et punir*, 32, *Knowledge/Power*, 80, *La Volonté*, 126, and *Politics*, 219.

CHAPTER VI

1. Richard Rorty, "Paroxysms and Politics," *Salgamundi* 97 (1993): 63–64.

2. Talmon, *Totalitarian Democracy*, 107, 115; Berlin, *Four Essays*, 162, 167; Furet, *Interpreting the Revolution*, 13; Isser Woloch, "Latent Illiberalism," 1452–70.

3. See Aron, *Opium*, xv; Paul Johnson, *Intellectuals* (New York: Harper Collins, 1988), 246; Judt, *Past Imperfect*, 11; Weightman, "Fatal Attraction." On the response to Foucault's support of the Iranian Revolution see Eribon, *Foucault*, 287–91. For a prosecutorial account of the ostensible link between intellectual radicalism and fascism in modern France, see Zeev Sternhell, *La Droite révolutionnaire 1885–1914* (Paris: Seuil, 1978).

4. Keith Baker, ed. *The Terror*, xiii. Dominick LaCapra has argued similarly that the Holocaust embodies a "limit-case" for contemporary historians, a traumatic event which activates a self-blinding range of Freudian defense mechanisms and thereby obstructs historical understanding (*Representing the Holocaust* [Ithaca: Cornell University Press, 1994], 14).

5. Quoted in David Caute, *Communism and the French Intellectuals, 1914–1960* (London: Andre Deutsch, 1964), 194; Foucault, *Politics*, 59, 79.

6. Alan Ryan, "Foucault's Life and Hard Times," *New York Review of Books*, 17 April 1993.

7. The classic theoretical work on totalitarianism remains Hannah Arendt's *The Origins of Totalitarianism*, rev. ed. (New York: Meridian Books, 1958). Its defining characteristics are detailed, for example, in Carl J. Friedrich and Zbignew K. Brezinski, *Totalitarian Dictatorship and Autocracy* (Cambridge, MA: Harvard University Press, 1965); and Michael Curtis, *Totalitarianism* (New Brunswick, NJ: Transaction Books, 1979).

8. See above, pp. 122–33, 136, 141, 151, 153, 157, 158, 161, 162.

9. See above, pp. 126–35.

10. Milan Kundera, *The Book of Laughter and Forgetting*, trans. Michael Henry Heim (New York: Penguin Books, 1981), 63.

11. On this point, see for example Merquior, *Liberalism*, 11. Stanley Hoff-

mann, by the same token, links the avoidance of "'face-to-face' compromises" in modern France to the "revolt against the bonds of personal dependency left behind by feudalism" (Hoffmann, *In Search of France*, 10).

12. See above, pp. 84, 111, 123, 128–30, 146, 158–59.

13. See above, pp. 142, 149–63.

14. See above, pp. 146–49.

15. Sa'adah, *Shaping of Liberal Politics*, 186. Sa'adah, detailing the mistrust of power and government in the discourse both of Robespierre and the Jacobins in general, makes a convincing case that neither anticipates totalitarianism in its twentieth-century form (154–55, 191–92, 152, 185).

16. On Foucault's fascination with Nietzsche, in light especially of "Dionysian" transgression and "limit-experiences," see Miller, *Passion*, 66–72, 231–39, 236. On French "Nietzscheanism" more generally—and that of Foucault and Deuleuze in particular—see Michael S. Roth, *Knowing and History: Appropriations of Hegel in Twentieth-Century France* (Ithaca: Cornell University Press, 1988), 189–224. For Nietzsche's sway over Bataille, Blanchot, Canguilhem, and Derrida, see Eribon, *Foucault*, 148–52; the German philosopher's importance for Georges Sorel, finally, would seem clear enough in *Reflections on Violence*, trans. T. E. Hulme and J. Roth (Glencoe, IL: The Free Press, 1950), 257–60.

17. See, for example, Caute, *Communism;* George Lichtheim, *Marxism in Modern France* (New York: Columbia University Press, 1966); and Tony Judt, *Marxism and the French Left* (New York: Oxford University Press, 1986).

18. Friedrich Nietzsche, *On the Genealogy of Morals/Ecce Homo*, ed. and trans. Walter Kaufmann (New York: Vintage Books, 1967), 35, 54.

19. Michel Crozier, *Bureaucratic Phenomenon*, and *Stalled Society.*

20. Crozier, *Bureaucratic Phenomenon*, 222 n, 219.

21. Ibid., 223, 224, 226, and *Stalled Society*, 96.

22. Ibid., 112, 132.

23. See above, chapter 3.

24. Crozier, *Stalled Society*, 120, 118, and "Cultural Revolution," 613–14.

25. Crozier, *Stalled Society*, 77, vii, 96, 123, 157. On the "end of the French exception," see François Furet, Jacques Julliard, and Pierre Rosanvallon, *La République du centre: la fin de l'exception française* (Paris: Calman-Lévy, 1988). For a historical account of the latter thesis in recent scholarship, see Khilnani, *Arguing Revolution*, 155–78.

26. Crozier, *Bureaucratic Phenomenon*, 223, 208.

27. I am grateful to my friend and colleague Susan Rosa, who first called my attention to this line of inquiry.

28. Ellery Schalk, *From Valor to Pedigree* (Princeton: Princeton University Press, 1986), 6, 21, 29, 195, 115.

29. While not disputing Schalk's definition of "noble virtue" in theory, Jonathan Dewald emphasizes its distance from noble practice under the Old Regime (*Aristocratic Experience and the Origins of Modern Culture: France, 1570–1715* [Berkeley: University of California Press, 1993], 10, 18, 45, 146, 207).

30. Tocqueville, *Old Regime*, 118–19.

31. Stendhal, *Le Rouge et le noir*, 490, 107, 100, 310, 460.

32. See above, pp. 39, 44–45, 63, 66–67; Sartre, *Les Mots,* 134, 137, 105, 142, and "À propos de l'existentialisme: Mise au point," in *Les Écrits de Sartre,* ed. Michel Contat and Michel Rybalka (Paris: Gallimard, 1970), 657.

33. See above, pp. 71–73, 74, 142, 149, 155–56; and Péguy, *Oeuvres complètes,* 3: 147, 151.

34. Norman Hampson, "The French Revolution and the Nationalisation of Honour," in *War and Society,* ed. M. R. D. Foot (New York: Barnes and Noble, 1973), 199–212; Robert A. Nye, *Masculinity and Male Codes of Honor in Modern France* (New York: Oxford University Press, 1993), 217.

35. Ibid., vii, 8.

36. Stendhal, *Le Rouge et le noir,* 49, 128, 442, 423.

37. See above, pp. 150–54, 156–57, 162; and Sartre, "À propos de l'existentialisme," 656; Foucault, *Politics,* 123, 12. Foucault's commentary on sadomasochistic practice is quoted in David Macey, *The Lives of Michel Foucault* (New York: Vintage Books, 1995), 369. It should be noted that Foucault explicitly championed what he called "the desexualization of pleasure" and renounced "the valorization of the genitalia"—and "particularly the male genitalia" (quoted in Miller, *Passion,* 263, 269). His account of sexual limit-experiences, however, would seem no less distinctively masculine, both symbolically and in practice.

38. See above, pp. 34, 43, 77.

39. See above, p. 43. Rousseau's comments are quoted by Dena Goodman in *Republic of Letters,* 55. On Rousseau's partitioning of society into masculine and feminine spheres, see also Nye, *Masculinity,* 48–49; and Joel Schwartz, *The Sexual Politics of Jean-Jacques Rousseau* (Chicago: University of Chicago Press, 1984).

40. See above, pp. 27, 75, 90, 100, 147–48. See also Robert Darnton, *The Kiss of Lamourette* (New York: Norton, 1990), 10; and Judt, *Past Imperfect,* 51. Ronald Hayman, one of Sartre's biographers, also remarks on his subject's tendency to "assume a polarity between consciousness (which he pictured as active, alert, male) and flesh (inert, flabby, clingy, female)," and to seek to "preserve" the former's "capacity" for "freedom" and "penetration" (see *Writing Against,* 193).

41. See, for example, Furet, *Interpreting the French Revolution,* 1; and Furet, Julliard, and Rosanvallon, *La République du centre.*

WORKS CITED

PRIMARY SOURCES

Bergson, Henri. *Essai sur les données immédiates de la conscience.* Paris: Presses Universitaires de France, 1927. [*Time and Free Will.* 1910. Translated by F. L. Pogson. New York: Harper, 1960.]

———. *L'Évolution créatrice.* Paris: Presses Universitaires de France, 1941. [*Creative Evolution.* Translated by Arthur Mitchell. New York: Henry Holt and Company, 1911.]

d'Alembert, Jean. "Essai sur la société des gens de lettres et des grands." In *Oeuvres complètes de d'Alembert.* Vol. 4. Paris: A. Belin, 1822.

Diderot, Dénis. "The Definition of an Encyclopedia." In *The Old Regime and the French Revolution.* Vol. 7 of *Readings in Western Civilization,* edited by Keith Michael Baker. Chicago: University of Chicago Press, 1987.

Foucault, Michel. *L'Archéologie de savoir.* Paris: Gallimard, 1969. [*The Archeology of Knowledge and the Discourse on Language.* Translated by M. Sheridan Smith. New York: Pantheon, 1972.]

———. *The Foucault Reader.* Edited by Paul Rabinow. New York: Pantheon, 1984.

———. *Language, Counter-Memory, Practice.* Edited by Donald F. Bouchard and translated by Donald F. Bouchard and Sherry Simon. Ithaca: Cornell University Press, 1977.

———. *Madness and Civilization: A History of Insanity in the Age of Reason.* Translated by Richard Howard. New York: Vintage Books, 1965.

———. *Les Mots et les choses.* Paris: Gallimard, 1966. [*The Order of Things: An Archaeology of the Human Sciences.* Edited by R. D. Laing. New York: Vintage Books, 1970.]

———. *Politics, Philosophy, Culture: Interviews and other Writings, 1977–1984.* Edited by Lawrence D. Kritsman and translated by Alan Sheridan. New York: Routledge, Chapman, and Hall, 1988.

———. *Power/Knowledge: Selected Interviews and Other Writings, 1972–1977.* Edited by Colin Gordon and translated by Colin Gordon et al. New York: Pantheon Books, 1980.

———. "The Subject and Power." In *Michel Foucault: Beyond Structuralism and Hermeneutics,* edited by Hubert L. Dreyfus and Paul Rabinow. Chicago: University of Chicago Press, 1982.

———. *Surveiller et punir.* Paris: Gallimard, 1975. [*Discipline and Punish: The Birth of the Prison.* Translated by Alan Sheridan. New York: Vintage Books, 1977.]

————. *La Volonté de savoir.* Vol. 1 of *Histoire de la sexualité.* Paris: Galli-mard, 1975. [*An Introduction.* Vol. 1 of *The History of Sexuality.* Trans-lated by Robert Hurley. New York: Vintage Books, 1978.]

Kundera, Milan. *The Book of Laughter and Forgetting.* Translated by Michael Henry Heim. New York: Penguin Books, 1981.

Michelet, Jules. *Écrits de jeunesse.* Edited by Paul Viallaneix. Paris: Galli-mard, 1959.

————. *Histoire de la révolution française.* 2 vols. Paris: Robert Laffont, 1979. [*History of the French Revolution.* Edited by Gordon Wright and translated by Charles Cocks. Chicago: University of Chicago Press, 1967.]

————. *Le Peuple.* Paris: Flammarion, 1974. [*The People.* Translated by John P. McKay. Urbana: University of Illinois Press, 1973.]

————. *Du Prêtre, de la femme, et de la famille.* Paris: Hachette, 1845. [*Spiri-tual Direction and Auricular Confession.* Philadelphia: James Campbell, 1845.]

Nietzsche, Friedrich. *On the Genealogy of Morals/Ecce Homo.* Edited and translated by Walter Kaufmann. New York: Vintage Books, 1967.

Péguy, Charles. *Le Choix de Péguy.* Paris: Gallimard, 1952.

————. *Oeuvres en prose 1898–1914.* 2 vols. Paris: Gallimard, 1957–59.

————. *Oeuvres en prose complètes.* 3 vols. Paris: Gallimard, 1992.

————. *Souvenirs.* Edited by Pierre Péguy. Paris: Gallimard, 1938.

Robespierre, Maximilien. *Oeuvres de Maximilien Robespierre.* 10 vols. Paris: Société des Études Robespierre, 1950–1967. [*The Ninth of Thermidor: The Fall of Robespierre.* Edited by Richard Bienvenu. New York: Oxford Univer-sity Press, 1968; *Robespierre: Great Lives Observed.* Edited by George Rudé. Englewood Cliffs, NJ: Prentice-Hall, 1967.]

Rousseau, Jean-Jacques. *Les Confessions.* Paris: Garnier, 1964. [*The Confes-sions.* Translated by J. M. Cohen. Harmondsworth, UK: Penguin Books, 1954.]

————. *Du Contrat social.* Paris: Garnier-Flammarion, 1966.

————. *Discours sur l'origine et les fondements de l'inégalité parmi les hom-mes/Discours sur les sciences et les arts.* Paris: Garnier-Flammarion, 1971. [*The Social Contract and Discourses.* Translated by G. D. H. Cole. London: J. M. Dent & Sons, 1973.]

————. *Discours sur les sciences et les arts/Lettre à d'Alembert sur les spec-tacles.* Paris: Garnier-Flammarion, 1987. [*Politics and the Arts: Letter to M. d'Alembert on the Arts.* Translated by Allan Bloom. Ithaca: Cornell Uni-versity Press, 1960.]

————. *Émile, ou de l'éducation.* Paris: Garnier-Flammarion, 1966. [*Émile.* Translated by Barbara Foxley. London: J. M. Dent & Sons, 1974.]

————. *Julie ou La Nouvelle Héloïse.* Paris: Garnier-Flammarion, 1967. [*La Nouvelle Héloïse: Julie, or the New Eloise.* Translated by Judith H. Mc-Dowell. University Park: Pennsylvania State University Press, 1968.]

Sartre, Jean-Paul. "À propos de l'existentialisme: Mise au point." In *Les Écrits de Sartre.* Edited by Michel Contat and Michel Rybalka. Paris: Gallimard, 1970.

————. *L'Age de raison.* Paris: Gallimard, 1945. [*The Age of Reason.* Trans-lated by Eric Sutton. New York: Vintage Books, 1974.]

———. *The Communists and the Peace.* Translated by Martha H. Fletcher and Phillip R. Beck. New York: George Braziller, 1968.

———. *Critique de la raison dialectique.* Paris: Gallimard, 1960. [*Critique of Dialectical Reason.* Edited by Jonathan Rée and translated by Alan Sheridan-Smith. London: NLB, 1976.]

———. *L'Etre et le néant.* Paris: Gallimard, 1943. [*Being and Nothingness.* Translated by Hazel E. Barnes. New York: Citadel Press, 1956.]

———. *L'Existentialisme est un humanisme.* Paris: Éditions Nagel, 1970. [*Existentialism and Human Emotions.* Translated by Bernard Frechtman and Hazel E. Barnes. New York: Philosophical Library, 1957.]

———. *Huis clos/Les Mouches.* Paris: Gallimard, 1947. [*No Exit and Three Other Plays.* Translated by Stuart Gilbert and Lionel Abel. New York: Vintage Books, 1976.]

———. *La Mort dans l'âme.* Paris: Gallimard, 1949. [*Troubled Sleep.* Translated by Gerard Hopkins. New York: Vintage Books, 1978.]

———. *Les Mots.* Paris: Gallimard, 1964. [*The Words.* Translated by Bernard Frechtman. New York: George Braziller, 1964.]

———. *La Nausée.* Paris: Gallimard, 1938. [*Nausea.* Translated by Lloyd Alexander. New York: New Directions Publishing, 1964.]

———. *Plaidoyer pour les intellectuels.* Paris: Gallimard, 1972.

———. Preface to *The Wretched of the Earth,* by Frantz Fanon. Translated by Constance Farrington. New York: Grove Press, 1963.

———. *Saint Genet, comédien et martyr.* Paris: Gallimard, 1952. [*Saint Genet: Actor and Martyr.* Translated by Bernard Frechtman. New York: George Braziller, 1963.]

———. *Sartre on Cuba.* New York: Ballantine Books, 1961.

———. *Situations.* 10 vols. Paris: Gallimard, 1948.

———. *Le Sursis.* Paris: Gallimard, 1972. [*The Reprieve.* Translated by Eric Sutton. New York: Vintage Books, 1947.]

Sorel, Georges. *Reflections on Violence.* Translated by T. E. Hulme and J. Roth. Glencoe, IL: The Free Press, 1950.

Stendhal. *Le Rouge et le noir.* Paris: Garnier-Flammarion, 1964. [*Red and Black.* Translated by Robert M. Adams. New York: Norton, 1969.]

———. *Vie de Henri Brulard.* Paris: Garnier frères, 1961. [*The Life of Henry Brulard.* Translated by Jean Steward and B. C. J. G. Knight. Chicago: University of Chicago Press, 1958.]

Voltaire. *Letters on England.* Translated by Leonard Tancock. New York: Penguin Books, 1981.

SECONDARY SOURCES

Arendt, Hannah. *The Origins of Totalitarianism.* Rev. ed. New York: Meridian Books, 1958.

Aron, Raymond. *The Opium of the Intellectuals.* Translated by Terence Kilmartin. New York: Doubleday, 1957.

Baker, Keith Michael. *Inventing the French Revolution.* Cambridge, UK: Cambridge University Press, 1990.

———, ed. *The Political Culture of the Old Regime.* Vol. 1 of *The French Revolution and the Creation of Modern Political Culture.* Oxford: Pergamon, 1987.

————. *The Terror.* Vol. 4 of *The French Revolution and the Creation of Modern Political Culture.* Oxford: Pergamon, 1994.

Barthes, Roland. *Michelet.* Translated by Richard Howard. New York: Hill and Wang, 1987.

Benichou, Paul. *Le Sacre de l'écrivain 1750–1830.* Paris: Libraire José Corti, 1973.

Berlin, Isaiah. *Four Essays on Liberty.* Oxford: Oxford University Press, 1969.

Blanchard, William H. *Rousseau and the Spirit of Revolt.* Ann Arbor: University of Michigan Press, 1967.

Blum, Carol. *Rousseau and the Republic of Virtue.* Ithaca: Cornell University Press, 1986.

Bourdieu, Pierre. *Distinction.* Translated by Richard Nice. Cambridge, MA: Harvard University Press, 1984.

————. *Homo Academicus.* Translated by Peter Collier. Stanford: Stanford University Press, 1988.

Brombert, Victor. *The Intellectual Hero: Studies in the French Novel, 1880–1995.* New York: J. P. Lippincott, 1960.

————. *Stendhal: Fiction and the Themes of Freedom.* New York: Random House, 1968.

Campbell, Joseph. *The Hero with a Thousand Faces.* Princeton: Princeton University Press, 1968.

Caute, David. *Communism and the French Intellectuals, 1914–1960.* London: Andre Deutsch, 1964.

Charle, Christophe. *Naissance des "intellectuels" 1880–1900.* Paris: Éditions de Minuit, 1990.

Chevalier, Jacques. *Henri Bergson.* Translated by Lilian A. Clare. New York: Macmillan, 1928.

Clark, Priscilla. *The Battle of the Bourgeois.* Paris: Didier, 1973.

————. *Literary France.* Berkeley: University of California Press, 1987.

Clark, Terry N. *Prophets and Patrons: The French University and the Emergence of the Social Sciences.* Cambridge, MA: Harvard University Press, 1973.

Cobban, Alfred. *Aspects of the French Revolution.* New York: George Braziller, 1968.

Cohen, Paul. "Heroes and Dilettantes: The Action Française, Le Sillon, and the Generation of 1905–14." *French Historical Studies* 4 (Fall 1988): 673–87.

————. *Piety and Politics.* New York: Garland Press, 1987.

Cohen-Solal, Annie. *Sartre: A Life.* Edited by Norman Macafee and translated by Anna Cancogni. New York: Pantheon Books, 1987.

Colletti, Lucio. *From Rousseau to Lenin.* Translated by John Merrington and Judith White. New York: Monthly Review Press, 1972.

Crouzet, Michel. *Nature et société chez Stendhal.* Lille: Presses Universitaires de Lille, 1985.

Crozier, Michel. *The Bureaucratic Phenomenon.* Translated by Michel Crozier. Chicago: University of Chicago Press, 1964.

————. "The Cultural Revolution: Notes on the Changes in the Intellectual Climate in France." In *A New Europe?* edited by Stephen R. Graubard, 604–29. Boston: Houghton Mifflin, 1964.

————. *The Stalled Society.* Translated by Michel Crozier. New York: Viking Press, 1973.

Curtis, Michael. *Totalitarianism.* New Brunswick, NJ: Transaction Books, 1979.

Darnton, Robert. *The Great Cat Massacre.* New York: Vintage Books, 1984.

————. *The Kiss of Lamourette.* New York: Norton, 1990.

Delhez-Sarlet, Claudette. "L'Académie Française et le Mécénat." In *L'Age d'or du Mécénat (1598–1661),* edited by Roland Mousnier and Jean Mesnard, 241–46. Paris: Éditions du Centre national de la recherche scientifique, 1985.

Derrida, Jacques. *Of Grammatology.* Translated by Gayatri Chakravorty Spivak. Baltimore: Johns Hopkins University Press, 1974.

de Tocqueville, Alexis. *The Old Regime and the French Revolution.* Translated by Stuart Gilbert. Garden City, NJ: Doubleday Anchor, 1955.

Dewald, Jonathan. *Aristocratic Experience and the Origins of Modern Culture: France, 1570–1715.* Berkeley: University of California Press, 1993.

Dieckmann, Herbert. "The Concept of Knowledge in the *Encyclopédie.*" In *Essays in Comparative Literature,* edited by Herbert Dieckmann, Harry Levin, and Helmut Motekat, 73–107. St. Louis: Washington University Studies, 1961.

Eribon, Didier. *Michel Foucault.* Translated by Betsy Wing. Cambridge, MA: Harvard University Press, 1991.

Fehér, Ferenc. *The Frozen Revolution: An Essay on Jacobinism.* Cambridge, UK: Cambridge University Press, 1987.

Friedrich, Carl J., and Zbignew K. Brezinski. *Totalitarian Dictatorship and Autocracy.* Cambridge, MA: Harvard University Press, 1965.

Furbank, P. N. "On Not Knowing Thyself: The Unresolved Conflict between Voltaire and Rousseau." *Times Literary Supplement* (London), 7 October 1994.

Furet, François. *Interpreting the French Revolution.* Translated by Elborg Forster. Cambridge, UK: Cambridge University Press, 1981.

Furet, François, Jacques Julliard, and Pierre Rosanvallon. *La République du centre: la fin de l'exception française.* Paris: Calman-Lévy, 1988.

Gay, Peter. *Voltaire's Politics: The Poet as Realist.* Princeton: Princeton University Press, 1959.

Gerassi, John. *Protestant or Protestor?* Vol. 1 of *Jean-Paul Sartre: Hated Conscience of his Century.* Chicago: University of Chicago Press, 1989.

Giraud, Raymond. *The Unheroic Hero in the Novels of Stendhal, Balzac and Flaubert.* New Brunswick, NJ: Rutgers University Press, 1957.

Goodman, Dena. *The Republic of Letters: A Cultural History of the French Enlightenment.* Ithaca: Cornell University Press, 1994.

Gordon, Daniel, David Bell, and Sarah Maza. "The Public Sphere in the Eighteenth Century: A Forum." *French Historical Studies* 17 (Fall 1992): 882–956.

Gossman, Lionel. *Between History and Literature.* Cambridge, MA: Harvard University Press, 1990.

Grogin, R. C. *The Bergsonian Controversy in France 1900–1914.* Calgary, Canada: University of Calgary Press, 1988.

Guy, Basil. "Rousseau Improv'd: The Prince de Ligne's *Fragments de l'histoire de ma vie.*" *Romanic Review* 71 (1980): 281–94.

———. "Notes on Péguy the Socialist." *French Studies* 15 (1961): 12–29.

Habermas, Jürgen. *The Structural Transformation of the Public Sphere: An Inquiry into a Category of Bourgeois Society.* Translated by Thomas Burger and Frederick Lawrence. Cambridge, MA: Harvard University Press, 1989.

Halévy, Daniel. *Péguy and the Cahiers de la Quinzaine.* Translated by Ruth Bethel. New York: Longman's, Green, and Co., 1947.

Hampson, Norman. "The French Revolution and the Nationalisation of Honour." In *War and Society,* edited by M. R. D. Foot. New York: Barnes and Noble, 1973.

———. *The Life and Opinions of Maximilien Robespierre.* London: Duckworth, 1974.

Harlan, David. "Intellectual History and the Return of Literature." *American Historical Review* 94 (June 1989): 581–609.

Hayman, Ronald. *Writing Against: A Biography of Sartre.* London: Weidenfeld and Nicolson, 1986.

Hayward, Jack. *After the French Revolution.* New York: New York University Press, 1991.

Hazareesingh, Sudhir. *Political Traditions in Modern France.* New York: Oxford University Press, 1994.

Helliung, Mark. *The Autocritique of the Enlightenment: Rousseau and the Philosophes.* Cambridge, MA: Harvard University Press, 1994.

Henri-Lévy, Bernard. *Les Aventures de la liberté: une histoire subjective des intellectuels en France.* Paris: Gallimard, 1991.

Hoffmann, Stanley. *Decline or Renewal? France since the 1930s.* New York: Viking Press, 1974.

———, ed. *In Search of France.* New York: Harper and Row, 1963.

Hunt, Lynn. *Politics, Culture, and Class in the French Revolution.* Berkeley: University of California Press, 1984.

Jardin, André. *Histoire du libéralisme politique: de la crise de l'absolutisme à la constitution de 1875.* Paris: Hachette, 1985.

Jaume, Lucien. *Le Discours jacobin et la démocratie.* Paris: Fayard, 1989.

Jennings, Jeremy, ed. *Intellectuals in Twentieth-Century France.* New York: St. Martin's Press, 1993.

Johnson, Paul. *Intellectuals.* New York: Harper Collins, 1988.

Jordan, David. *The Revolutionary Career of Maximilien Robespierre.* Chicago: University of Chicago Press, 1985.

Judt, Tony. *Marxism and the French Left.* New York: Oxford University Press, 1986.

———. *Past Imperfect: French Intellectuals 1944–1956.* Berkeley: University of California Press, 1992.

Julliard, Jacques. *La Faute à Rousseau: essai sur les conséquences historiques de l'idée de souveraineté populaire.* Paris: Seuil, 1985.

Kettering, Sharon. *Patrons, Brokers, and Clients in Seventeenth-Century France.* New York: Oxford University Press, 1986.

Khilnani, Sunil. *Arguing Revolution: The Intellectual Left in Postwar France*. New Haven: Yale University Press, 1993.

Kippur, Stephen A. *Jules Michelet*. Albany: State University of New York Press, 1981.

Klaits, Joseph, and Michael H. Halzel, eds. *Liberty/Liberté: The American and French Experiences*. Baltimore: Johns Hopkins University Press, 1991.

Koselleck, Reinhart. *Critique and Crisis*. Translated by Berg Publishers. Cambridge, MA: Harvard University Press, 1988.

Krieger, Leonard. *The German Idea of Freedom*. Chicago: University of Chicago Press, 1957.

LaCapra, Dominick. *Representing the Holocaust*. Ithaca: Cornell University Press, 1994.

———. "Rethinking Intellectual History and Reading Texts." In *Modern European Intellectual History*, edited by Dominick LaCapra and Stephen Kaplan, 47–85. Ithaca: Cornell University Press, 1982.

Lejeune, Philippe. *L'Autobiographie en France*. Paris: Armand Colin, 1971.

Lichtheim, George. *Marxism in Modern France*. New York: Columbia University Press, 1966.

Lottman, Herbert R. *The Left Bank*. Boston: Houghton Mifflin, 1982.

Lough, John. *Writer and Public in France*. Oxford: Oxford University Press, 1978.

Lucas, Colin, ed. *The Political Culture of the French Revolution*. Vol. 2 of *The French Revolution and the Creation of Modern Political Culture*. Oxford: Pergamon Press, 1988.

Macey, David. *The Lives of Michel Foucault*. New York: Vintage Books, 1995.

Maritain, Raissa. *Les Grands Amitiés*. Paris: Desclée de Brouwer, 1958.

May, Gita. *Stendhal and the Age of Napoleon*. New York: Columbia University Press, 1977.

McDonald, Joan. *Rousseau and the French Revolution*. London: Athlone Press, 1965.

Merquior, J. G. *Liberalism Old and New*. Boston: Twayne, 1991.

———. *Rousseau and Weber: Two Studies in the Theory of Legitimacy*. London: Routledge, 1980.

Miller, James. *The Passion of Michel Foucault*. New York: Simon and Schuster, 1993.

———. *Rousseau, Dreamer of Democracy*. New Haven: Yale University Press, 1984.

Mornet, Daniel. *Les Origines intellectuelles de la révolution française*. Paris: Armand Colin, 1933.

Nicolet, Claude. *L'Idée républicaine en France (1789–1924)*. Paris: Gallimard, 1982.

Nye, Robert A. *Masculinity and Male Codes of Honor in Modern France*. New York: Oxford University Press, 1993.

Orr, Linda. *Jules Michelet: Nature, History, Language*. Ithaca: Cornell University Press, 1976.

Ozouf, Mona. *Les Mots des femmes*. Paris: Fayard, 1995.

Petrey, Sandy. *Realism and Revolution*. Ithaca: Cornell University Press, 1988.

Polin, Raymond. *La Politique du solitude.* Paris: Sirey, 1970.

Porter, Dennis. *Rousseau's Legacy.* New York: Oxford University Press, 1995.

Poster, Mark. *Critical Theory and Poststructuralism.* Ithaca: Cornell University Press, 1989.

———. *Existential Marxism in Postwar France: From Sartre to Althusser.* Princeton: Princeton University Press, 1976.

———. *Foucault, Marxism, and History.* Cambridge, UK: Polity Press, 1984.

Prost, Antoine. *Histoire de l'enseignement en France, 1800–1967.* Paris: Armand Colin, 1968.

Ranum, Orest. *Artisans of Glory: Writers and Historical Thought in Seventeenth-Century France.* Chapel Hill: University of North Carolina Press, 1980.

Reader, Keith. *Intellectuals and the Left in France since 1968.* London: Macmillan, 1987.

Rémond, René. *L'Anticléricalisme en France.* Paris: Fayard, 1976.

Rigney, Ann. "Icon and Symbol: The Historical Figure Called Maximilien Robespierre." In *Representing the French Revolution,* edited by James Heffernan, 106–22. Hanover: Dartmouth University Press, 1992.

Ringer, Fritz K. *Education and Society in Modern Europe.* Bloomington, IN: University of Indiana Press, 1979.

———. *Fields of Knowledge.* Cambridge, UK: Cambridge University Press, 1992.

Rorty, Richard. "Paroxysms and Politics." *Salgamundi* 97 (Winter 1993): 60–69.

Rosenblum, Nancy. *Another Liberalism.* Cambridge, MA: Harvard University Press, 1987.

Roth, Michael S. *Knowing and History: Appropriations of Hegel in Twentieth-Century France.* Ithaca: Cornell University Press, 1988.

Rudé, George. *Robespierre, Portrait of a Revolutionary Democrat.* New York: Viking Press, 1975.

Ryan, Alan. "Foucault's Life and Hard Times." *New York Review of Books,* 8 April 1993.

———, ed. *The Idea of Freedom: Essays in Honor of Isaiah Berlin.* Oxford: Oxford University Press, 1979.

Sa'adah, Anne. *The Shaping of Liberal Politics in Revolutionary France.* Princeton: Princeton University Press, 1990.

Schalk, Ellery. *From Valor to Pedigree.* Princeton: Princeton University Press, 1986.

Schwartz, Joel. *The Sexual Politics of Jean-Jacques Rousseau.* Chicago: University of Chicago Press, 1984.

Shklar, Judith. *Men and Citizens.* Cambridge, UK: Cambridge University Press, 1969.

Sirinelli, Jean-François, and Pascal Ory. *Les Intellectuels en France de l'affaire Dreyfus à nos jours.* Paris: Armand Colin, 1986.

Smith, Robert. *The École Normale Supérieure and the Third Republic.* Albany: State University Press of New York, 1982.

Starobinski, Jean. *Jean-Jacques Rousseau: Transparency and Obstruction.*

Translated by Arthur Goldhammer. Chicago: University of Chicago Press, 1988.

Sternhell, Zeev. *La Droite révolutionnaire 1885–1914*. Paris: Seuil, 1978.

Stuart Hughes, H. *Consciousness and Society*. New York: Vintage Books, 1958.

Talmon, J. L. *The Rise of Totalitarian Democracy*. Boston: Beacon Press, 1952.

Taylor, Marjorie. *The Arriviste*. Wales, UK: Dragon Books, 1972.

Tharaud, Jean, and Jérome Tharaud. *Notre cher Péguy*. Paris: Plon, 1927.

Toews, John E. "Intellectual History after the Linguistic Turn: The Autonomy of Meaning and the Irreducibility of Experience." *American Historical Review* 92 (October 1987): 879–907.

Trahard, Pierre. *Les Maîtres de la sensibilité française au XVIIIe siècle (1715–1789)*. Vol. 1. Paris: Boivin, 1931.

Van Kley, Dale, ed. *The French Idea of Freedom: The Old Regime and the Declaration of Rights of 1789*. Stanford: Stanford University Press, 1994.

Viala, Alain. *Naissance de l'écrivain*. Paris: Éditions de Minuit, 1985.

Weightman, John. "Fatal Attraction." *New York Review of Books,* 11 February 1993.

Weisz, George. *The Emergence of Modern Universities in France, 1863–1914*. Princeton: Princeton University Press, 1983.

White, Hayden. *Metahistory*. Baltimore: Johns Hopkins University Press, 1973.

———. "Method and Ideology in Intellectual History: The Case of Henry Adams." In *Modern European Intellectual History: Reappraisals and New Perspectives,* edited by Dominick LaCapra and Stephen L. Kaplan, 280–310. Ithaca: Cornell University Press, 1982.

———. *Tropics of Discourse*. Baltimore: Johns Hopkins University Press, 1978.

Woloch, Isser. "On the Latent Illiberalism of the French Revolution." *American Historical Review* 95 (December 1990): 1452–70.

Zeldin, Theodore. *Intellect and Pride*. Vol. 2 of *France 1848–1945*. Oxford: Oxford University Press, 1977.

INDEX